Putting Metaclasses to Work

A New Dimension in Object-Oriented Programming

Ira R. Forman
Scott H. Danforth

ADDISON-WESLEY

An imprint of Addison Wesley Longman, Inc.

Reading, Massachusetts • Harlow, England • Menlo Park, California
Berkeley, California • Don Mills, Ontario • S
Bonn • Amsterdam • Tokyo • Mexico C

Many of the designations used by manufacturers and sellers to distinguish their products are claimed as trademarks. Where those designations appear in this book, and Addison Wesley Longman Inc. was aware of a trademark claim, the designations have been printed in initial caps or all caps.

SOMobjects and System Object Model (SOM) are trademarks of International Business Machines Corporation.

The authors and publisher have taken care in the preparation of this book, but make no expressed or implied warranty of any kind and assume no responsibility for errors or omissions. No liability is assumed for incidental or consequential damages in connection with or arising out of the use of the information or programs contained herein.

The publisher offers discounts on this book when ordered in quantity for special sales. For more information, please contact:

AWL Direct Sales
Addison Wesley Longman, Inc.
One Jacob Way
Reading, Massachusetts 01867
(781) 944-3700

Visit AW on the Web: www.awl.com/cseng/

Library of Congress Cataloging-in-Publication Data

Forman, Ira R.
    Putting metaclasses to work : a new dimension in object-oriented
programming / Ira R. Forman, Scott H. Danforth.
        p.   cm.
    Includes bibliographical references and index.
    ISBN 0-201-43305-2
    1. Object-oriented programming (Computer science) I. Danforth,
Scott. II. Title.
QA76.64.F68   1998
005.1'17--dc21   98-38783
                                                                  CIP

ISBN 0-201-43305-2
Text printed on recycled and acid-free paper.
1 2 3 4 5 6 7 8 9 10—MA—0201009998
First printing, September 1998

To our parents
Dean and Caroline Danforth
Nathan and Sylvia Forman
who taught us that which is most important in life,
and
to our wives
Kasey Goss
Janet Forman
who have encouraged and supported us.

Contents

Chapter 4   **Dynamic Aspects of Our Object Model** **59**

Chapter 5   **DTS C++** **85**

Preface

In object-oriented programming, objects are created as instances of classes. This book deals with the kind of object model in which classes are themselves objects (that is, classes are created as instances of other classes). We have discovered the key to designing such a model so as to improve markedly the levels of composability and reusability attainable in object-oriented programming. Our goal in writing this book is to convey our discovery to others interested in object-oriented programming.

If one thinks of objects as cookies, then classes are analogous to cookie cutters. Cookie cutters are templates that are used to make and determine the properties of cookies; classes make and determine the properties of objects. But how are cookie cutters themselves made? Let us say that they are pressed from sheet metal using a cookie cutter press (a piece of heavy machinery). So, if a cookie cutter press is used to make cookie cutters, what is used to make classes? The answer is a **metaclass.** Although a cookie cutter press does not directly make cookies (because it makes cookie cutters), it does determine properties of cookies. In a very similar way, a metaclass can determine the properties of objects, because it builds a class that makes objects. Our solution for greater reusability is based on the use of metaclasses to isolate and implement object properties.

Metaclasses alone are not enough to attain the improved levels of composability and reusability. This book introduces a new kind of object model called a **monotonic reflective class-based model.** In this new model, inheritance extends beyond instance variables and methods into a new dimension in which the relationship between a class and its metaclass is also inherited. This extension, called **inheritance of metaclass constraints,** is our key discovery. In the resulting technology, not only can metaclasses isolate and implement individual properties, but the composition of the metaclasses isolates and implements the composite property. That is, if one metaclass implements property P while another implements property Q, the composite metaclass implements the property P and Q. This degree of composability does not happen by accident; it is engineered by the proper design of metaclasses and other primitive capabilities within our technology.

In the course of developing the abovementioned ideas, this book explains concepts that are generally useful to and appreciated by anyone interested in object-oriented programming. This book develops object technology from first principles. In doing so, it motivates and demystifies metaclasses, shows how to construct them and compose them, and presents examples of their use. By reading this book, you will learn not only our technology but also the general principles of reflection in object technology.

This book returns to the source of power of object-oriented programming — the synergy of knowledge representation and programming — to yield a major improvement. Consider the following linguistic interpretation of the evolution of computer programming. In the 1950s and 1960s, programming was about commanding the computer — verbs. In the 1970s, this approach proved deficient. A new paradigm arose in which the specification of abstract data types and then classes — nouns — became foremost for the programmer. This paradigm, object-oriented programming, has evolved throughout the 1980s and 1990s. Although powerful and useful, object-oriented programming has proved deficient in isolating properties of objects — adjectives — so that the code that implements a property can be reused. Our technology has an abstraction for adjectives (metaclasses) to complement the nouns (classes) and verbs (methods) of today's object technology. Furthermore, as we will show, composition of metaclasses is as easy as putting a sequence of adjectives in front of a noun when we speak.

Organization of This Book

- Chapter 1 motivates our work with a compelling story for both individual programmers and the organizations for which they work.

- Chapter 2 introduces our theory of reflective class based object-oriented models. The theory is built up from first principles (for example, every object has a class, all classes are objects, and so on).

- Chapter 3 introduces a new semantic concept for object models: inheritance of metaclass constraints. This concept implies a new invariant on the class structure of an object model with metaclasses. Inheritance of metaclass constraints is fundamental to ensuring proper class composition.

- Chapters 4 and 5 together explain how the object model becomes object-oriented programming by binding the structures developed in Chapter 2 to programming language constructs (in particular, we use C++). This book is about a new way of looking at object-oriented programming in general; we purposefully do not introduce a new programming language syntax.

- Chapter 6 presents the basic metaobject protocol for our object model. The metaobject protocol is used to program new metaclasses that isolate reusable properties.

- Chapter 7 uses the metaobject protocol to create a new abstraction, the cooperative metaclass, which is used to attain composability of metaclasses. The combination of Chapters 6 and 7 is the entire metaobject protocol; the separation is for pedagogical purposes.

- Chapters 8, 9, and 10 contain useful examples of metaclasses that can be built with our metaobject protocol and the cooperative metaclass. These are examples of commonly needed object properties that cannot be isolated and reused in the current programming languages.

- Chapter 11 presents and solves the problem of release-to-release binary compatibility. Subclassing between separately compiled units has been troublesome in object-oriented programming. We formalize and solve the problem, and state the implications of the solution for object models with metaclasses.

Basis for Claims

This book presents new techniques in object-oriented programming, and you have the right to ask our basis for claiming that these techniques are effective. We developed and used these techniques over a four-year period in the evolution of IBM's SOMobjects Toolkit. Most of the important metaclasses described in this book are based on metaclasses implemented in IBM's SOMobjects Toolkit 3.0, although not all of them have publicly available interfaces (those without public interfaces are used to program other parts of the toolkit). All of these metaclasses have been used by the authors or other SOM programmers to write real programs.

The metaclasses of IBM's SOMobjects Toolkit 3.0 are written using the toolkit's metaobject protocol. To make this book as readable as possible, we have simplified that protocol. In addition, we have taken the opportunity in writing this book to improve the toolkit's metaobject protocol. Because of these two factors, our metaobject protocol (the one in this book) is SOM-like, but is not SOM.

Because we have deviated from IBM's SOMobjects Toolkit 3.0 in this book, we have provided a simulation of the object model, our metaobject protocol, and an implementation of all metaclasses in this book that runs on the object model simulation. This is programmed in Java (because of its portability) and can be downloaded from the following URL http://www.awl.com/cseng/titles/0-201-43305-2. Consult the "readme" file for further information about the simulation.

Audience

This book is intended for programmers, researchers in object-oriented programming, and students in computer science. It is written at the level of senior undergraduates studying computer science. There are two prerequisites for reading this book:

- An aquaintance of the basic ideas of object-oriented programming, because we do not go into detail as to why encapsulation, polymorphism, and inheritance are important

- A minimal understanding of discrete mathematics, which can be obtained from any number of books (in particular, [53] is an excellent choice)

Acknowledgments

Throughout the six years of work that led to this book, we have benefited from discussions with and comments from many friends and colleagues. We thank Liane Acker, Govind Balakrishnan, Arindam Banerji, Michael Cheng, Ravi Condamoor, Mike Conner, George Copeland, Diane Copenhaver, Brad Cox, Nissim Francez, Ted Goldstein, Kevin Greene,

Mike Heytens, Duane Hughes, Shmuel Katz, Gregor Kiczales, Donovan Kolbly, Hillel Kolodner, Vinoj Kumar, John Lamping, Rene Llames, Hari Madduri, Andy Martin, Simon Nash, Harold Ossher, Andy Palay, Tom Pennello, Jim Platt, Larry Raper, Cliff Reeves, Charlie Richter, Brian Ritter, Frederick Rivard, Kim Rochat, Jerry Ronga, Roger Sessions, Erin Shepler, Marc Smith, Robert Stroud, Brian Watt, and Cun Xiao for their aid in achieving our goal. Special thanks go to Derek Beatty, David Boles, Michael Cheng, Nate Forman, John Lamping, Doug Lea, Charlie Richter, Leick Robinson, Brett Schuchert, Kent Spaulding, and Gerhart Werner for their comments on the draft of this book. Special acknowledgment must go to the designers and implementors of the original version of SOM: Mike Conner, Andy Martin, and Larry Raper.

Glossary of Symbols

Sets

Symbol	Meaning	Example
$\{v1, ...\}$	set constructor	$\{a,b,c\}$
$\cup$	set union	$\{a,b,c\}\cup\{c,d\} = \{a,b,c,d\}$
$\cap$	set intersection	$\{a,b,c\}\cap\{c,d\} = \{c\}$
$\varnothing$	empty set	$\{a,b\}\cap\{c,d\} = \varnothing$
$\subseteq$	subset of	$\{a\}\subseteq\{a,b,c\}$
$\in$	set membership	$a\in\{a,b,c\}$
$-$	set difference	$\{a,b,c\}-\{c,d\} = \{a,b\}$
$\times$	Cartesian product	$\{a,b\}\times\{c,d\}=$ $\{<a,c>,<a,d>,$ $<b,c>,<b,d>\}$
member	select a random member of the set	a and b are possible values of *member*($\{a,b\}$)

Relations

Symbol	Meaning	Example
$\circ$	composition	$\{<a,1>,<b,2>\}\circ\{<2,B>\} =$ $\{<b,B>\}$
-1	inverse	$\{<a,1>,<b,2>,<c,3>\}^{-1} =$ $\{<1,a>,<2,b>,<3,c>\}$
$*$	reflexive transitive closure	$\{<a,b>,<b,c>,<c,c>\}^{*} =$ $\{<a,a>,<a,b>,<a,c>,$ $<b,b>,<b,c>,<c,c>\}$

Lists

Operator	Meaning	Example
<v1, ...>	list constructor	<a,b,c>
<>	empty list	<> ^ <a,b,c> ^ <> = <a,b,c>
^	append	<a,b,c> ^ <c,d> = <a,b,c,c,d>
◁	list merge (unique)	<a,b,c>◁<c,d> = <a,b,c,d>
◀	conservative merge	see page 65
−	list difference	<a,b,c,c> − <c,d> = <a,b>
.aNonnegative	list element	<a,b>.0 = a
#	length	#<a,b,c> = 3
∈	list membership	a∈ <a,b,c>
aList[i,j]	the subsequence of aList from i'th to j'th element	<a,b,c,d>[3,4] = <c,d>

Dictionaries (also see Section 1.2)

Symbol	Meaning	Example
{k1=v1, ...}	dictionary constructor	{a=2,b=4} see page 4
◁	dictionary merge (unique)	{a=2,b=4}◁{b=2,c=4} = {a=2,b=4,c=4}
◀	recursive dictionary merge (unique)	see page 5
{}	empty dictionary	{}◁{a=2,b=4}◁{} = {a=2,b=4}
.key	dictionary lookup	{b=2,c=4}.c = 4
∈	dictionary membership	c∈ {b=2,c=4}
α	random list of the keys in a dictionary	α{a=2,b=4,c=4} = <b,c,a>
#	number of slots	#{a=2,b=4,c=4} = 3
delete	delete the member of the dictionary with a key	delete({b=2,c=4},b) = {c=4}

Object Environments

Symbol	Meaning	Example
◯	ordinary object	myCheckingAccount
◎	ordinary class	CheckingAccount
◉	metaclass	JointlyOwned
⟶	subclass of	CheckingAccount is a subclass of BankAccount
┄┄▶	instance of	myCheckingAccount is an instance of BankAccount

Typographic Conventions

Font	Meaning	Example
Times bold	definition of English terms	**instance variable**
Times italic	object model primitives and object references (they can be used in specifications but not in programs)	*Class, Object, X, ThreadSafe, respondsTo*
Times italic bold	single character symbols for sets	***O, C, M***
Helvetica	instructions that make up a program	x := x + 1;

Chapter 1
Introduction

One interpretation of the history of programming is that progress is made by providing abstractions for ever larger entities and by ensuring the composability of those abstractions. In the beginning, assembly language instructions were gathered into control structures. Subsequently, control structures were gathered into procedures, and this was followed by the gathering of procedures into abstract data types. Now we have arrived at object-oriented programming, where abstract data types become classes and are gathered into an inheritance hierarchy. This book contributes to the next step in this progression by showing how useful class behavior can be gathered into instance relationships mediated by metaclasses, and how this behavior can be composed. In short, we show how metaclasses can be put to practical use.

In object-oriented programming, the class of a class object is called a metaclass. If you have encountered metaclasses before reading this book, they probably seemed to be endowed with magical powers. After all, "A sufficiently advanced technology is indistinguishable from magic" [23]. In this book we will demystify metaclasses for you. While doing so, we will contribute to the progress of programming technology.

1.1   A Fable

Let us begin with a fable about a programmer named George.

George works for Menagerie Class Libraries, Inc. George is responsible for the world's greatest *Dog* class. There is only one problem with this class: it works only in single-threaded applications. Early one morning, George's manager decrees that to win a big contract the *Dog* class must work in multithreaded applications by 8 AM the next morning. We have all been in George's shoes and know that he must do the following to the source code of his *Dog* class.

1. At the beginning of each method, a semaphore must be acquired.

2. He must ensure the release of the semaphore at all return points of each method.

3. He must discover all inherited methods and override them: in each override, he must acquire the semaphore, invoke the parent method, and then release the semaphore.

George is in for a long night. To make matters worse, if during the night a colleague adds a new method to an ancestor of the *Dog* class (after George has examined the ancestor), the thread-safeness of George's *Dog* class will be in jeopardy.

The task of making the *Dog* class thread safe is both arduous and mechanical. Yet this task cannot be simplified, because none of our programming languages (for example, C++) can make a reusable module for the property of thread safety. Now imagine how much better it would be if the property of thread safety could be embodied in a module (in particular, a metaclass) so that George could do this task by writing something like this:

class ThreadSafeDog is subclass of Dog and is ThreadSafe;

The result would be the required thread-safe *Dog* class. George could take the afternoon off and attend his son's basketball game. If Martha, George's office mate, got the same assignment for her *Cat* class, she could reuse the metaclass by writing a similar line of code.

Now consider the plight of George's employer, Menagerie Class Libraries, Inc. It has developed a class library of n classes. There are p properties that they wish their classes to have in all combinations. Both the number of classes and the number of properties are growing as the company evolves to meet the increasing needs of its customers. Menagerie Class Libraries, Inc. is facing the possibility of having a class library of $n2^p$ classes. Instead, if each property could be isolated in a metaclass and if the metaclasses could be composed (so that the properties compose), the class library would be of size $n+p$. This would represent an enormous savings to the company.[1]

To impart a property such as thread safety requires the capability of querying about the class that is to receive the property and the capability of modifying that class (imparting the property). We usually think of such capabilities as the domain of the programmer, because the required information usually disappears after the compiler has finished its job. But if classes are objects (instances of metaclasses), then important semantic structures of

---

1. George Copeland of IBM has pointed out to us that this is a real problem. He has observed that when an object-oriented database is first brought into a programming shop, the number of classes doubles (in this case, there is one property — persistence — and $p=1$).

a program can be retained after compilation and can be available at runtime. Furthermore, because metaclasses actually construct their class objects, this allows one part of a program to adjust itself on the basis of the structure of another. In turn, this yields the ability to isolate a programming concept (such as thread safety) so that it can be reused. The retention of semantic structures and the capability of modifying them at runtime combine to create an **open** programming system.

Openness has a degree of risk, which is the lack of structure and safety. We manage this risk by using this openness only to construct metaclasses. The metaclass provides us with a programming abstraction that can be easily understood and reused. This yields a particular kind of program module in which a property is isolated, and further yields an accompanying discipline.

Finally, in addition to the ability to isolate and reuse object properties, the fact that the metaclasses can be composed to create metaclasses with composite properties is of extraordinary importance, because one can obtain a large number of properties with a small number of metaclasses.

With *openness tempered by discipline and magnified by composability* in mind, let us introduce a few preliminary concepts.

1.2 Dictionaries

Let us reconsider our fable. George's task of making his *Dog* class thread safe is so deceptively simple that George might consider writing a program that will do it and thus provide a valuable utility for his colleagues. The input of this program would be the source code for the *Dog* class (or any other class), and the output would be the source code for a thread-safe version of the input class. Although the specification seems simple enough, such a program is quite difficult to write. In addition to the difficulties that we have already mentioned (for example, changes to ancestor classes), there is the difficulty of parsing the programming language so that the *Dog* class can be read as input.

Now imagine that George's programming system made the representation of the *Dog* class available at runtime. Then it is conceivable that George could write such a program, because all of the work of parsing the input has been done for him. This is one aspect of why a metaclass can be so valuable: it can act as a programming agent as it constructs class objects, doing things that a programmer would do. One prerequisite for accomplishing this goal is that we must have a way of representing the bindings of names to program parts. A dictionary is a good way to represent such bindings.

To understand this book, it is essential that you understand our dictionary data type. Objects will be defined in terms of dictionaries. Classes will be defined in terms of dictionaries. Inheritance will be defined in terms of dictionary operations. This section provides a sufficient introduction to dictionaries (other data types such as sets and lists are described in the Glossary of Symbols on pages xv to xvii).

Definition 1. A **dictionary** is a (finite) set of key-value pairs in which the keys are distinct. Each pair is called a **slot.**

If k is a key and v is a value, a slot is written $k=v$ (rather than the usual $<k,v>$). A dictionary is written like this:

$$\{ k_0=v_0, k_1=v_1, ..., k_{n-1}=v_{n-1} \}$$

The dictionary key has two uses. Sometimes a dictionary key is data and sometimes it is programming language literal. The duality of usage is fundamental to why you are reading this book: you want the capability of doing things at runtime that in most programming languages you can do only at compile time. It is not necessary for a key to have a string value. For example,

$$\{ \text{"x"} = 30, \text{"y"} = 50, 321 = 70 \}$$

is a dictionary.

Because this book does not deal with sets of equations as data, there is no ambiguity in the notation between dictionary constants and set constants. Note that $\{\}$ denotes the empty dictionary while $\varnothing$ denotes the empty set. There are several operations that are important with respect to dictionaries.

Definition 2. Let D_1 and D_2 be dictionaries, and let k be a key.
- $k \in D_1$ is a Boolean expression that is true if and only if D_1 has a k slot
- $D_1.k$ is an expression that denotes the value of the slot in D_1 with key k
- αD_1 is a list of the keys for the dictionary D_1; α is a nondeterministic operator (that is, any permutation of the set of keys is a possible result of using this operator)
- $D_1 \triangleleft D_2$ is the addition to D_1 of those slots of D_2 that do not have keys in D_1

Example.

Let D_1 be the dictionary
```
{   "title" = "Structured Programming",
    "authors" = "Dahl, Dijkstra, and Hoare",
    "locations" = {    "Dahl" = "University of Oslo",
                       "Dijkstra" = "University of Texas",
                       "Hoare" = "Oxford University" }
}
```
Note that the value of the locations slot is also a dictionary. Then

$\text{"title"} \in D_1$ is true,

$D_1.\text{"title"}$ has the value "Structured Programming"

and

αD_1 has $<\text{"title"},\text{"authors"},\text{"locations"}>$ as a possible value (or any of the other five permutations). Note that the quotation marks are mandatory here.

Let D_2 be the dictionary
    {   "publisher" = "Academic Press",
        "locations" = {   "North America" = "New York",
                  "Europe" = "London"}
    }

The value of $D_1 \triangleleft D_2$ is
    {   "title" = "Structured Programming",
        "authors" = "Dahl, Dijkstra, and Hoare",
        "locations" = {   "Dahl" = "University of Oslo",
                  "Dijkstra" = "University of Texas",
                  "Hoare" = "Oxford University" }
        "publisher" = "Academic Press"
    }

As shown above, a dictionary can be nested inside of another dictionary.

Definition 3. $D_1 \blacktriangleleft D_2$ is the **recursive merge** of the dictionaries. That is, if the values of slots $D_1.k$ and $D_2.k$ are dictionaries, then $(D_1 \blacktriangleleft D_2).k = D_1.k \blacktriangleleft D_2.k$; otherwise the slots of $D_1 \blacktriangleleft D_2$ are just like those of $D_1 \triangleleft D_2$.

Example.
Let D_1 and D_2 be as in the previous example. The value of $D_1 \blacktriangleleft D_2$ is
    {   "title" = "Structured Programming",
        "authors" = "Dahl, Dijkstra, and Hoare",
        "locations" = { "Dahl" = "University of Oslo",
                "Dijkstra" = "University of Texas",
                "Hoare" = "Oxford University",
                "North America" = "New York",
                "Europe" = "London"}
        "publisher" = "Academic Press"
    }

1.3 Procedural Specifications

This book is about new concepts in programming. This requires us to write programs. On the other hand, these concepts are programming language independent; this implies that we wish to avoid designing a new programming language. We resolve these contradictory goals by writing procedural specifications in this book. The specification language is divided between an **outer syntax** and an **inner syntax** [83].

- The outer syntax deals with control structure, data structure, and system/module structure.
- The inner syntax deals with operations and tests on data.

Choosing a current programming language for our outer syntax relieves us of the burden of defining the semantics of many program structures. Our outer syntax is C++. Our inner syntax comes from a range of entities and operations much wider than the range that exists in C++. For example, it is acceptable to use dictionary operations such as recursive merge in the inner syntax. All such entities and their operations are defined in the Glossary of Symbols. So how does one tell if one is looking at C++ or at a specification? It is easy. All C++ is written in Helvetica font, while inner syntax (that is not C++) is written in italics or uses special symbols. In addition, methods and procedures are specified by a precondition and an action. The template for the specification of a method or a procedure is given in Figure 1-1. A method is a procedure in which the target object is an implied parameter that is accessed with the special variable this.

<method-or-procedure-signature>
{ /* Specification */
Precondition:
    <Boolean-expression>
Action:
    <procedural-code>
}

Figure 1-1. Specification template for a method or procedure.

To illustrate this specification technique, let us consider the problem of topological sorting. Given a directed acyclic graph, a **topological sort** is a list of the vertices of the graph such that no vertex v is listed behind any vertex that can be reached with a path that begins with v. Our representation for a graph is a dictionary in which, for each slot, the key is a vertex identifier and the value is a list of the vertex identifiers of the successors to the vertex mentioned in the key. Below is the specification of an algorithm for topologically sorting such a dictionary. The basic idea is that topSort calls findMinimalVertices to get a list of those vertices with no predecessors. It appends the list of remaining minimal vertices to the result and removes them from the list of vertices. This continues until all the vertices are in the result list.

list **topSort**(*dictionary acyclicDirectedGraph*)
{ /* Specification */
Precondition:
    true
Action:
    list vlist = α *acyclicDirectedGraph*; // this list of keys is the list of vertices
    list result = <>;
    while (*vlist* ≠ <>) {
      list minimals = findMinimalVertices(*vlist, acyclicDirectedGraph*);
      if (*minimals* == <>) {
        printf("The graph is NOT acyclic\n");
        return NULL;
        }
      result = *result* ◁ *minimals*;
      vlist = *vlist* − *minimals*;
    }
    return *result*;
}

list **findMinimalVertices**(*list vlist, dictionary edges*)
{ /* Specification */
Action:
    list result = *vlist*;
    int i;
    for (i=0; i<#*vlist*; i++) {
      result = *result* − *edges*.(*vlist*.i);
    }
    return *result*;
}

There are several points to add about this specification technique.

- If the precondition is omitted, it is the same as saying it is *true*.

- Non-C++ data types are written in italics and so are the variables of those types.

- Variables of non-C++ data types can be assigned the value NULL, which indicates no value and is different from the empty dictionary, empty list, empty set, and so on, as the case may be.

- Because C++ uses the equal sign (=) for assignment, we use the double equal sign (==) to indicate an equality test in the inner syntax.

If the precondition for a method or procedure is not true when it is invoked, we do not specify what happens. For all examples in this book, a precondition is true when a method or procedure is invoked. This has two advantages. First, we do not burden our readers with the details of error handling, which would be a digression from our goal of putting metaclasses to work. Second, all of our metaclasses are underspecified, which means that the results in this book can be easily transferred to other settings.

Example.
    Consider the following directed graph.

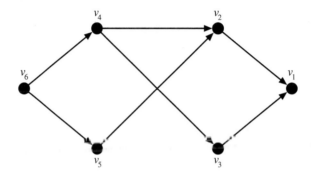

Its encoding as a dictionary appears as
    $\{v_1=<>, v_2=<v_1>, v_3=<v_1>, v_4=<v_2,v_3>, v_5=<v_2>, v_6=<v_4,v_5>\}$
where the v_i's are arbitrary distinct values. topSort produces a topological sort for the directed graph represented by this dictionary. One of the possible results is
    $<v_6,v_4,v_5,v_2,v_3,v_1>$.
                                                                                               □

The procedures topSort and findMinimalVertices show how inner syntax and outer syntax are interwoven to produce a succinct specification. There are minor syntactic ambiguities in mixing the inner syntax with the outer syntax, but we do not expect these ambiguities to be a problem for the reader.

1.4 Exercises

1.1   Let X be the dictionary
            {   "name" = "Abraham Lincoln",
                  "home" = "Springfield",
            }
          Let Y be the dictionary
            {   "position" = "President",
                  "home" = "Washington, D.C."
            }
          Compute the values of $X \triangleleft| Y$ and $Y \triangleleft| X$.

1.2   Let X be the dictionary
             {   "Edit" = { "Cut" = xCutFunction,
                             "Copy" = xCopyFunction,
                             "Paste" = xPasteFunction },
                   "File" = { "New" = xNewFunction,
                              "Open" = xOpenFunction,
                              "Save" = xSaveFunction },
             }
             Let Y be the dictionary
             {   "Edit" = { "Cut" = yCutFunction,
                              "Copy" = yCopyFunction,
                              "Paste" = yPasteFunction },
                   "File" = { "New" = yNewFunction,
                              "Open" = yOpenFunction,
                              "Save" = ySaveFunction,
                              "SaveAs" = ySaveAsFunction },
             }
             Compute the values of $X \vartriangleleft Y$, $Y \vartriangleleft X$, $X \blacktriangleleft Y$, and $Y \blacktriangleleft X$.

1.3   Prove that $\blacktriangleleft$ is associative but not commutative.

1.4   Let Z be the dictionary
             {   "color" = "blue",
                   "tireStatus" = {   "leftFront" = "okay",
                                       "rightFront" = "about 1000 miles to go",
                                       "leftRear" = "worn out",
                                       "rightRear" = "okay"
                                  }
             }
             a) Write the expression for the value of Z's left rear tire.
             b) Write the expression for a dictionary that has the status of the spare tire in addition to Z's slot values.

1.5   Disprove the following
             $$\alpha(D_1 \vartriangleleft D_2) = \alpha D_1 \vartriangleleft \alpha D_2$$

1.6   Write a specification for each of the dictionary operations described in Definition 2 and Definition 3. (As you read this book, ensure that your specification is not violated. If it is, rewrite your specification.)

1.7   Implement dictionaries in your favorite programming language.

1.8   The result of topSort is nondeterministic because of the specification of the α operator. Is every topological sort of a graph a possible result of topSort?

Chapter 2
The Elements of
Reflective Class-Based Models

Our first task is to produce a model of objects. This chapter does part of the job by producing a model of the static aspects of objects. This chapter defines object, class, metaclass, and inheritance. Chapter 4 completes the job by defining instance variable access, method invocation, and class construction. In the presentation below, some statements are declared to be postulates. Taken together, these statements characterize the area of study we title **reflective class-based models,** a term that will be clear when you have finished reading this chapter.

2.1　The Set of Objects

> **Postulate 1.** Each member of the nonempty, finite set of objects is identified by a value called an **object reference.**

The set of objects is denoted O. It may seem strange to introduce object references before defining objects, but there are important results to be derived before defining the structure of an object. We do not further define object reference. Like "point," "line," and "plane" in Euclidean geometry, object reference is a primitive and is not further defined. We do require that object references can be compared for equality.

Objects are depicted as in Figure 2-1, with either a circle or a rounded rectangle (when we need more space to write something inside the object). Object references are written in Times italic. The object reference is written in the center of a circle or at the top center of a rounded rectangle.

Figure 2-1. X_1 and X_2 are object references.

Figure 2-2 depicts a set of objects. A structure such as that depicted in Figure 2-2 is called an **environment.** Figure 2-2 depicts an environment in which there are five objects: X_1, X_2, X_3, X_4, and X_5. Note that O is a symbol for writing about the environment but is not part of the environment itself. Such symbols are very handy for succinctly expressing concepts and writing specifications.

Postulate 2. Every object has a uniquely associated entity called a **class.**

The set of all classes is denoted C. Figure 2-3 depicts the correspondence between a set of objects and their associated classes. Classes are drawn with a double boundary, and the relation between a class and its instances is drawn with a dashed arrow from an object to its class. Postulate 2 implies that the mapping of objects to classes is a function. This yields the following definition.

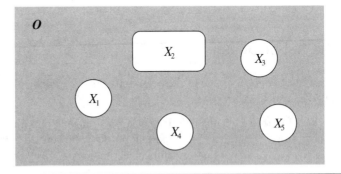

Figure 2-2. A set of objects.

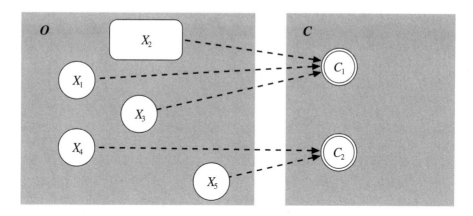

Figure 2-3. C is the set of classes.

Definition 4.
- *class* is the function $O \rightarrow C$ that defines the class associated with an object
- *isClassOf* is the relation over $C \times O$ such that Y *isClassOf* X
  if and only if $Y = class(X)$
- *isInstanceOf* is the relation *isClassOf*$^{-1}$
- *extentOf*$(Y) = \{X \in O$ such that $class(X) = Y\}$

Although we give formal definitions for relational symbols (such as *isInstanceOf*), most of this book is written using the natural forms of such phrases (for example, "is an instance of").

2.2   A Class Is an Object

Postulate 3. Every class is an object.

In other words, $C \subseteq O$. We subsequently use the term **class reference** to indicate the object reference of a class. This postulate implies that the environment must look like the one shown in Figure 2-4, where the set of classes is drawn inside the set of objects. Now, if a class is an object, a class must have a class, which in turn must have a class, and so on. This confusing situation is remedied by the following theorem.

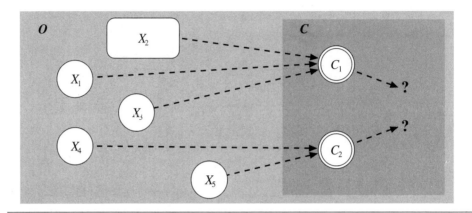

Figure 2-4. Classes are objects.

Theorem 1. Every finite acyclic directed graph must have a vertex of out-degree zero (that is, a vertex with no arrows leaving it).

Proof.([57] page 200).

> Because the graph is finite and acyclic, the paths can be listed. Consider any maximal path P. The last vertex of P can have no successor because P is maximal. Therefore, the graph has a vertex with no arrows leaving it.

$\square$

Because every object has a class and all classes are objects, either the graph (of the *class* function) must be infinite or the graph must have a cycle. To implement the entire object model, there must be a cycle. To minimize the complexity of our design, the cycle is chosen to be a class pointing to itself. This yields the existence of a special class that must exist, which we name *Class*; it is drawn with a triple boundary, as shown in Figure 2-5.

Theorem 1 yields significant insight into three distinct approaches taken by object models with respect to metaclasses. There is the approach taken by certain object-oriented database projects [49,98] in which the class of a class is not among the set of objects. The second approach is the infinite tower that is used in one kind of reflection [116]; in this approach, although the graph is infinite, only the needed levels are generated. Finally, there is the kind of reflection in which the graph has a cycle. This last approach is the one that this book takes.

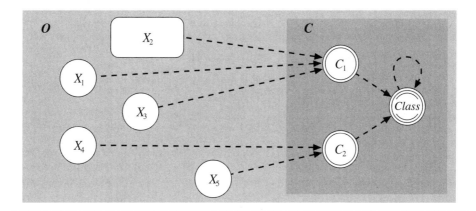

Figure 2-5. The class *Class*.

Definition 5. A **metaclass** is an object whose instances are classes.

Class is a metaclass; the set of all metaclasses is denoted **M.** Figure 2-6 depicts a sample environment with the set of metaclasses, which we intend to populate with useful abstractions later in this book.

Smalltalk [50] has two metaclasses in its cycle, whereas IBM SOM [63], CLOS [104], ObjVlisp [24], Dylan [2], and Proteus [108] each have single metaclasses in their cycles, as we have done. Our presentation uses ideas and techniques from all of these languages, which have all contributed much to object-oriented programming.

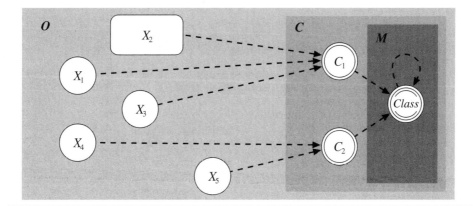

Figure 2-6. The set of metaclasses **M.**

The phrase "*Y* is the **metaclass of** *Z*" means *Y=class(class(Z))*, where *Z* is an object, while the phrase "*Y* is the **metaclass for** *Z*" means *Y=class(Z)*, where *Z* is a class. This is a bit subtle, but the meaning is usually clear from the context; where necessary, we use the formal counterparts to ensure that there is no confusion.

Definition 6. The members of *O − C* are called **ordinary objects,** and the members of *C − M* are called **ordinary classes.**[1]

Note that the extent of an ordinary object is defined and always empty, because only classes have instances.

Properties of an object model can be classified as **intrinsic** or **extrinsic.** An intrinsic property is one that can be computed from information available within the objects. Extrinsic properties cannot be so computed. At this point in our exposition, all properties are extrinsic, because there is no data in our objects. The remainder of this chapter defines our object model so that the data contained in the objects makes certain desired properties intrinsic.

2.3   Structure of an Object

An object is structured by the following two definitions.

Definition 7. A **data table** is a dictionary whose keys are class references and whose slot values are dictionaries whose keys are strings.

Here is an example of a data table.
```
{ Location = {     "x" = 23,
                   "y" = 100 },
  Velocity = {     "deltax" = 1,
                   "deltay" = 2 }
}
```
With this understood, we can finally give the definition of an object.

Definition 8. An **object** with object reference *iX* is a dictionary that is the merge of a slot named class (whose value is *class(iX)*) and a data table.

By asserting that every object has a slot named class whose value is *class(iX)*, we change an extrinsic property into an intrinsic one. The *class* function represents the organization of *O,* whereas the class slot means that this organization can be computed from information within the objects of *O*. On the other hand, *iX ∈ O* is an extrinsic property in this book and remains so, because there is no place in the environment where the existing

---

1. The notation here is set difference. For example, *O − C* represents the members of *O* not in *C*.

objects are tracked and we do not add sufficient structure to the environment to determine this from the contents of the objects.

Example.

Let *Book* be a class. If *iBook* is an instance of *Book*, one possible value of *iBook* is

```
{   "class" = Book,
        Book = {   "title" = "Structured Programming",
                   "authors" = "Dahl, Dijkstra, and Hoare"}
}
```

This says that the value of the object *iBook* is a dictionary with two slots, class and *Book*. The value of the slot class is the class reference *Book*. The value of the slot *Book* is a dictionary with two slots where "Structured Programming" is the value of the slot named title. The value of the title slot is accessed with the expression

$$iBook.Book."title"$$

which has the value "Structured Programming". Note that the value of the object *iBook* can be expressed by

```
{"class" = Book} ◁ {Book = {   "title" = "Structured Programming",
                                "authors" = "Dahl, Dijkstra, and Hoare"}
                   }
```

which Definition 8 demands. Further note that the data table portion of the object may have multiple slots with keys of different class references.

□

Definition 9. An **instance variable** is a pair of the form <class reference, name> (which represents the successive keys required to access a value from a data table).

In the example above, the instance of *Book* has two instance variables, <*Book*,"title"> and <*Book*,"authors">. By Definition 9, the class slot is not an instance variable. This is done so that instance variable access cannot be used to change the class of an object. The definition of instance variable may seem a bit strange because of your experience with programming languages, but we are not designing a programming language. Chapter 5 discusses binding of this model to a programming language to ease the writing of programs.

Postulate 4. The data table of an object is determined by its class.

Every class X contains the instance variable <*Class*,"ivs">, which is a data table used to create instances of X. In particular, when an instance iX of class X is first created, the value of iX is

$$\{class=X\} \quad ◁ \quad X.Class."ivs"$$

Although <*Class*,"ivs"> is used as a template to create instances of class X, the values stored in the instance variable slots are allowed to change subsequently.

Example.

The *Book* class in the previous example in part looks like this:

    {   "class" = *Class*,
        Class = { "ivs" = { *Book* = { "title" = "",
                                          "authors" = "" } }
        }
        ...
    }

assuming that *Book* is an instance of *Class*. Note how, with the exception of the class slot, the *<Class*,"ivs"> instance variable in *Book* contains all the slots of *iBook*.

□

The following two functions are helpful in expressing the important relationship between an object and its class.

Definition 10. Let X be a class and let iX be an object.
- *supportedIVs*(X) = { $<c,n>$ such that $X.Class."ivs".c.n$ is defined }[2]
- *containedIVs*(iX) = { $<c,n>$ such that $iX.c.n$ is defined }

With these two expressions defined, we can state that, for all objects iX,

$$containedIVs(iX) = supportedIVs(class(iX))$$

is always true. This statement is the formal interpretation of Postulate 4. It is subtly profound, because it implies that the structure of an object cannot change without changing its class (in either sense of the notion of changing the class — that is, either the class slot must change or the class object must change).

2.4 Methods

This section continues the elaboration of our object model by introducing the part of the structure of classes that relates to the behavior of objects.

A **code pointer** identifies an executable procedure. Just as with object reference, the notion of a code pointer is primitive and is not further defined. A code pointer is a value that can be used to start the execution of a procedure. Code pointers are written in the Helvetica font. Analogous to the situation with instance variables, we have the following two definitions.

---

2. For a recursive dictionary D,
    { $<c,n>$ such that $D.c.n$ is defined } means $\bigcup_{c \in \alpha D} \{c\} \times \{n$ such that $n \in \alpha(D.c) \}$.

Definition 11. A **method table** is a dictionary whose keys are class references and whose values are dictionaries whose keys are **method names** (strings) and whose values are code pointers.

An example of a method table is

> { *Location* = { "inPolarCoordinates" = CodePtr_inPolarCoordinates
>   },
>   *Velocity* = {   "getSpeed" = CodePtr_getSpeed,
>   "locationEstimate" = CodePtr_locationEstimate }
> }

where the strings with prefix CodePtr_ stand for code pointers.

Definition 12. A **method** is a pair of the form <class reference, name> (which represents the successive keys required to access a code pointer from a method table).

Postulate 5. The methods to which an object responds are determined by its class.

This postulate is very inclusive; any object model in which dispatching of methods is determined by the classes of objects involved in a method invocation satisfies this postulate. In our object model, we ensure that behavior is intrinsic by having every class X contain the instance variable <*Class*,"mtab">, which is a method table for the methods to which instances of X respond.

Definition 13. Let iX be an instance of class X.
- *supportedMethods*(X) = { <c,m> such that $X.Class.$"mtab".$c.m$ is defined }
- *respondsTo*(iX) = { <c,m> such that $class(iX).Class.$"mtab".$c.m$ is defined }

Our formal interpretation of Postulate 5 is that for all $iX \in \boldsymbol{O}$,

> *respondsTo*(iX) = *supportedMethods*$(class(iX))$

which is the fundamental property of class-based object models.

Example.

> Suppose the *Book* class introduces a method named isAuthor whose implementation is defined by the code pointer isParamSubstringOfAuthors. Then
>
> > *Book.Class.*"mtab".*Book.*"isAuthor" = isParamSubstringOfAuthors.
>
> This means that
>
> > <*Book*,"isAuthor"> $\in$ *supportedMethods*(*Book*)
>
> and
>
> > <*Book*,"isAuthor"> $\in$ *respondsTo*(*iBook*)
>
> where *iBook* is an instance of class *Book* (that is, *class(iBook)=Book*).

□

2.5 Inheritance

Once the decision has been made to accumulate information about objects in classes, there is a strong impetus to organize the classes into a hierarchy, as is done in knowledge representation. This is an ancient idea attributed to Aristotle, who first organized knowledge in a hierarchy. Object-oriented programming makes simple but effective use of this venerable concept by employing the class hierarchy to facilitate incremental class definitions. Subclassing allows a class to inherit the instance variables and methods defined by other classes, and allows the class to introduce new instance variables and methods incrementally.

Postulate 6. There is a relation on the set of classes called the **inheritance graph.**

In addition, we require the inheritance graph to be acyclic. The inheritance graph in our model is determined as follows.

Definition 14. Every class X has an associated list of parent classes denoted by $parents(X)$ and an instance variable $<Class,$"parents"$>$ that contains this list. That is,

$$parents(X) = X.Class."parents"$$

In our diagrams, a solid arrow indicates that the class at the tail of the arrow is a subclass of the class at the head of the arrow. In Figure 2-7, C_1 is a parent of C_2 (that is, $C_1 \in parents(C_2)$).

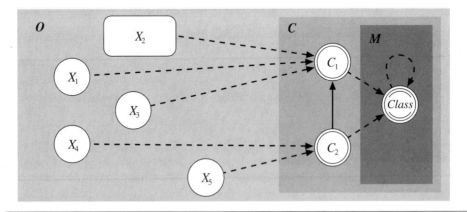

Figure 2-7. C_1 is a parent of C_2.

Some object models (such as those of Smalltalk and Java) restrict the parents list to at most one element. This is called **single inheritance.** Object models that allow the parents list to have more than one element (such as those of C++ and CLOS) are said to support **multiple inheritance.**

The function *parents*(X) yields a list, which means that the parents of a class are ordered. When drawing inheritance graphs, we adopt the convention that the left-to-right ordering of the arrows emanating from a class is the order of the parents list. If this is not the case, the arrows are numbered (beginning with zero).

Definition 15. The following relations and functions are defined for convenience.
- *isSubclassOf* = {<X,Y> such that Y∈ *parents*(X) }
- *isParentOf* = *isSubclassOf* $^{-1}$
- *isAncestorOf* = *isParentOf* *
- *isDescendantOf* = *isSubclassOf* *
- *isA* = *isInstanceOf* ° *isDescendantOf*
- *ancestors*(X) = {Y such that Y *isAncestorOf* X}
- *descendants*(X) = {Y such that Y *isDescendantOf* X}
- *strictAncestors*(X) = {Y such that Y *isAncestorOf* X and Y ≠ X}
- *strictDescendants*(X) = {Y such that Y *isDescendantOf* X and Y ≠ X}

The first five items in Definition 15 are relations. If the expressions on the right-hand side are unfamiliar, see the sections on sets and relations in the Glossary of Symbols. Note that for all classes X, X is an ancestor of itself and a descendant of itself.

Postulate 7. The supported instance variables and supported methods of a class are the respective accumulated instance variables and methods defined by itself and its ancestors.

Every class X contains the instance variables <*Class*,"ivdefs"> and <*Class*,"mdefs">.

- <*Class*,"ivdefs"> is a data table that contains the instance variables defined by X.

- <*Class*,"mdefs"> is a method table for the behavior defined by X.

To summarize, the structure of the metaclass *Class* looks like this:
```
{     "class" = Class,
      Class = {     "ivdefs" = ...,
                    "mdefs" = ...,
                    "ivs" = ...,
                    "mtab" = ...,
                    "parents" = ...}
}
```
which means (as we will see) that part of every class looks like the structure above.

Now that the subclass relation has been introduced, inheritance can be defined. In the definition below, the order of the terms on the right sides of the equations is called the **method resolution order.** The method resolution order for class X, denoted by *MRO*(X), is a topological sort[3] of the subgraph of the inheritance hierarchy that contains *ancestors(X)*. We defer a definition of method resolution order to Chapter 4. At this time, it is important to understand that the ancestors of a class are placed in a linear order with which recursive dictionary merge can be used to define inheritance.

Definition 16. Let *X* be a class.

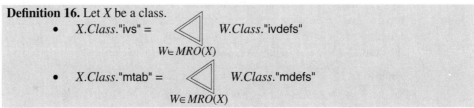

- $X.Class."ivs" = \underset{W \in MRO(X)}{\triangleleft}\ W.Class."ivdefs"$

- $X.Class."mtab" = \underset{W \in MRO(X)}{\triangleleft}\ W.Class."mdefs"$

Definition 16 is the definition of inheritance, and as such is a formalization of Postulate 7.[4] We need to keep in mind that recursive dictionary merge is not commutative; therefore, the order of terms is important.

Definition 17. Let *X* be a class.
- *definedIVs(X)* = { <*c,n*> such that *X.Class*."ivdefs".*c.n* is defined }
- *definedMethods(X)* = { <*c,m*> such that *X.Class*."mdefs".*c.m* is defined }

Definition 16 defines how classes are formed. However, it is more common to talk in the terms of Definition 17. The analogous result is given in the following theorem.

Theorem 2.

$$supportedIVs(X) = \underset{W \in ancestors(X)}{\bigcup}\ definedIVs(W)$$

$$supportedMethods(X) = \underset{W \in ancestors(X)}{\bigcup}\ definedMethods(W)$$

Proof.

Let us consider the proof for *supportedMethods(X)*; the proof for *supportedIVs(X)* is similar. By Definition 13,

   supportedMethods(X) = { <*c,m*> such that *X.Class*."mtab".*c.m* is defined }

By Definition 16,

   supportedMethods(X)

   = { <*c,m*> such that (... $\triangleleft$ *W.Class*."mdefs" $\triangleleft$ ...).*c.m* is defined }

---

3. A topological sort for a partially ordered set is a linear ordering (a list) of the elements of that set such that no element appears in the list ahead of a predecessor in the partial ordering. A partial order may have multiple distinct topological sorts. See Section 1.3 for an example of an algorithm that computes a topological sort.

4. Definition 16 provides for the notion of overriding an instance variable, but this is a notion that we do not explore.

This can be rewritten

supportedMethods(X)

$\qquad$ = { <*c,m*> such that ... or (*W.Class*."mdefs".*c.m* is defined) or ... }

$\qquad$ = ... $\cup$ { <*c,m*> such that *W.Class*."mdefs".*c.m* is defined } $\cup$ ...

$\qquad$ = ... $\cup$ *definedMethods*(W) $\cup$ ...

$\qquad\qquad\qquad\qquad\qquad\qquad\qquad\qquad\qquad\qquad\qquad$ □

In some sense, Theorem 2 is the definition of inheritance common to all object models, where as Definition 16 is our specific version. If one takes this view, Theorem 2 is a correctness result for Definition 16.

Example.

$\qquad$ Let *Book* be a class such that

$\qquad$ *parents*(X) = <*Object*>

$\qquad$ *Book.Class*."ivdefs" = { *Book* = { "title" = "", "authors" = "" }}

$\qquad$ *Book.Class*."mdefs" = { *Book* = { "isAuthor" = isParamSubstringOfAuthors } }

$\qquad$ and suppose that the *Book* class has a subclass, *Biography*, as follows:

$\qquad$ *parents*(*Biography*) = <*Book*>

$\qquad$ *Biography.Class*."ivdefs" = { *Biography* = { "subject" = "" } }

$\qquad$ *Biography.Class*."mdefs" = { *Biography* =

$\qquad\qquad\qquad\qquad\qquad\qquad$ {"isSubject" = stringCompareWithSubject}

$\qquad\qquad\qquad\qquad\qquad$ }

$\qquad$ An instance of *Biography* might appear as

$\qquad$ { "class" = *Biography*,

$\qquad\qquad$ *Book* = { "title" = "Passions of the Mind",

$\qquad\qquad\qquad\qquad$ "authors" = "Stone"}

$\qquad\qquad$ *Biography* = {"subject" = "Sigmund Freud"}

$\qquad$ }

$\qquad\qquad\qquad\qquad\qquad\qquad\qquad\qquad\qquad\qquad\qquad$ □

$\qquad$ The inherited, introduced, and overridden methods and instance variables of a class can be defined as follows.

Definition 18.

- *inheritedMethods*(X) = $\bigcup\limits_{W \in strictAncestors(X)} definedMethods(W)$

- *inheritedIVs*(X) = $\bigcup\limits_{W \in strictAncestors(X)} definedIVs(W)$

- *introducedIVs*(X) = *definedIVs*(X) - *inheritedIVs*(X)

- *introducedMethods*(X) = *definedMethods*(X) - *inheritedMethods*(X)

- *overriddenIVs*(X) = *definedIVs*(X) $\cap$ *inheritedIVs*(X)

- *overriddenMethods*(X) = *definedMethods*(X) $\cap$ *inheritedMethods*(X)

Overriding a method means changing the inherited implementation (that is, the code pointer associated with the method). In this model, overriding an instance variable means changing the value with which it is initialized. Although defined for the sake of completeness in Definition 16, overriding an instance variable is not used anywhere in this book. We formally close off this possibility with the requirement: a class only introduces instance variables — that is, *overriddenIVs*(X)=$\varnothing$ for all $X \in C$.

Example.

> Consider the class *Autobiography*, a subclass of *Biography* (defined above). Suppose
>
> *Autobiography.Class*."mdefs"
>
> > = { *Biography* = {"isSubject" = stringCompareWithAuthors} }
>
> This specifies that the method <*Biography*,"isSubject"> uses the code pointer stringCompareWithAuthors instead of using stringCompareWithSubject. From the naming of the code pointers, we can infer that for an instance of *Autobiography*, the subject instance variable is not used, which forces the subject and the author to be the same.

$\square$

Now that inheritance has been defined, we can best explain why instance variables and methods are defined to be pairs of the form <class reference, name> rather than just plain names. By qualifying the name with the class reference, each class is given a separate name space in which to introduce new instance variables and new methods. Encapsulation makes this a natural choice for instance variables. As with instance variables, we consider the purpose of a method to be determined by its introducing class. Thus, if two classes each introduce a method that has the same name, we consider these to be different, unrelated methods. They may expect different arguments and have entirely different semantics. Including the introducing class reference in our definition of method ensures that there are no accidental conflicts, and allows programmers to specify unambiguously what methods they intend to invoke.

2.6   The Top of the Inheritance Hierarchy

Our inheritance hierarchy has at its top a single class named *Object*; it is an instance of *Class*, *Class* is a subclass of *Object*, and *Object* has no parents. That is, we require a structure such as that shown in Figure 2-8. All usable classes are descendants of *Object*. Therefore, all objects respond to any method introduced by *Object*. There is no postulate for introducing *Object*, because its existence is not a fundamental requirement of class-based object-oriented programming. Object models can be designed that do not have a single class at the top of the inheritance hierarchy. It is convenient to have a place to put methods to which all objects respond.

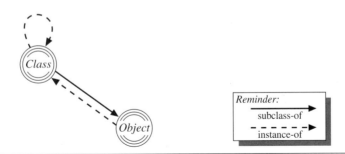

Figure 2-8. A minimal environment with the class *Object* added.

When first seen, Figure 2-8 makes everyone uncomfortable because in elementary school we are all taught that circular definitions are bad. However, as programmers, we use recursion and simultaneous linear equations, which are both circular definitions. Indeed, as we see in the next section, Figure 2-8 dictates a set of equations to which the initial environment must adhere.

2.7   An Initial Environment

In our object model, an initial environment comes into existence, and then, as the result of method invocations on its objects, the environment evolves until it is destroyed. This is illustrated in Figure 2-9. An **invariant** of the environment is a condition that is true when no method introduced by *Class* or *Object* is executing. For example, in the previous section, we required that the defined instance variables of a class not be overrides. This is an example of an invariant that can be formally stated as follows.

Invariant. For all $X \in$ **C,** $overriddenIVs(X) = \varnothing$.

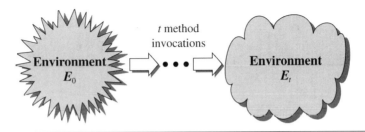

Figure 2-9. The evolution of the environment.

Figure 2-8 specifies that for the initial environment,

Class."class" = *Class*
Object."class" = *Class*
Class.Class."parents" = *<Object>*
Object.Class."parents" = *<>*

In addition, Figure 2-8 and Definition 16 lead to the following set of equations that govern the initial environment.

Class.Class."mtab" = *Class.Class*."mdefs" ◁ *Object.Class*."mdefs"
Object.Class."mtab" = *Object.Class*."mdefs"
Class.Class."ivs" = *Class.Class*."ivdefs" ◁ *Object.Class*."ivdefs"
Object.Class."ivs" = *Object.Class*."ivdefs"

These equations tell us that the values of

Class.Class."mdefs"
Object.Class."mdefs"
Object.Class."ivdefs"

are independent variables. With respect to *Class.Class*."ivdefs" there are two more equations to take into consideration:

containedIVs(*Class*) = *supportedIVs*(*class*(*Class*))
containedIVs(*Object*) = *supportedIVs*(*class*(*Object*))

which are consequences of Definition 10.

Figure 2-10 depicts the objects *Class* and *Object* and a minimal set of initial values that satisfy the equations above. Note that the data tables of both *Class* and *Object* have the instance variables that are in the template of *Class* — that is, *Class.Class*."ivs". As our presentation progresses, this figure evolves by populating the two mdefs instance variables above with methods.

Figure 2-10 illustrates an interesting fact. Because the value of *<Class*,"ivdefs"> in *Object* is empty, the only space overhead associated with all objects is the class slot.

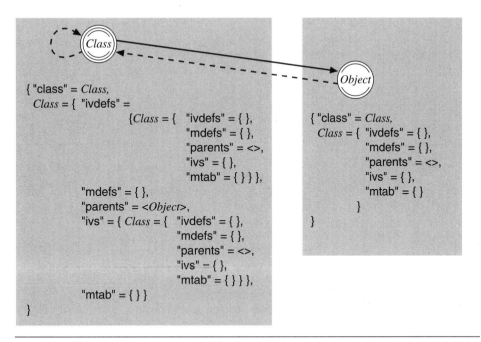

Figure 2-10. Initial environment with instance variables of *Class* and *Object*.

2.8 Creating Objects

Postulate 8. There exists a method that creates new objects as instances of its target.

Let us carry the process of setting up the initial environment one step further by adding one method, the method that creates new instances of a class.

Definition 19. There is a method named makeInstance in *definedMethods*(*Class*) that when invoked on a class *X* adds a new object to the environment of the form
$$\{\text{"class"}=X\} \lhd X.Class.\text{"ivs"}$$

Postulate 4 specifies instance creation. Figure 2-11 shows the initial environment where *Class* binds the name makeInstance to a code pointer newImpl, which implements the method for creating objects.

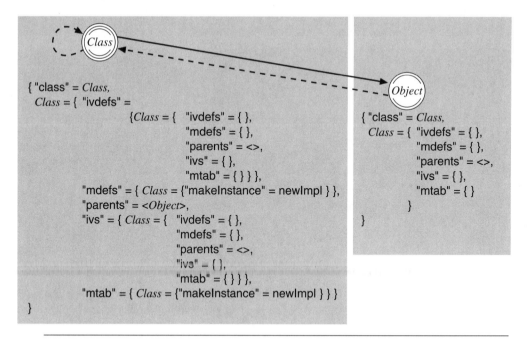

```
{ "class" = Class,
  Class = { "ivdefs" =
                {Class = {  "ivdefs" = { },
                            "mdefs" = { },
                            "parents" = <>,
                            "ivs" = { },
                            "mtab" = { } } },
            "mdefs" = { Class = {"makeInstance" = newImpl } },
            "parents" = <Object>,
            "ivs" = { Class = {  "ivdefs" = { },
                                 "mdefs" = { },
                                 "parents" = <>,
                                 "ivs" = { },
                                 "mtab" = { } } },
            "mtab" = { Class = {"makeInstance" = newImpl } } }
}
```

```
{ "class" = Class,
  Class = { "ivdefs" = { },
            "mdefs" = { },
            "parents" = <>,
            "ivs" = { },
            "mtab" = { }
          }
}
```

Figure 2-11. Initial environment with makeInstance added to mdefs of *Class*.

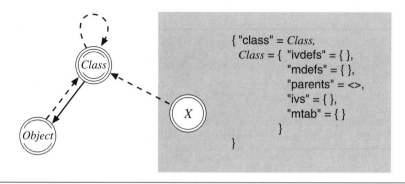

```
{ "class" = Class,
  Class = { "ivdefs" = { },
            "mdefs" = { },
            "parents" = <>,
            "ivs" = { },
            "mtab" = { }
          }
}
```

Figure 2-12. An instance of *Class*.

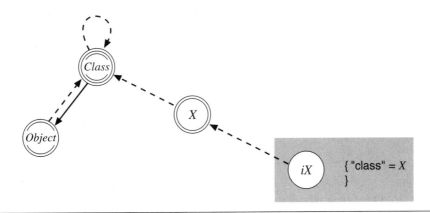

Figure 2-13. An instance of *X*.

The class *Class* introduces makeInstance. If the method named makeInstance is invoked on *Class*, the result is a class object, as depicted in Figure 2-12. Because

$$Object.Class."ivdefs" = \{\,\}$$

no object has a key that corresponds to instance variables introduced by *Object* (that is, the expression *iX.Object* is meaningless for any object *iX*).

Note that *X* (Figure 2-12) also responds to <*Class*,"makeInstance">, because it is an instance of *Class*. So invoking makeInstance on *X* yields an ordinary object, as depicted in Figure 2-13. The object *iX* is not a class, and its class *X* does not support the <*Class*,"makeInstance"> method; so *iX* cannot be used to create other objects.

The next two theorems yield interesting insights about the object model. Theorem 3 states that all classes create objects. Theorem 4 states that any descendant of *Class* is a metaclass.

Theorem 3. If *X isA Class*, then *X* responds to <*Class*,"makeInstance">.

Proof.　　*X isA Class*
　　　　　implies *class(X) isDescendantOf Class*　　　　　　　　(by Definition 15)
　　　　　implies *supportedMethods(Class)* ⊆ *respondsTo(X)*　　(by Theorem 2)
　　　　　<*Class*,"makeInstance"> ∈ *supportedMethods(Class)*　(by Definition 19)
　　　　　Therefore, <*Class*,"makeInstance"> ∈ *respondsTo(X)*

　　　　　　　　　　　　　　　　　　　　　　　　　　　　　　□

Theorem 4. Let $X \in C$. If X *isDescendantOf Class*, then $X \in M$. (That is, if a class is a descendant of *Class*, the class is a metaclass.)

Proof.

> If X *isDescendantOf Class*, for all instances Y of X, Y *isA Class*. By Definition 5, $X \in M$.
>
> $\square$

Theorem 4 prescribes how new metaclasses are created — that is, new metaclasses are created by subclassing *Class*. This becomes important later, when new metaclasses are created that isolate object properties for reuse.

2.9 Drawing Class Structures

An object structure such as the one shown in Figure 2-11 contains much redundancy. For example, there is a slot giving the class of the object and a dashed arrow with the same meaning. We streamline the drawing by removing the redundancy and, when necessary, writing the values of instance variables inside the object. An expanded rationale for these drawing conventions is given in Appendix C.

Example.

> Assuming that the class *Book* is a subclass of *Object*, the book object *iX*
> $\{$ "class" = *Book*,
>   *Book* = $\{$ "title" = "Structured Programming",
>   "authors" = "Dahl, Dijkstra, and Hoare"$\}$
>
> $\}$
> can be drawn as follows:

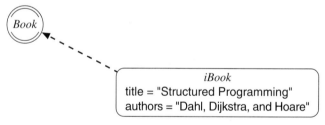

When there is no ambiguity, the name of an instance variable is not qualified by its introducing class. Note that the quotation marks around the variable name are not necessary; these diagrams are a graphical syntax in which the placement of a name can imply that it is quoted.

$\square$

Now that we have shown how instance variables are written inside an object, let us consider the special instance variable <*Class*,"ivs">. This instance variable of a class is special because it is the template for the creation of an object. So when drawing a class object, ivs has the special distinction of being drawn as an object inside the class object. Inside this boundary, we write the introduced instance variable names. Outside the boundary, we write the introduced method names and the overridden methods (the implication of this wording is that the overridden methods are fully qualified).

Example.

The class *Book* is drawn as follows. Only the introduced instance variables are displayed, because inherited instance variables are displayed in the introducing ancestor.

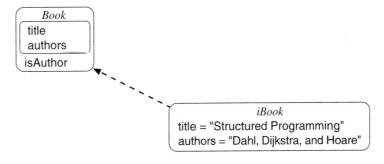

To summarize, a class object is drawn as follows:

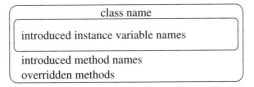

When a metaclass object is drawn, an empty inner shape is drawn inside the ivs shape. This represents the value of <*Class*,"ivs"> inherited from *Class*, which contains an empty ivs template for class objects. In other words, the inner shape represents the ivs template within the ivs values of the metaclass. To summarize, a metaclass is drawn as follows.

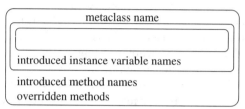

With this new convention, Figure 2-11 can be redrawn as we have done in Figure 2-14. Note that Figure 2-14 is not equivalent to Figure 2-11 and is not a complete specification, because of the information that is not included (for example, code pointers for method implementations).

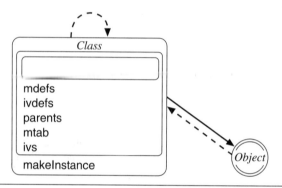

Figure 2-14. The initial environment as minimally drawn.

2.10 Metaobject Protocols

An ordinary class is a **metaobject** because it contains a description of its instances (ordinary objects). A metaclass is also a metaobject, but because a metaclass describes a class, the term "metaobject" is almost never used when talking about a metaclass. The interface to the metaobjects is called the **metaobject protocol.** In our model, the set of methods in *Class.Class.*"mtab" embodies this interface. Note that our metaobject protocol therefore includes the methods introduced by *Object*. Classes are not the only kind of metaobject, nor is it necessary that all of the metaobject protocol consist of methods (in programming systems such as C++, parts can be ordinary functions). If more information about method implementation were needed than mere code pointers, we could have chosen to have metaobjects for methods, too (see [69] for a metaobject protocol that does this).

There is an area of computer science called **reflection,** which is closely related to object models such as the one we have just developed. Generally, reflection [116] is an operation that a program P_0 executes and that turns the program and its current state into a data structure and turns execution over to another program P_1. The program P_1 can examine and change P_0, or it can reflect and turn execution over to P_2, or it can turn control back to P_0, which is called **reification.** One requirement of reflection is that P_i's program be expressible as data structures in P_{i+1}'s programming language. This brief description is meant only to establish the relationship between that area and our object model. When one gets the class of an object, it is similar to reflection, because one then has a representation of the structure of the object and its behavior. Once the method to get the class of an object is introduced, our metaobject protocol becomes reflective.

Postulate 9. There is an operation for retrieving the class of an object.

2.11 Summary

This chapter has established a set of postulates (Table 2-1) that characterize all reflective class-based object-oriented models, which we have shortened to reflective class-based models. In addition, we have produced a concrete realization of these postulates on which the rest of the book depends.

Table 2-1. Summary of Postulates for Reflective Class-Based Models

Postulate 1. Each member of the nonempty, finite set of objects is identified by a value called an object reference.

Postulate 2. Every object has a uniquely associated entity called a class.

Postulate 3. Every class is an object.

Postulate 4. The data table of an object is determined by its class.

Postulate 5. The methods to which an object responds are determined by its class.

Postulate 6. There is a relation on the set of classes called the inheritance graph.

Postulate 7. The supported instance variables and supported methods of a class are the respective accumulated instance variables and methods defined by itself and its ancestors.

Postulate 8. There exists a method that creates new objects as instances of its target.

Postulate 9. There is an operation for retrieving the class of an object.

This completes the first phase of our exposition plan. We have defined the static aspects of our object model, and we have placed sufficient data in the objects of the environment to compute the properties that we will need in subsequent chapters to present, and later use, our metaobject protocol. We have not strived for completeness in doing so — that is, not all properties of the model have been made intrinsic, but only those that are required for putting metaclasses to work.

2.12 Exercises

2.1   If class X has the value

$$\{ \quad \text{"class"} = Class,$$
$$Class = \{ \quad \text{"parents"} = < Object >,$$
$$\text{"ivdefs"} = \{ X = \{ \text{"xvar"} = 0 \} \},$$
$$\text{"ivs"} = \{ \quad X = \{ \text{"xvar"} = 0 \} \},$$
$$\text{"mdefs"} = \{ X = \{ \text{"xmethod"} = \text{xcodePtr} \} \},$$
$$\text{"mtab"} = \{ X = \{ \text{"xmethod"} = \text{xcodePtr} \} \}$$
$$\}$$
$$\}$$

and class Y has the value

$$\{ \quad \text{"class"} = Class,$$
$$Class = \{ \quad \text{"parents"} = < Object >,$$
$$\text{"ivdefs"} = \{ Y = \{ \text{"yvar"} = 0 \} \},$$
$$\text{"ivs"} = \{ Y = \{ \text{"yvar"} = 0 \} \},$$
$$\text{"mdefs"} = \{ Y = \{ \text{"ymethod"} = \text{ycodePtr} \} \},$$
$$\text{"mtab"} = \{ Y = \{ \text{"ymethod"} = \text{ycodePtr} \} \}$$
$$\}$$
$$\}$$

what is the value of the class Z that is an instance of *Class* and a subclass of both X and Y? (Hint: use Definition 16.)

2.2   Prove:
$$supportedMethods(X) = definedMethods(X) \cup \bigcup_{P \in parents(X)} supportedMethods(P)$$

$$supportedIVs(X) = definedIVs(X) \cup \bigcup_{P \in parents(X)} supportedIVs(P)$$

2.3   Prove that the converse of Theorem 4 holds if one assumes that the only valid objects are created by $<Class,$makeInstance$>$.

2.4   Prove
           For all $X \in \boldsymbol{C}$, *overriddenIVs*$(X) = \varnothing$
           from the invariant
           For all $X \in \boldsymbol{C}$, $\alpha(\text{*definedIVs*}(X)) = \{X\}$.

2.5   Write a program for creating the initial environment.

2.6   The environment is such that all objects respond to the methods introduced by *Object* and
           all classes respond to the methods introduced by *Class*. However, there are no methods to
           which only metaclasses respond. Redesign the environment so that there are methods to
           which only metaclasses respond.

2.7   Consider the following environment.

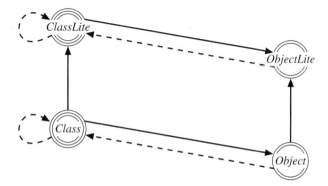

           The purpose of such an initial environment is to allow one to implement a submodel of our
           model. That is, a subset of the methods defined for *Class* could be moved to *ClassLite*. A
           similar action could be taken for *Object*. Evaluate this design. That is, if a subset of the
           methods of *Class* is moved to *ClassLite* and a subset of the methods of *Object* is moved to
           ObjectLite, what properties of the model remain invariant and what properties have
           changed? In addition, are there any constraints on the subsets of methods that are moved?

2.8   The Java initial environment [65] looks like our initial environment (Figure 2-8). Java has
           the notion of an interface. It uses instances of its class Class to represent interfaces at
           runtime. Of course, Java's class Class introduces the method newInstance, which creates
           objects. Because one cannot make instances of an interface, Java has to turn off
           newInstance for interfaces. Structure an initial environment that has *Object, Class,
           Interface*, and possibly others such that interfaces do not respond to makeInstance.

2.9   We asserted that the inheritance graph is a directed acyclic graph. Under what conditions
           is it possible to have cycles in the inheritance graph and still adhere to Definition 16?

2.10   Formalize the postulates of reflective class-based models (Table 2-1).

2.11   Under what conditions can the converse of Theorem 3 be proved?

Chapter 3
Inheritance of Metaclass Constraints

All of the features of the object model developed in Chapter 2 have counterparts in the object models implicit in many of today's programming languages. In this chapter, we add the property that makes our object model unique: the metaclass for a class must be a descendant of the metaclass for each of its parents. The effect of this property is that the metaclass for a parent is a constraint that is inherited by its descendants. This property is an additional postulate on the class hierarchy and is so important that we devote an entire chapter to its explanation and justification.

3.1 Fundamental Guarantee of Object-Oriented Programming

In object-oriented programming, any attempt to invoke a method on an instance of X not in *supportedMethods*(X) is called a **method resolution failure.** The following guarantee is required of object-oriented programming systems.

> If class Y is a descendant of X, then code that executes without method resolution failure on instances of X should also execute without method resolution failure on instances of Y.

This guarantee (which is also called the principle of substitutivity [117]) enables the construction of generic code by object-oriented programmers. Often this guarantee is referred to as **polymorphism.** There are, of course, many object-oriented programming systems, each with a different distinct notion of polymorphism. But this guarantee, as illustrated in Figure 3-1, lies at the heart of all of these object-oriented programming systems, because it matches the intuitive desire that the class hierarchy be an "is a" hierarchy.

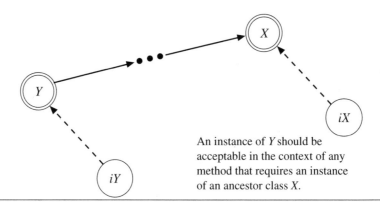

An instance of Y should be acceptable in the context of any method that requires an instance of an ancestor class X.

Figure 3-1. The fundamental guarantee — part 1.

The semantics of inheritance given in Chapter 2 guarantees that any method supported by X in Figure 3-1 is also supported by Y. However, this alone is not enough for our model to support the fundamental guarantee of object-oriented programming, because our model allows the implementation of a method for accessing the class of an object and then invoking methods on this class (that is, methods supported by the metaclass of the object). As a result, to support the fundamental guarantee in the context of Figure 3-1, it is necessary to ensure that the metaclass for Y inherits from the metaclass for X, as shown in Figure 3-2. Not doing this has the consequence described in the next section.

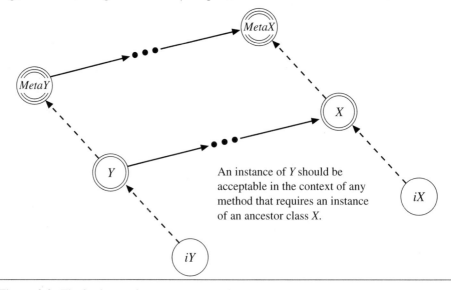

An instance of Y should be acceptable in the context of any method that requires an instance of an ancestor class X.

Figure 3-2. The fundamental guarantee — part 2.

3.2 Metaclass Incompatibility

Let us look at an example of the unconstrained use of metaclasses to see how things can go wrong. Consider the situation in Figure 3-3. Suppose the method named foo has the following implementation, which we express in C++-like syntax:

```
X::foo()
{    Class* classObject;
     classObject = getClass(this);
     classObject->MX::bar();
}
```

where getClass is a function of the metaobject protocol that computes the class of an object and the fourth line is a method invocation in our object model (that is, the method <*MX*,"bar"> is resolved against the method table of the target object).

The method foo can be invoked successfully on *iX* (an instance of *X*). The class *X* supports foo; so foo begins execution. The assignment command sets a local variable to the object reference of the class object. The last line invokes bar on the class object. This succeeds because the class *X* responds to bar (because its metaclass *MX* introduces bar). We are not concerned with what bar does, but only that it is introduced by *MX*.

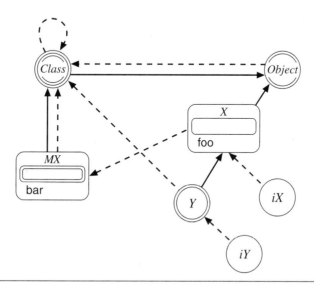

Figure 3-3. Metaclass incompatibility.

However, the situation in Figure 3-3 is far different in the case of invoking foo on *iY* (an instance of *Y*). The method foo cannot successfully execute on *iY*, because its class does not respond to the method bar (because its class, *Class*, does not support bar). This situation was first addressed by Nicolas Graube [52] and we refer to such a situation as a **metaclass incompatibility.** Put simply, the metaclass for *Y* (which is *Class*) is not compatible with the requirements placed on *Y*'s metaclass by the parent of *Y*. The problem that is addressed in this chapter is attainment of a programming model in which metaclass incompatibilities do not arise.

Clearly, in Figure 3-3, the metaclass for *Y* should be *MX*. In general, however, the choice of an appropriate metaclass is not so simple. Sometimes one has to create an appropriate metaclass; we refer to this process as **deriving a metaclass.** Another example in which derivation of a new metaclass is necessary is provided in Figure 3-4. Here, a new class *Y* is being created using multiple inheritance from two other classes, *W* and *X*, whose classes are, respectively, *MW* and *MX*. The appropriate choice of a metaclass for *Y* is unclear. Neither *MW* nor *MX* is appropriate, because the metaclass for *Y* must have the interfaces of both *MW* and *MX*.

The most general choice for the metaclass for *Y* in Figure 3-4 is *DerivedMetaY*, which is the multiple inheritance join of the metaclasses of *W* and *X*, as shown in Figure 3-5.

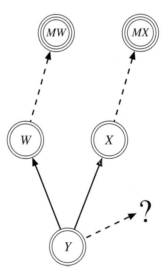

Figure 3-4. Of what metaclass should *Y* be an instance?

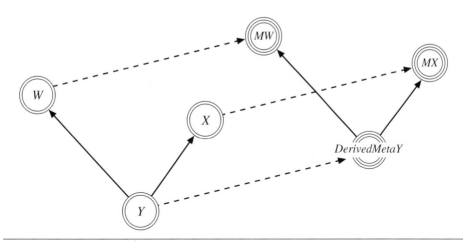

Figure 3-5. The solution: *Y*'s metaclass can be derived from the metaclasses for *W* and *X*.

It is interesting to note the conditions under which metaclass incompatibility can arise. Figure 3-4 shows how a metaclass incompatibility can arise in the case of multiple inheritance models. In addition, some programming languages allow the class declarations to specify a metaclass: this is called an **explicit metaclass** declaration. In CLOS, for example, one can write

```
(defclass <name> ( <parent-list> )
      ...
           (:metaclass <explicit-metaclass-name>)
      ...
)
```

or, in the interface definition language of IBM's SOMobjects Toolkit, one can write

```
interface <name> : <parent-list> {
      ...
      <method-declarations>
      ...
      metaclass = <explicit-metaclass-name>;
      ...
};
```

An important issue in the design of such languages is the meaning of the explicit metaclass declaration. One choice is to treat the declaration as an imperative — that is, the metaclass for the declared class is the explicit metaclass. The implication of this choice is that metaclass incompatibilities are designed into the language. We prefer to design metaclass incompatibilities out of programming languages. For this reason, an explicit metaclass should be treated as an additional constraint. This also leaves open the possibility that class declarations may have multiple explicit metaclasses in some yet-to-be-designed programming language. In the case of single-inheritance models, metaclass incompatibilities can arise, too, if explicit metaclass declarations are allowed.

The metaclass incompatibility problem must be solved by all class-based models.

- C++ solves the metaclass incompatibility problem by not having metaclasses.
- Java solves the problem by not allowing its class *Class* to be subclassed; Java has a single metaclass *Class*, of which all classes are instances.
- Smalltalk solves it by not having explicit metaclasses and by not allowing multiple inheritance.
- CLOS solves the problem by detecting the possibility of a metaclass incompatibility at runtime and raising an exception.

Only by deriving the appropriate metaclass, as is done in our model, is the metaclass incompatibility problem solved without further constraining the programmer.

3.3 Metaclass Constraints

As explained above, to ensure the fundamental guarantee (and eliminate metaclass incompatibilities) within an object-oriented programming system, it is necessary for the environment to adhere to the following postulate.

Postulate 10.
   The metaclass for a class must be equal to or a descendant
   of the metaclass for each of its parents
or, equivalently,[1]
   If *X isAncestorOf Y*, then *class*(*X*) *isAncestorOf class*(*Y*).

The effect of this postulate is that when multiple inheritance is used to create a new class, the metaclass for each parent becomes a constraint on the metaclass for that new class. The ten postulates of this book characterize a **monotonic reflective class-based model,** because the function *class* is monotonic.[2]

---

1. Reminder: The relation *isAncestorOf* is reflexive.

2. Let P and Q be ordered sets. A function $f:P{\rightarrow}Q$ is monotonic, if $x{\le}y$ in P implies $f(x){\le}f(y)$ in Q. In our case, both P and Q are the set of classes C ordered by the inheritance graph.

In our model, when necessary, a new metaclass can be created to satisfy the constraints imposed by parent classes and explicit metaclass declarations; we call this a **derived metaclass** because a multiple-inheritance class derivation is used to solve the constraints. The general approach to satisfying the metaclass constraints is illustrated in Figure 3-6. Note that the explicit metaclasses are placed at the beginning of the parent list of the derived metaclass. This reflects the view that because the programmer explicitly declared the metaclass constraint, it is more important.

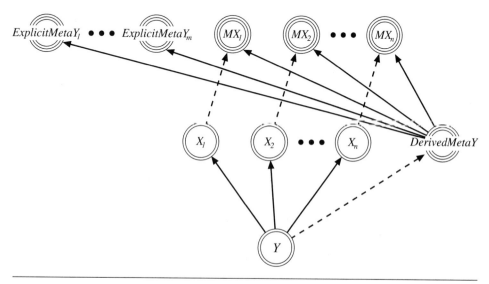

Figure 3-6. A general solution for metaclass compatibility.

Example.

Suppose we have classes *PersistentSpreadSheet* and *ThreadSafeSpreadSheet* and we want to create a subclass of both — that is, a *PersistentThreadSafeSpreadSheet*. Before the class *PersistentThreadSafeSpreadSheet* can be instantiated, an appropriate metaclass must be created as is shown in Figure 3-7. Note that neither *Persistent* nor *ThreadSafe* is appropriate.

□

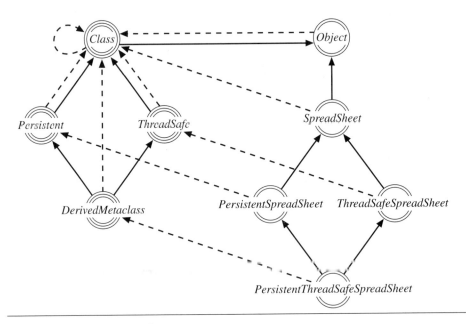

Figure 3-7. Deriving a metaclass.

Now let us go back to Figure 3-6, because one detail is missing from that figure. That detail is the class of *DerivedMetaY*. The class of *DerivedMetaY* must also adhere to Postulate 10. This leads to a repeated process, as depicted in Figure 3-8. This process must stop, because there are a bounded number of "instance of" links to *Class* and because *Class* is an instance of itself. So, if the constraint-satisfying process does not stop sooner, it must surely stop with *Class* as the appropriate metaclass. The process can stop with a solution that is a strict descendant of *Class*, if at any level all of the constraints are the same. An algorithm to implement this process is given as part of our metaobject protocol in Chapter 6.

In Chapter 6, the metaobject protocol for our object model is defined such that metaclass constraints are always satisfied when new classes are constructed. This is done by providing a method for computing derived metaclasses and by refusing to construct classes whose metaclasses fail to satisfy the necessary constraints.

By specifying that an implementation of our object model must solve the metaclass constraints and automatically create an appropriate metaclass, a new facility is added to object-oriented programming: **inheritance of metaclass constraints.** Normally, classes inherit methods and instance variables. In our model, metaclass constraints are also inherited. This is a direct consequence of Postulate 10.

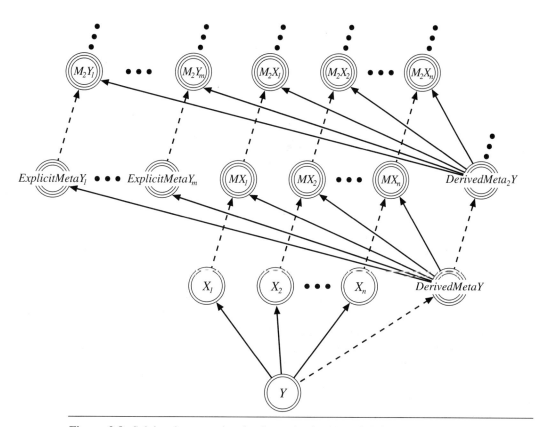

Figure 3-8. Solving the constraints for the appropriate metaclass is recursive.

3.4 Importance of Inheriting Metaclass Constraints

Our approach has a very important consequence. It allows explicit metaclasses to capture object properties without associating them with any particular class. Examples of such metaclasses are *Persistent* and *ThreadSafe*; let us assume that neither is an ancestor of the other. A useful way to view such metaclasses is that they are mappings of the set of class objects into itself. That is, if *SpreadSheet* is a class, then so is *Persistent*(*SpreadSheet*); let us view such an expression as an abstraction for the syntax in any programming language that states "declare a class that has *SpreadSheet* as a parent and *Persistent* as an explicit metaclass." Consider the situation in Figure 3-9, where

   PersistentSpreadSheet = *Persistent*(*SpreadSheet*)

Now consider

   ThreadSafePersistentSpreadSheet = *ThreadSafe*(*PersistentSpreadSheet*)

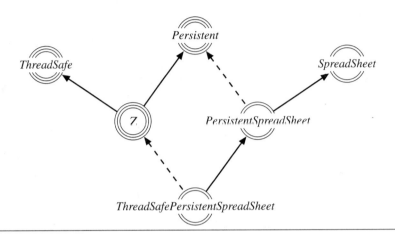

Figure 3-9. Z must be the class that is both *ThreadSafe* and *Persistent*.

and ask what must be true of its metaclass Z. By our Postulate 10, Z must be a descendant of *Persistent*. This means that Z cannot be the metaclass *ThreadSafe*. On the other hand, Z must be able to impart the thread-safe property to its instances (otherwise, the explicit metaclass declaration has no meaning). Inheritance is the most direct way for Z to obtain the ability to impart a property, and so we conclude that Z must be a descendant of *ThreadSafe*. If Z is a descendant of both *ThreadSafe* and *Persistent* and there are no other considerations to be taken into account, the simplest solution is to conclude that Z must be equivalent to the join of *ThreadSafe* and *Persistent*.

This informal argument makes a very strong claim: in models in which metaclass constraints are inherited, composition of metaclasses (viewed as mappings of classes into classes) is equivalent to the multiple-inheritance join of the metaclasses.

Thus, we have been led from a simple desire (elimination of metaclass incompatibilities) to an important result: the ability to equate composition of properties expressed as metaclasses with multiple inheritance in the metaclass hierarchy. If $\sqcup$ represents multiple-inheritance join, then

$$F(\,G(X)\,) = (F \sqcup G)(X)$$

where X is an arbitrary class and F and G are arbitrary metaclasses. (We have been somewhat cavalier in our use of symbols such as F and G to denote both metaclass objects and metaclass mappings. Formalization is left for the future.)

A similar argument yields another desirable result:

$$(F \sqcup G)(X) = F(X) \sqcup G(X)$$

— that is, application of metaclass mappings distributes over the join operation.

3.5   From the Programmer's Point of View

Now let us examine what inheritance of the metaclass constraint means to programmers Aaron (the programmer of class *A*) and Beth (the programmer of class *B*, which is a subclass of *A*).

Consider the example depicted in Figure 3-10, where Beth wishes to create class *B* as a single-inheritance subclass of *A* (which is an instance of the metaclass *F*). Without inheritance of the metaclass constraint, Beth is faced with the problem of determining the metaclass for *B*.

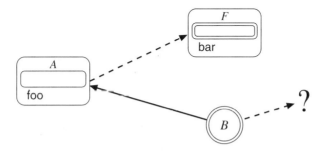

Figure 3-10. Programmer convenience example.

In this example, things are simple as a result of the absence of multiple inheritance and an explicit metaclass for *B*. The right answer is *F*. Thus, it might not be too unreasonable in this case to require this information from Beth. However, when multiple inheritance and explicit metaclasses are available, arriving at the right answer is not as simple as in Smalltalk (as we have seen, the general solution requires recursion to determine the class of the metaclass, and the class of the metaclass's class, and so on [30]). Thus, from the standpoint of programmer convenience, it is even more important to provide an automatic solution as part of the semantics of subclassing.

Let us pursue this idea further by considering what happens if Beth wishes *B* objects to have a property that is implemented by the explicit metaclass *G* (see Figure 3-11). We argued above that a composition of *G* with *F* is necessary in this case. But is this really necessary? Suppose Beth wishes to avoid the overhead of composing *G* and *F*. What must she know to do so safely? Among other things, she must know that no method of *A* is implemented reflectively, in terms of any method of *F* — but this is information that Beth should not have in general; subclasses should not need to know how methods of ancestors are implemented. Moreover, as we have explained, our interest is in allowing inheritance of reflective code. Thus, Beth must compose *G* and *F*. It is the only safe thing to do when reflective code can be used to implement methods.

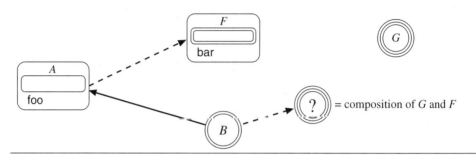

Figure 3-11. Programmer needs to include property implemented by *G*.

Therefore, from Beth's point of view (as the programmer of *B*), the programming system should provide inheritance of metaclass constraints and automatic composition. The composition needs to be done, it can be done automatically, and, because of the complexity of the solution in general, there seems nothing to gain and much to lose if the programmer is required to do it explicitly.

Now let us consider Aaron's point of view. Suppose Aaron is considering a change in *A*. Figure 3-12 depicts a change in which *A* is to be reimplemented with the explicit metaclass *F'*, a new subclass of *F*. If inheritance of metaclass constraints is not included in the semantics of subclassing, Aaron cannot make this change, because *B* (and all other existing descendants of *A*) may then suffer from metaclass incompatibility.

Ultimately, the implications of this (for maintaining consistency within class libraries and between different class libraries) are simply unacceptable. One reason why object-oriented programming is successful is that it makes sense in terms of its real-world benefits for software engineering. Correctness-perserving changes in the implementation of an ancestor class must not require explicit source changes in the declaration of descendant classes. This topic is further addressed in Chapter 11, where we enumerate the safe transformations that must be supported. Specifically, a programmer should be able to migrate the metaclass for a class downward in the metaclass inheritance hierarchy. Asserting that this transformation must preserve the correctness of descendants implies that the metaclass constraint must be inherited. That is, on the right side of Figure 3-12, the programming environment must make *F'* the metaclass for *B* when that class object is created.

Note that we have been giving the impression that Aaron and Beth are different people, but the problems presented here are just as troublesome if there is only one person involved. Although our examples have shown *B* to be a direct subclass of *A*, all of these problems are still present when *B* is some distant descendant of *A*. Thus, given enough distance between the classes and enough time between their development, no programmer can be expected to manage the problem of inferring that the metaclass for *B* needs to be changed.

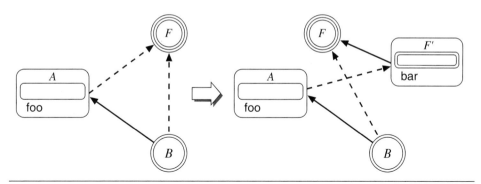

Figure 3-12. Evolution of a class.

Solving the metaclass constraints is a burden too complex, tedious, and error prone to place on programmers, especially because the solution is so easily calculated by a computer. If you are not yet convinced, let us consider a real example. Figure 3-13 shows an abstraction of the classes required to re-create a traced proxy class for the *SpreadSheet* class in the IBM SOMobjects Toolkit (Version 2.1). The figure separates what is part of the toolkit from what the user of the toolkit writes, and uses light-colored thick lines to highlight those portions of the derivation that result from use of derived metaclasses. In a programming system that enforces Postulate 10 by deriving appropriate metaclasses automatically, the user needs to write only three lines of code, which in the SOMobjects Toolkit happen to look like this:

```
interface TracedProxyForSpreadSheet : ProxyForObject, SpreadSheet {
    metaclass = Traced;
};
```

Now imagine the user's problem in a system where metaclass declarations are treated as imperatives. In this case, the user has to understand all of the toolkit portion of Figure 3-13 in order to compute the metaclass for *TracedProxyForSpreadSheet* (which in turn returns its metaclass to be constructed). This is an arduous task, which is complicated by the fact that some metaclasses are instances of other metaclasses.

It is too early in our presentation to show a more concrete example of how complex it can be to solve the metaclass constraints, but the message should be clear. When a class object is being created, the process of finding an appropriate metaclass (one that satisfies all the inherited constraints) is both complex and computable. This makes the process ideal for incorporation into a metaobject protocol.

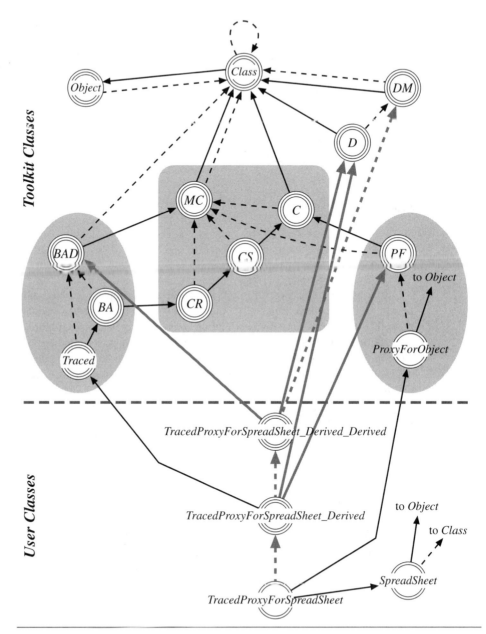

Figure 3-13. The complexity of creating a traced proxy for *SpreadSheet*.

3.6 Epistemological Argument for Inheritance of Metaclass Constraints

In addition to its support for encapsulation and code reuse, an important contribution of object-oriented programming to software engineering is that object-oriented programming is a synthesis of programming and knowledge representation. In standard object-oriented programming, a class corresponds to a noun representing a set of objects with some common properties. The introduction of the abstractions from knowledge representation (such as inheritance of object properties) into programming languages greatly narrows the gaps between problem analysis and software implementation, between customer and software provider, and between model and program.

Roughly speaking, in the 1950s programming language design was concerned with the modeling of verbs (in COBOL, procedures are called "verbs"). In the 1970s, the concern shifted to the modeling of nouns (with the invention of abstract data types and object-oriented programming). Now, based on our experience with IBM SOMobjects Toolkit, we perceive the possibility of further strengthening the connection with knowledge representation by using metaclasses to model adjectives.

A metaclass can be used to modify a class so as to impart a property to its objects (instances). Consider the situation depicted in Figure 3-14. The metaclass illustrated here modifies a class object to give its instances a thread-safe property. This is most easily done using the Before/After Metaclasses described in Chapter 8, but the use of Before/After Metaclasses is not necessary to our argument — it just grounds our claim that such metaclasses can be built. Continuing with Figure 3-14, we ask what is X? The answer is that X is the class of thread-safe spreadsheets.

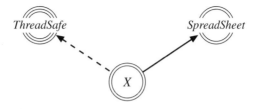

Figure 3-14. Modifying a class with a metaclass.

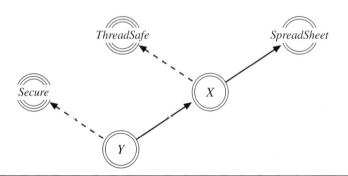

Figure 3-15. Implicitly composed metaclasses.

Now let us take this one step further. Consider Figure 3-15 and ask what is Y? If X is the class of thread-safe spreadsheets, then Y must be the class of secure, thread safe spreadsheets. This argument declares that if the classes and their instances are to form a proper "is a" hierarchy, an instance of Y must be a proper instance of X. This again implies that the metaclass constraint must be inherited. Furthermore, Figure 3-15 may appear to express the desire that Y also have the secure property, but the figure is not properly drawn because the dashed arrow is supposed to represent the actual instance relation (not the explicit metaclass) and we know that Y must be an instance of the composition of *Secure* and *ThreadSafe*.

Let us reexamine the phrase "Y must be the class of secure, thread-safe spreadsheets." This means that instances of Y are secure and thread-safe, where "and" corresponds to a union[3] of properties when we intend that classes represent a set of objects. In class structures, multiple inheritance is used to express such unions. This must also hold on the metaclass level, because metaclasses are classes. Therefore, when metaclasses are composed, it is proper to use multiple inheritance on the metaclasses; in this context, "proper" refers to the viewpoint of knowledge representation. Therefore, Figure 3-16 is the appropriate way to represent that Y is a secure and thread-safe spreadsheet class, where M is the metaclass whose instances are classes that are both secure and thread-safe.

---

3. We are all taught that if $A = \{x | P(x)\}$ and $B = \{x | Q(x)\}$, then $A \cap B = \{x | (P(x) \wedge Q(x))\}$. But if $\{p_0,...,p_n\}$ is a set of predicates each of which is true for all elements of set A and $\{q_0,...,q_m\}$ is a set of predicates each of which is true for all elements of set B, then $\{p_0,...,p_n\} \cup \{q_0,...,q_m\}$ is the set of known predicates each of which is true for all elements of set $A \cap B$.

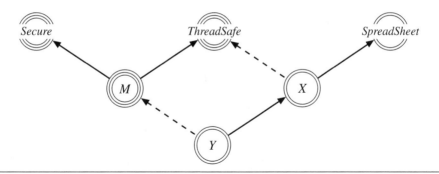

Figure 3-16. Explicit composition of metaclasses.

Not all metaclasses correspond to adjectives; some metaclasses are not meant to be instantiated. But those that impart properties to instances of ordinary classes are normally amenable to being named with adjectives. A minor issue arises here as to whether metaclasses should be named with adjectives alone or with adjectives prepended to the word "*Class*." Using the word "*Class*" at the end of every metaclass distinguishes classes from metaclasses, but using adjectives alone is useful for indicating that the metaclass is intended to be instantiated.

Conversely, not all adjectives make good metaclasses. Inheritance of the metaclass constraint implies that metaclasses should add properties rather than take them away. It is observed in [96] that if one uses a metaclass to implement the "must be abstract" class property (that is, no class instances can exist), inheritance of the metaclass constraint means that the property passes to all descendant classes. Clearly, this is not a useful constraint to be inherited. A preferable alternative (which is presented in Chapter 10) is to confer classes with the inherited ability to determine abstractness individually (on a per-class basis). In other words, one can usefully introduce and inherit a "can be abstract" property, as opposed to a "must be abstract" property.[4]

---

4. In our opinion, inheritance of the metaclass constraint and the use of multiple inheritance as the composition mechanism have such great value (when compared with the alternatives) that the lack of special support for metaclasses that subtract properties seems of little consequence. Certainly there are good examples of the utility of nonmonotonic logic in knowledge representation (particularly as regards exceptions to inheritance of properties) [108,113]. But our feeling is that in the engineering of class hierarchies, the benefits of compositionality (as provided by inheritance of metaclass constraints) outweigh the benefits of nonmonotonic capabilities.

3.7 On Metaclasses That Invoke Instance Methods

Inheritance of metaclass constraints ensures that the interface of the metaclass for a class contains all the methods required by that class. Method invocation also occurs in the other direction. If care is not taken, method resolution failures can occur in this direction, too. For example, consider the situation (from [14]) depicted in Figure 3-17, where bar invokes hook (in order to do so, the call to bar must acquire the reference of an ordinary object, but we are not concerned here with how this comes about). Now, when bar is invoked in the context of iX, the invocation of hook works fine. However, when bar is invoked in the context of iY, the invocation of hook produces a method resolution failure, because the class Y does not support hook.

One might consider the situation depicted in Figure 3-17 to be another type of metaclass incompatibility. However, we do not choose to do so, because the situation in Figure 3-17 is much less troublesome than that in Figure 3-3. The reason is quite simple. All ancestors of the metaclass for a class participate in the construction of the class. This is an important part of class construction in our metaobject protocol (described in Chapter 4 and specified in Chapter 6). Thus, while participating in the construction of class Y, the metaclass MX can ensure that hook is supported by Y (probably by raising an exception if Y is not a descendant of X). The important point here is that the check can be arranged by the programmer of the metaclass MX, who knows that bar is invoking hook. Section 10.1 presents a metaclass that must make this kind of check.

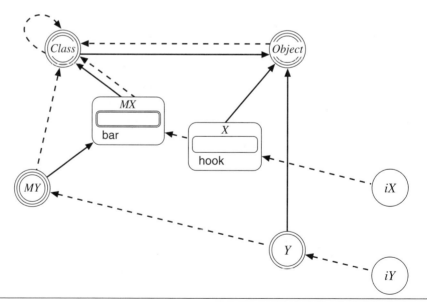

Figure 3-17. Another possible source of method resolution failures.

Refer to [31] for an explanation of how instances such as *iX* are normally made available to "implicit" metaclasses (such as those provided by Smalltalk) for which no such check is necessary. As noted there, access control can be used to restrict explicit metaclass use to a single class, as with implicit metaclasses, and thereby safely reproduce the functionality of implicit metaclasses. The purpose of runtime validation is to allow more general reuse of such metaclasses and to produce a runtime error in cases where it is not appropriate.[5]

3.8 Summary

This chapter has shown how our model implicitly supports inheritance of metaclass constraints through use of derived metaclasses, and has explained why we believe that this is the only reasonable approach in object-oriented programming models that support multiple inheritance and explicit metaclasses. Our examples have focused on considerations that relate to practical requirements of software engineering in the real world, and have also illustrated a strengthened relationship between object-oriented programming and knowledge representation.

Ultimately, we expect that the most important aspect of our approach may relate to the benefits offered by information hiding. The fewer things about ancestor classes that subclass designers need to know and depend on, the better. We therefore exclude metaclasses of ancestors from the list of things that a subclass programmer needs explicitly to consider. Without the concept of deriving the appropriate metaclass, dealing with metaclass constraints would be difficult enough in static situations, but real software is not static. It grows and evolves. As we worked with the IBM SOMobjects Toolkit class library, we were continually reminded of how important it is to be able to make major changes without breaking clients. If reflective programming is to be useful in this context (and to us, it certainly seems to be), requiring subclasses to be explicitly modified when ancestor classes use different metaclasses is simply not a workable solution.

---

5. Exercise 5.8 concerns how static typechecking can be used to achieve the same result while avoiding runtime errors.

3.9 Exercises

3.1   In the figure below, what is the metaclass for *Z*?

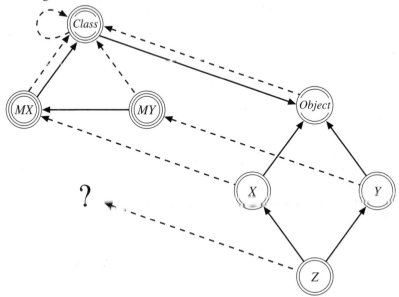

3.2   Correct the metaclass for *Z*.

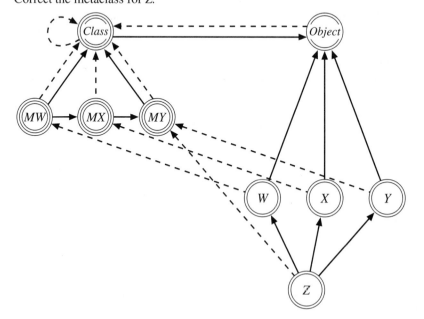

3.3   Show that if a class reference X appears more than once in a parent list of another class Y, only the first appearance has any impact on the mtab and ivs of Y. Use this fact to justify our statement that the constraint imposed by an explicit metaclass is more important than the constraint imposed by a parent class.

Chapter 4
Dynamic Aspects of
Our Object Model

Chapters 2 and 3 present the static aspects of our object model but do not explain how this model is to be used by programs. This chapter addresses dynamic issues such as method invocation and instance variable access. Another important topic covered in this chapter is method resolution order, which was left unspecified in Chapter 2. In addition, Section 2.10 defined a metaobject protocol as the methods supported by *Class*, but that section introduced only the method makeInstance. In this chapter, we informally introduce those methods of our metaobject protocol that are required for an understanding of the basic interplay between the object model and programming languages. At the end of this chapter, you will understand how computation is done with our object model and how it can be used by a programming language. The goal of our book is to state clearly the principles and techniques for putting metaclasses to work. The only positions taken with respect to programming language design are those necessary to achieve our goal.

4.1 Method Invocation

A method invocation has three syntactic parts:

- A designation of the **target object**
- An indicator of the method to be executed
- A list of parameters

    Among object-oriented programming languages, the syntax for method invocations are not all identical; listed below are a few examples in which the value of iBook is an object reference.

Smalltalk   iBook isAuthor: "Dijkstra"
C++   iBook->isAuthor("Dijkstra")
Java   iBook.isAuthor("Dijkstra")
CLOS   (isAuthor iBook "Dijkstra")
Dylan   (isAuthor iBook "Dijkstra")

When executed, a method invocation must perform four steps:

1. Retrieve the appropriate code pointer of the method based on the class of the target object.

2. Arrange the parameters and the target object reference for the method implementation (usually, push the target object reference and parameters on the call stack).

3. Transfer control to the method implementation.

4. If necessary, arrange for proper transfer of return values.

In our object model, to invoke the method $<X,m>$ on a target object with reference iY, the target object reference and other parameters of the method are passed to the code pointer returned by the expression

iY."class".$Class$."mtab".$X.m$

This expression states that the code pointer is retrieved from the method table of the class of iY. The metaobject protocol must provide a method for retrieving the abovementioned code pointer (a process called **method resolution**). The method that retrieves a code pointer is called resolveMethod; its specification is given in Chapter 6. Note that the code pointer is chosen using the method table of the class of the target object. This supports **polymorphism,** which refers to the fact that by using method invocations, the same code can be used to handle different classes of objects.

Example.

If *Book* is a class such that

$parents(Book) = <Object>$
$Book.Class$."mdefs" = { $Book$ = { "isAuthor" = isParamSubstringOfAuthors } }
$Book.Class$."mtab" = { $Object$ = { },
                                    $Book$ = { "isAuthor" = isParamSubstringOfAuthors }
                            }

where isParamSubstringOfAuthors is a code pointer and *Book* has an instance *iBook* indicated as

{   class = *Book*,
     $Object$ = { },
     $Book$ = {   "title" = "Structured Programming",
                          "authors" = "Dahl, Dijkstra, and Hoare"}
}

then the instance *iBook* responds to the method $<Book,$"isAuthor"$>$. Let us assume that our object model is implemented in C where an object reference is a C pointer, a method implementation is a C function whose first parameter is the target object reference, and a code pointer is a C function pointer. A method invocation for method <*Book*,"isAuthor"> could be implemented with a C block that looks like this:

```
{   typedef void*(MethodImpl*)( void*, char* );
    MethodImpl impl = iBook."class".Class."mtab".Book."isAuthor" ;
    void* target = iBook;
    char* param1 = aStringFromOutsideOfThisBlock;
    returnValueOutsideOfThisBlock = impl( target, param1 );
}
```

The first line declares the type for a code pointer that implements the method, and the second line retrieves the correct code pointer. The second line of the block would normally be written with resolveMethod instead of using the representational structures of the model. But our point here is to illustrate how resolveMethod is explained in terms of the model. The third and fourth lines marshal the parameters. The fifth line is the call to the method implementation.

□

The example above shows code that explicitly does method resolution by assuming that a method implementation is a C function in which the first formal parameter is the target object reference, and by using a function pointer typedef to provide the C compiler with the information needed to pass arguments from the **method invocation site** to the method implementation. Object-oriented programming languages normally hide these details, and specially distinguish the method target both at the method invocation site and within the method implementation.

4.2 Instance Variable Access

A method implementation must be able to

- Retrieve the value of an instance variable
- Set the value of an instance variable

Access to the instance variable <*X*,*v*> within a target object with reference *iY* translates to a computation of the value

  iY.X.v

or the assignment of a new value to that cell. The metaobject protocol must provide a method for access to instance data (a process called **data resolution**). Now, keeping in mind that this book is independent of programming language design, we need to formulate an abstraction for instance variable access. Our metaobject protocol requires two methods for data resolution. One is named getIV and the other is named setIV. If *iY* is an object that contains the instance variable $<X,v>$, then getIV returns the value $iY.X.v$ whereas setIV changes the value of $iY.X.v$. The signatures for getIV and setIV are given in Chapter 6; we need not worry about them for now.

Example.

If *Book* is a class such that
   $parents(Book) = <Object>$
   $Book.Class.$"ivdefs" = { $Book$ = { "title" = "", "authors" = "" }}
and *Book* has an instance *iBook* indicated as
   {   "class" = $Book$,
       $Object$ = { },
       $Book$ = {   "title" = "Structured Programming",
                    "authors" = "Dahl, Dijkstra, and Hoare"}
   }
then the object *iBook* contains the instance variable $<Book,$"authors"$>$. Let us again assume that our object model is implemented in C, where the data table is implemented as a C structure. Then the instance variable layout for *iBook* might look like this:
   struct {
       char* title;
       char* authors;
   }
In this kind of implementation, the object *iBook* might be initialized as follows:
   void* bookData = $iBook.Book$;
   bookData->title = "Structured Programming";
   bookData->authors = "Dahl, Dijkstra, and Hoare";

□

The example above assumes that instance variable access is mapped to C structure access in this C implementation. One might assume that a metaobject protocol could be properly designed with one method named getDataTable, which returns a reference to the dictionary within an object that contains the instance variables introduced by a particular class (that is, getDataTable computes the $iY.X$ part of $iY.X.v$). Once getDataTable returns a pointer to the appropriate structure, instance variable access is just like structure item access. This is simply an example of how our model can be implemented. It is not a recommendation, for two reasons: it breaks encapsulation of the object model, and it does not allow metaclasses to intercede in instance variable access.

In object-oriented programming, **encapsulation** refers to the degree to which the instance variables of a class X can be accessed from the method implementations defined for other classes. In a **completely encapsulated** programming system, no access whatsoever is allowed outside of the method implementations defined for *X*. Complete encapsulation has the advantage of hiding the structure of the data within instances of the class *X*; this implies that structure can be changed without impacting other classes.

In some programming systems, an instance variable can be declared **public,** which means that the methods for any other class may access the instance variable. Another degree of control is to allow access to descendants only; in C++, this is called **protected.**

When one wants to be pejorative, the granting of data access to methods defined by other classes is referred to as **breaking encapsulation.** Here are two examples.

- Smalltalk has the concept of a class variable, which is an instance variable of a metaclass. Methods defined by the instance of that metaclass have access to the class variables.

- C++ has the concept of declaring a class to be the friend of another class. This grants data access to the friend to all private data.

The getIV and setIV methods completely encapsulate our object model in that the representation of objects is hidden, but our metaobject protocol is neutral with respect to breaking encapsulation at the level of a programming language that uses this protocol. The facility is there to do so; it all depends on where getIV and setIV are used in the implementation of the programming language.

The second reason for not using the getDataTable approach is the capability to intercede in data access. **Intercession** refers to the ability of the metaobject protocol to affect the action being taken by an application program. A metaclass programmer may need to know when an instance variable is accessed in order to succeed in imparting a property to a class. By requiring that instance variable access be accomplished through getIV and setIV, not only do we encapsulate objects, but we also create the metaobject interface by which data access intercession is done. That is, a metaclass may intercede in data access by overriding the getIV and setIV methods inherited from *Object*.

4.3   Instance Initialization

To review, the method for creating an object is makeInstance, and Definition 19 on page 27 specifies what makeInstance does. From the viewpoint of practical programming, it is useful to be able to initialize the instance variables of an object without having to override makeInstance, which would require a new metaclass. To accomplish this, our metaobject protocol specifies that all objects respond to the method initialize, which is introduced by *Object*. We require that makeInstance invoke initialize as part of its object creation process. Thus, the programmer of an ordinary class can initialize the instance variables of an instance with a simple override.

4.4 Conservative Merge

As specified in Definition 16, the implementation of an inherited method[1] for a class X is determined by the first ancestor to define the method, where "first" is determined by the **method resolution order** of the class X (denoted $MRO(X)$). In other words, the method resolution order of a class must be known in order to determine its method table. The $MRO(X)$ is computed by starting with an initial method resolution order that contains only the class reference X and then by successively merging the method resolution orders of the parents of X, in left-to-right order. This section defines the merge operation, and Section 4.5 defines the algorithm for computing the method resolution order. A **linearization** for a class X is a list of the ancestors of X (that contains no duplicates). Our method resolution order is a special kind of linearization. Appendix A provides additional background material on linearization of inheritance hierarchies.

The **conservative merge** operation takes two lists, *leftList* and *rightList*, and produces a single list as a result. The result contains all elements that appear in either list, contains no duplicates, and preserves the order of the two lists (if possible).

The operation is easy to understand as series of insertions of elements from *rightList* into *leftList*. Figure 4-1 illustrates this process. Undirected lines in this diagram locate merge points in *leftList*. Arrows represent insertions. Not all lists can be conservatively merged so easily.

Definition 20. An **order disagreement** exists between two lists L_1 and L_2 if there are two elements X and Y such that X precedes Y in L_1 and Y precedes X in L_2.

By adding X just after Y in *leftList* in Figure 4-2, we create an example of two lists that have an order disagreement. In this case, the position of X in *leftList* takes precedence.

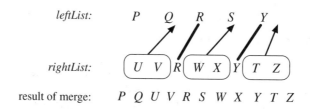

leftList: P   Q   R   S   Y

rightList: U V   R   W X   Y   T Z

result of merge: P   Q   U   V   R   S   W   X   Y   T   Z

Figure 4-1. Abstract example of the conservative merge operation.

---

1. Definitions 13 and 18 give the meanings of defined methods, inherited methods, and introduced methods.

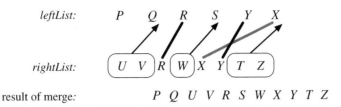

leftList: P   Q   R   S   Y   X

rightList: U   V   R   W   X   Y   T   Z

result of merge: P   Q   U   V   R   S   W   X   Y   T   Z

Figure 4-2. Example of two lists with an order disagreement.

With some intuition about conservative merge having been established, let us look at the algorithm that computes it. Below is the algorithm in the notation described in the Glossary of Symbols; the algorithm computes the conservative merge operation. Note that if *L* is a list, then *L*[i,j] is the subsequence of the i'th element to the j'th element, inclusive.

list **conservativeMerge**(*list leftList, list rightList*)
{ /* Specification */
Action:
    int i,j,r;
    list rightInsertions;
    for (i=0; i < #*leftList*; i++)
      for (j=0; j < #*rightList*; j++)
        if (*leftList*.i == *rightList*.j) { // found a merge point
          for (r=0; r < j; r++)
            if (*rightList*.r ∉ *leftList*)
              rightInsertions = rightInsertions ◁ *rightList*.r;
          return conservativeMerge(
                leftList[0,i-1] ◁*rightInsertions* ◁*leftList*[i,#*leftList*-1],
                rightList[j+1,#*rightList*-1]);

        }
    return *leftList* ◁ *rightList*;
}

We have defined conservativeMerge to be a total function (that is, it returns a list for all pairs of input lists). For our object model, all method resolution orders end with *Object*, so the last return statement never gets executed. However, reflective class-based models (see Table 2-1 on page 33) do not require the inheritance hierarchy to have a unique top; our definition of conservativeMerge accommodates such reflective class-based models.

Theorem 5 (below) shows that conservativeMerge is a feasible basis on which to create an algorithm for computing the method resolution order. This is an area in which one must be very cautious: there are algorithms that are quite similar to conservativeMerge for which Theorem 5 does not hold (see Exercise 4.4).

Theorem 5. The conservativeMerge of the linearizations of two classes in an inheritance hierarchy does not violate the precedence of the inheritance hierarchy.

Proof.

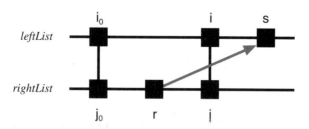

The diagram above shows the state of the indices of the algorithm when a merge point is found. The two input lists are represented by the horizontal lines, and the vertical connections represent identical entries. The connection on the right (*leftList*.i and *rightList*.j) is the pair of identical elements just found; the connection on the left (*leftList*.i_0 and *rightList*.j_0) represents the pair of identical elements found in the calling execution of conservativeMerge (remember that this is a recursive algorithm). At this point in the execution, each element *rightList*.r ($0 \leq r < j$) is tested to see if it is in *leftList* to the right of the merge point. Note that *rightList*.r cannot appear before the merge point, because if this were the case, it would be the previous merge point. There are two cases to consider:

Case 1: *rightList*.r does not appear in *leftList* to the right of the merge point.
In this case, *rightList*.r should be inserted before the merge point, because it is possible that *rightList*.r is a descendant of the merge point class.

Case 2: *rightList*.r appears in *leftList* to the right of the merge point.
In this case, *rightList*.r is not a descendant of the merge point class, because their counterparts in *leftList* occur in the reverse order. Thus, in this case, *rightList*.r is ignored (not put in the list *rightInsertions*), because it is already in *leftList*. Note that if *rightList*.r appears in *leftList*, so does every ancestor of *rightList*.r.

□

4.5 Method Resolution Order

Below are some examples chosen to provide intuition regarding how the method resolution order of a class relates to its inheritance graph.

Example. Single inheritance

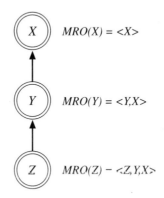

$MRO(X) = <X>$

$MRO(Y) = <Y,X>$

$MRO(Z) - <Z,Y,X>$

Example. Multiple inheritance

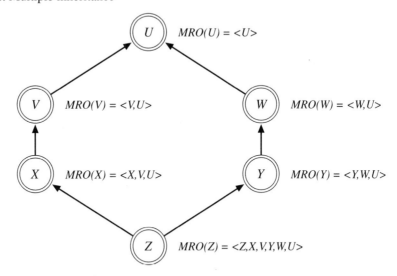

$MRO(U) = <U>$

$MRO(V) = <V,U>$

$MRO(W) = <W,U>$

$MRO(X) = <X,V,U>$

$MRO(Y) = <Y,W,U>$

$MRO(Z) = <Z,X,V,Y,W,U>$

Example. Multiple inheritance with multiple join points

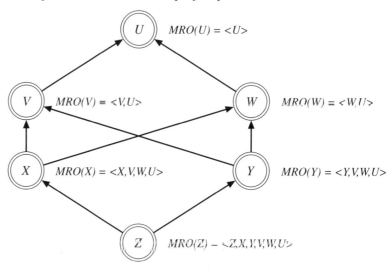

The computation of method resolution order is defined by the following algorithm.

```
list MRO( Z )
{ /* Specification */
Precondition:
      Z ∈ C   // (that is, Z is a class reference)
Action:
      int i;
      list result = <Z>;
      for ( i = 0; i < #Z.Class."parents"; i++ ) {
         list parentMRO = MRO( Z.Class."parents".i );
         if ( noSeriousOrderDisagreements( result, parentMRO ) )
            result = conservativeMerge( result, parentMRO );
         else
            return NULL;
      }
      return result;
}
```

To ensure that there is no misunderstanding, the primitive *MRO* (which was left undefined in Chapter 2) is computed by the MRO algorithm. MRO returns NULL if an order disagreement (Definition 20) is discovered and is considered serious. The algorithm for discovering order disagreements is given below. For the moment, we assume that isDisagreementSerious always returns TRUE — that is, that all order disagreements are serious enough to cause a NULL return. Later in this chapter, we identify those situations in which an order disagreement can be ignored. The algorithm below is written in terms of two primitives, firstIndexOf and lastIndexOf, which are defined after the algorithm.

boolean **noSeriousOrderDisagreements**(*list leftList, list rightList*)
{ /* Specification */
Action:
```
    int i,j,r;
    for ( i=0; i < #leftList-1; i++ ) {
        if ( (r = firstIndexOf( rightList, leftList.i, 0 )) >= 0 ) {
            for ( j=i+1; j< #leftList; j++ ) {
                if ( lastIndexOf( rightList, leftList.j, r ) >= 0 ) {
                    // Found an order disagreement
                    if ( isDisagreementSerious( leftList.i, leftList.j ) )
                        rcturn FALSE;
                }
            }
        }
    }
    return TRUE;
}
```
where

firstIndexOf(l,x,i) - searches the list l forward from the i'th entry and returns the index of the first appearance of x in the list l. -1 is returned if x does not appear in that part of l.

lastIndexOf(l,x,i) - searches the list l backward from the i'th entry and returns the index of the last appearance of x in the list l. -1 is returned if x does not appear in that part of l.

Assuming that there are no serious order disagreements, if we think of conservative merge as a binary operation denoted as $\lessdot$, then MRO has the following algebraic specification:

$$\text{MRO}(Object) = <Object>$$
$$\text{MRO}(Z) = <Z> \lessdot \text{MRO}(P_0) \lessdot ... \lessdot \text{MRO}(P_n)$$

where $P_0,...,P_n$ are the elements of *parents(Z)* (that is, $P_i = parents(Z).i$). Note that $\lessdot$ is not associative and that the second equation is evaluated from left to right.

Here are some other important properties of the MRO algorithm.

- All ancestors of a class appear after it in the resulting method resolution order.

- The result produced by MRO depends only on the inheritance hierarchy.

- If class Y is a descendant of class X, the procedure isDisagreementSerious always returns TRUE, and MRO(X) and MRO(Y) return non-NULL, then the relative order of MRO(X) is preserved in MRO(Y).

The first property states that the algorithm produces a topological sort. The second property states that the MRO algorithm is **language independent** (that is, it produces linearizations that depend only on the structure of the inheritance hierarchy of the ancestors of the class being constructed). The last property states that if all order disagreements are considered serious and the MRO algorithm does not return NULL, then it computes a **monotonic linearization** (the linearization of each ancestor is a subsequence of the computed linearization, where s' is a subsequence of s if s' can be derived from s by eliminating items from s).

It would be ideal to have a linearization algorithm that is monotonic for all possible inheritance hierarchies. Unfortunately, there are no language-independent linearizations that are monotonic for all inheritance hierarchies. This is a theorem that was first presented in [35], and we reproduce the proof in Appendix A. (This is a good time to read Appendix A.) The theorem tells us that if we want a language-independent, monotonic linearization algorithm (which we do), there will be some inheritance hierarchies that the algorithm must not linearize. At this point, our MRO algorithm does not produce a linearization in those cases where an order disagreement is discovered (because we temporarily assume that isDisagreementSerious always returns TRUE). This is too restrictive for our purposes, because we are promoting composition of classes. Later in this chapter, we redefine isDisagreementSerious so that it returns TRUE only in cases where the order disagreement really matters.

4.6 Class Construction

There is no single "create subclass" operation in our metaobject protocol. Instead, subclassing is achieved by a dynamic process that uses successive operations to construct the desired class object. The methods of *Class* that are used during this overall process, and the order in which they are used, represent a key aspect of our metaobject protocol.

The process of subclassing begins by creating a new class object. This is done by invoking makeInstance on a metaclass that does not violate Postulate 10 in Chapter 3. This metaclass is found by using a function called solveMetaclassConstraints, which is provided by our metaobject protocol. The resulting **nascent class** has no parents and defines no methods, so it supports no methods. A class is nascent until the class construction protocol is completed, at which time the class becomes **usable.** In Chapter 2, we stated that every usable class is a descendant of *Object*, which is not necessarily true for a nascent class, because the parent list is specified during the class construction process. However, as all objects do, a nascent class responds to the methods supported by its metaclass, which supports the methods introduced by *Class*. These methods are then invoked on the nascent class object, first to perform inheritance from a specified set of parent classes according to Definition 16 (using initializeClass), and then to introduce new methods and override inherited methods (using addMethod and overrideMethod). The process ends with the invocation of readyClass to indicate that the process is complete and the class is ready to be used (for instance creation, or as a parent of some other class). The distinction between nascent and usable is necessary, because the protocol does not immediately create a usable class.

In order for initializeClass to use Definition 16, the method resolution order for the nascent class must be computed with the MRO algorithm. It is possible for the MRO algorithm to return NULL. This means that the programmer requested the multiple-inheritance joining of two classes that have a serious order disagreement (which is explained later in this chapter). This may seem odd at first, but it is really no different from any other runtime check. Further, for a programming language that uses our model, static analysis can discover serious order disagreements for statically declared inheritance hierarchies.

Figure 4-3 depicts a path expression constraining the use of these methods. A **path expression** is a regular expression over an alphabet of procedure names that represents a temporal constraint on the order of execution. Figure 4-3 states that after creating a nascent class, there is first a single invocation of initializeClass, which is followed by a set of invocations of overrideMethod and addMethod, which is followed by a single invocation of readyClass, which changes a class from nascent to usable. More formal descriptions of these methods are given in Chapter 6. As described above, makeInstance is invoked on a metaclass to instantiate a class object, whereas the other methods are invoked on the newly instantiated class object to construct it properly.

---

makeInstance initializeClass (overrideMethod+addMethod)* readyClass

---

Figure 4-3. Path expression for class construction.

4.7 Parent Method Call

Let W introduce method $<W,"m">$, let X be a descendant of W, let Y be a descendant of X, let X and Y both override $<W,"m">$, and let Z be a descendant of Y. This situation is diagramed in Figure 4-4. The implementation of method $<W,"m">$ is the accumulated implementations of W, X, and Y. Together they form the **implementation chain** for $<W,"m">$ belonging to Z. The order of the implementation chain is determined by the method resolution order. Because W introduced the method, its implementation is last and is called the **base implementation.** Y made the last override; its implementation is in the method table and is the one that gets control when the method is invoked.

A **parent method call** (or just **parent call** for short) can be made from within the implementation of a method override to invoke the next implementation in the implementation chain. That is, from within Y's override for the method $<W,"m">$, parent method resolution invokes the implementation denoted by $X.Class."mdefs".W."m"$, where X is the next class after Y in $MRO(Z)$ that defines $<W,"m">$.

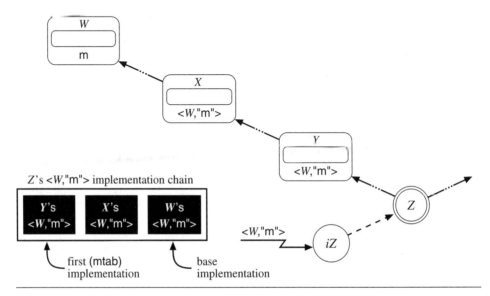

Figure 4-4. Example of an implementation chain.

Example.

Figure 4-5 does not explicitly show the implementation chain; instead, the class structure diagram is drawn in gray so that the sequence of parent method calls may be distinctly seen (the parent method calls are drawn as black arrows). The diagram shows that U introduces the method $<U,"m">$ and is overridden by V and Y. An invocation of $<U,"m">$ on an instance of Z causes Y's implementation of $<U,"m">$ to execute, because Y is the first class in $MRO(Z)$ that defines the method. When Y's implementation of $<U,"m">$ executes a parent method call, V's implementation of $<U,"m">$ is executed because V is the next class in $MRO(Z)$ that defines the method. Finally, when V's implementation of $<U,"m">$ executes a parent method call, U's implementation of $<U,"m">$ is executed. The result is that the implementations corresponding to all definitions of $<U,"m">$ by Z and its ancestors get to execute.

□

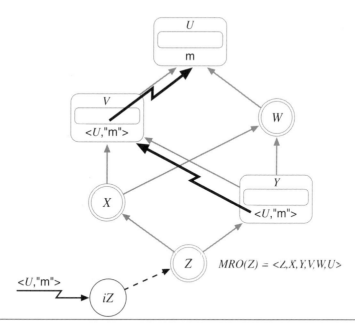

Figure 4-5. Sequence of parent method calls when <*U*,"m"> is invoked on *iZ*.

Example.

> If all of the classes in the preceding example were to define <*U*,"m"> and all overrides were to make a parent method call, then the overall result of invoking <*U*,"m"> on *iZ* would be the execution of each of these implementations as determined by visiting each class in *MRO(Z)* according to this ordering, as shown in Figure 4-6.   □

Programming languages must provide a special syntax for doing parent method calls. For example, suppose one wishes to make a parent method call for a method named updateWith, which takes one parameter; here is how it would look in several different programming languages.

Java	super.updateWith (param)
Smalltalk	super updateWith: param
DTS C++	__parent->updateWith(param)
CLOS	(call-next method param)
Dylan	(next-method)

In Java, Smalltalk, and DTS C++, there is a key word indicating that this is a parent method call, the method name, and the parameters. In CLOS, the method name is not necessary, whereas Dylan makes the parameter list unnecessary (unless one wishes to change the values of parameters).

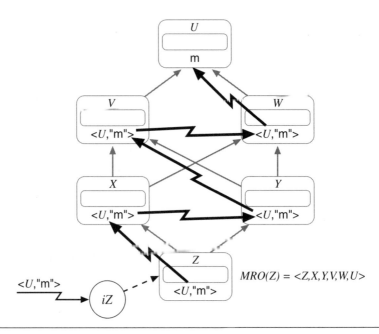

Figure 4-6. Sequence of parent method calls when <*U*,"m"> is defined by all ancestors of *Z*.

4.8 Cooperative Override Methods

We are progressing toward a definition of when an order disagreement is serious. Toward this end, we must now examine how method overrides are written and how they use parent method calls.

Definition 21. A cooperative override is one that has the form
> S′; parent-method-call; S″

where the semicolon represents sequential composition and the prime and double prime letters represent the parts of the override before and after the parent method call. A **cooperative override method** is a method for which all overrides must be cooperative.

For a cooperative override method, we need to ensure that once a class fixes the order of execution in the implementation chain it cannot be changed by a descendant class. Consider Figure 4-7, where *V* and *W* have overrides for the method named foo. Invocations of foo on instances of *X* execute the overrides in the reverse order of invocations of foo on instances of *Y*. There is nothing necessarily wrong with this. Now suppose that the programmer of *X* introduces method xbar, which invokes foo, and the programmer of *Y* introduces method ybar, which invokes foo. The correct execution of xbar requires *X*'s order of execution for the foo overrides, whereas the correct execution of ybar requires Y's order of execution for the foo overrides. There is still no problem as long as descendants of either X or Y (but not both) execute xbar and ybar correctly. That is, descendants of X see V's override executed before W's override, and vice versa for Y.

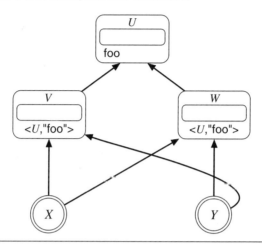

Figure 4-7. Class X and class Y have method resolution orders that disagree.

Now suppose that a programmer tries to create Z with parents X and Y. It is an error to try to create Z because of the order disagreement between X and Y. There is no linearization that executes the overrides of foo in the correct order for both xbar and ybar.

We can also ask the question "Under what circumstances can the overrides of foo be executed in either order?" Let V's override of foo be of the form

  (f′; parent-method-call; f″)

and let W's override of foo be of the form

  (g′; parent-method-call; g″)

Asking if these overrides can be executed in either order is the same as asking

  Is (f′; g′; parent-method-call; g″; f″) equivalent to (g′; f′; parent-method-call; f″;g″)?

Now, on seeing such a question, one's first thought is that proving equivalence of programs is not a solvable problem [86]. However, this is going a little too deep into the theory of computing. The important issue is that the overrides need only perform externally visible actions for there to be nonequivalence. For example, if f′ turns on the bedside wake-up alarm and g′ monitors the making of your morning coffee, who is to say that they can be executed in either order? After all, f′;g′ implies that you have time to dress while the coffee is brewing, and g′;f′ implies that you wake up to freshly brewed coffee.

The next question is whether there are any reasonable conditions under which the order of execution does not matter. It turns out that there are. Not surprisingly, the ability to execute the before parts and the after parts in parallel is a sufficient condition. Consider just f' and g'. The basic idea is that if both are limited to making changes in main memory (no input or output) and neither interferes with the other (that is, they access nonintersecting sets of memory locations), they can be executed in either order (or in parallel). The technical details can be found on page 195 in [45].

> **Definition 22.** A cooperative override f − (f'; parent-method-call; f") is called **highly cooperative** if both f' and f" access only the instance variables introduced by the class that defines f.

Now if the only actions that need to be performed in overrides yield highly cooperative overrides, there is no need to discuss the order of execution of overrides. Unfortunately, this is a very strong definition. It implies that a highly cooperative method cannot make method invocations. It is possible to relax this definition — for example, to allow the creation of objects whose class is an instance of *Class* and whose initialize is highly cooperative. However, we are not going to play that game, because it does not lead to overrides that can produce externally visible actions, and this is too limiting. Instead, we will concentrate on making effective use of the order of execution of overrides.

4.9 Serious Order Disagreements

Earlier we left unanswered the question "When is an order disagreement serious?" The MRO algorithm is defined in terms of the procedure noSeriousOrderDisagreements, which in turn is defined with the procedure isDisagreementSerious, which was temporarily assumed always to return TRUE. That is, all order disagreements were considered serious enough that the MRO returns NULL, thus preventing the class from being constructed. Now let us reconsider Figure 4-7. Suppose *V* and *W* do not both override foo. In this case, although there is an order disagreement between *V* and *W*, there is no common cooperative override. Thus the relative ordering of these two classes in the MRO can have no effect on the overall execution of foo (specifically, the ordering of the different implementations executed by the parent call chain) and there is no need to take the order disagreement between *X* and *Y* seriously when forming the multiple inheritance join. This observation forms the basis of the following algorithm for isDisagreementSerious.[2]

---

2. Section 2.5 closed off the possibility that the initial values of instance variables could be overridden in the inheritance process (on page 24 we declared that *overriddenIVs(X)*=∅ for all *X*∈ *C*). If this were not so, ancestor classes could also disagree over the initialization of instance variables. This alternative would require redefinition of isDisagreementSerious to account for this source of disagreement.

```
boolean isDisagreementSerious( X, Y )
{ /* Specification */
```
Precondition:
    X, Y ∈ *C*
Action:
    int i;
    // The assignment below coerces a set into a list.
    list commonMdefs = (*list*) (*definedMethods*(X) ∩ *definedMethods*(Y));
    for (i=0; i < #*commonMdefs*; i++) {
        if (isCooperative(*commonMdefs*.i)) {
            if (!isHighlyCooperative(*commonMdefs*.i))
                return TRUE;
        }
        else
            return TRUE;
    }
    return FALSE;
}
```
where

        isCooperative( m ) is a Boolean procedure that returns TRUE if and only if m is supposed to be a cooperative method

        isHighlyCooperative( m ) is a Boolean procedure that returns TRUE if m is determined to be a highly cooperative method.

The two functions isCooperative and isHighlyCooperative are parameters of our object model. For the remainder of this book, we can consider isCooperative always to return TRUE for all methods except *<Object,*"dispatch"*>* (a special method to be introduced in Chapter 6) and isHighlyCooperative to return TRUE only for the method *<Object,*"initialize"*>* (that is, initialize is the only method in this book that is required to be highly cooperative).

To ensure that *<Object,*"initialize"*>* is highly cooperative, it is sufficient to dictate that an implementation of initialize can only

    1. assign to the instance variables introduced by the class that defines the override
    2. create objects whose class is an instance of *Class*

We take this approach because we expect initialize to be overridden often, and, if initialize were not highly cooperative, overrides of initialize would likely interfere with composability. Non–highly cooperative initialization necessary to support specific types of objects can be accomplished by introducing a cooperative method in the corresponding class. Also, as we will see, metaclasses can perform object initializations by overriding the makeInstance method.

**Theorem 6.** Under the assumptions above, all initialize overrides are highly cooperative.
```

4.10   A Simple Programming Model

A programming model represents a set of conventions and expected patterns within which one programs. Most class frameworks (including our metaobject protocol) have an associated programming model whose aspects are not necessarily enforced by either compiler or runtime environment. In this book, we assume a programming model in which methods are cooperative, because this allows us to focus on the efficacy of metaclass programming. Further, we have discussed various aspects of how this model would be enforced at runtime (without going into great detail concerning the metadata required for this purpose). However, a realistic programming model must also allow for noncooperative methods, which we discuss in this section.

Parent method calls allow the overall execution of a method to proceed through the implementation chain for that method. This is a powerful and important capability, because it allows incremental extension of a method's functionality. But, in many cases, parent method calls are not required to implement the desired semantics of a method.

Definition 23. A replacement override is an override that does not make a parent method call.

Replacement overrides, when they occur, provide complete replacement of the inherited implementation. This is an important special case for noncooperative method implementations that might initially seem simpler than cooperative overrides (because it avoids issues related to parent method call semantics). But replacement overrides create other problems for construction of extendable object-oriented programming systems, and they require an analysis different from identification of serious order disagreements to prevent unexpected and difficult-to-diagnose runtime failures. To understand why, consider Figure 4-8, in which the class Z does not override <W,"foo">.

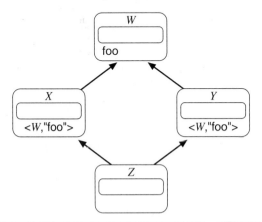

Figure 4-8. A dominance violation.

If the overrides are cooperative, all of the overrides and the base implementation get executed. However, if <*W*,"foo"> is meant to be overridden with replacements (for example, <*W*,"foo"> may be an abstract method), then only *X*'s replacement is executed (because of our definition of method resolution order). There is little reason to believe that the behavioral requirements of both *X* and *Y* are met by the execution of *X*'s replacement only.

In C++, this situation is called a **dominance violation,** based on the fact that a method override is said to **dominate** the implementations of its ancestors. The reasoning is that an override can be assumed to know about and replace the behavioral characteristics of its ancestors. In Figure 4-8, because *X* and *Y* are unrelated by inheritance, neither *X*'s nor *Y*'s override of <*W*,"foo"> dominates the other. So there is no good choice for which implementation should be used for *Z*. To avoid this, *Z* must override the method.

Note that this issue has nothing to do with order disagreements among *Z*'s ancestors. Certainly there are none in the example above. However, because the method resolution order is used to determine the inherited implementation of a method, the MRO computation seems to be a natural place to add an additional runtime check for dominance violations on noncooperative methods.

4.11 Monotonicity of Implementation Chains

This chapter has developed a very sophisticated approach to inheritance hierarchies with respect to method resolution order and the overriding of methods. The reasons for this approach are not obvious and need to be explained.

For the purposes of software engineering (rather than knowledge representation), one characteristic of a good inheritance hierarchy is the monotonicity of properties. That is, if we know that a property is true for a class, it is desirable that the property also be true for its descendants. This criterion stems from the view that the investment made in studying a class in the inheritance hierarchy should not be devalued as we move down the hierarchy. In particular, as object-oriented programmers, we are most interested in the behavioral properties of our objects. For a class *Y* that has a descendant *Z*, knowing whether *MRO(Y)* is a subsequence of *MRO(Z)* can be sufficient (but not necessary) for understanding the behavioral properties of instances of *Z* in terms of *Y*. This is true mainly because the implementation chain for each method belonging to *Z* is a subsequence of the implementation chain for that same method belonging to *Y*.

Because the MRO algorithm is parameterized by isDisagreementSerious, a spectrum of possibilities arises. At one end of the spectrum, if order disagreements are ignored (that is, if isDisagreementSerious always returns FALSE), it is not the case that *MRO(Y)* must be a subsequence of *MRO(Z)*, as the counterexample in Figure 4-9 shows. This is unacceptable, because implementation chains are not necessarily monotonic. At the other end of the spectrum, if all order disagreements are considered serious (that is, if isDisagreementSerious always returns TRUE), one cannot construct many multiple-inher-

itance combinations of classes even though the order disagreement has no impact on the
behavioral properties of ordinary objects. The elaboration of isDisagreementSerious that
considers whether methods are cooperative and further whether methods are highly cooperative permits our object model to stand in a middle ground. In this middle ground, an
order disagreement is considered serious only if it impacts the order of execution of implementation chains (with the exception of highly cooperative methods, for which order does
not matter) [3]

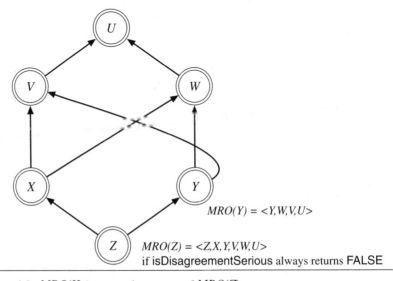

$MRO(Y) = <Y,W,V,U>$

$MRO(Z) = <Z,X,Y,V,W,U>$
if isDisagreementSerious always returns FALSE

Figure 4-9. $MRO(Y)$ is not a subsequence of $MRO(Z)$.

To address completely the issue of taking the middle ground (in the computation of
isDisagreementSerious), we must examine all of the uses of method resolution order in
our object model. This examination must ensure that permitting classes to be constructed
in the presence of order disagreements has no impact on the behavioral properties of the
instances of those classes. We have made two uses of method resolution order thus far.

---

3. There are many ways to use a metaobject protocol to implement a method whose behavior
depends on the structure of the class hierarchy. For such a method, an order disagreement might be
problematic even though isDisagreementSerious does not define the disagreement as serious. We
are, of course, excluding such implementations in this discussion. The good metaclass programmer
creates metaclasses that support monotonicity of behavioral properties.

- Method resolution order is required to define inheritance (that is, to determine mtab and ivs according to Definition 16 on page 22). For ivs in Definition 16, whether or not $MRO(Y)$ is a subsequence of $MRO(Z)$ can be of no consequence because we do not allow the overriding of variables (as was stated on page 24).

- Of equal importance, method resolution order determines which class's override is invoked by a parent method call, as explained in Section 4.7. Because we disallow the construction of a class that has a serious order disagreement among its parents (except in the cases of methods that are highly cooperative), implementation chains are monotonic where necessary. Note that because the first entry of the implementation chain is the mtab entry, we have also examined the mtab portion of Definition 16.

This second point is characterized by the following theorem.

Theorem 7. Let class Z be a descendant of class Y. If $<W,"m">$ is a method introduced by an ancestor of Y that is cooperative but not highly cooperative, the implementation chain for $<W,"m">$ belonging to Y is a subsequence of the implementation chain for $<W,"m">$ belonging to Z.

Proof.

> Because Z is a descendant of Y, $ancestors(Y) \subseteq ancestors(Z)$. This means that every item of $MRO(Y)$ appears in $MRO(Z)$. This implies that every item of the implementation chain for $<W,"m">$ belonging to Y is also an item of the implementation chain for $<W,"m">$ belonging to Z. Because Z is a constructed class, there are no serious order disagreements between $MRO(Y)$ and $MRO(Z)$ for any method that is cooperative but not highly cooperative. Therefore, the implementation chain for $<W,"m">$ belonging to Y is a subsequence of the implementation chain for $<W,"m">$ belonging to Z.

$\square$

When viewed properly (in terms of implementation chains), our version of multiple inheritance is consistent with recent trends. For example, Java achieves monotonicity of implementation chains by allowing implementations on only one inheritance path (which is distinguished by the keyword extends). In addition, this scheme implies that the implementation chain of an ancestor is a subsequence that is a suffix. Dylan [7] has enforced monotonicity of linearizations, which implies monotonicity of implementation chains. It is instructive to compare the trade-offs between the course taken in Java and the one we propose here. For example, linearizations produced by our MRO algorithm are harder to understand than the obvious linearization of single inheritance. Unfortunately, Java achieves its relative simplicity by restricting application solutions. We believe that the reasons for such restrictions (primarily dominance violations) are better addressed by an enhanced multiple-inheritance model that includes cooperative methods. This approach allows a simple solution to the problem we wish to solve (inheritance of metaclass constraints) and is useful for application solutions in general.

4.12 Summary

Chapter 3 established the importance of inheritance of metaclass constraints. The inheritance of metaclass constraints requires construction of derived metaclasses, which are computed with multiple inheritance. Multiple inheritance is an object-oriented programming feature that has fallen into disfavor recently, because multiple inheritance cannot provide all the compositionality that can be imagined. Furthermore, languages with multiple inheritance that use linearizations (such as CLOS) have some disturbing problems when order disagreements arise (see [34]), whereas languages that avoid linearization (such as C++) have problems with inheritance along multiple paths between classes (see Subsection 5.4.4). Chapter 4 has presented a new form of multiple inheritance, based on the concept of monotonic implementation chains, that overcomes these previously encountered problems. Multiple inheritance is still union-like joining of classes, and again, to get beyond this basic fact, we have introduced inheritance of metaclass constraints.

This concludes the exposition of the basics of our object model, in which we have explained both static and dynamic aspects of objects, classes, class construction, and method invocations. We have done this in a language-independent manner so as to emphasize that our approach to putting metaclasses to work transcends any particular programming language. The next chapter introduces DTS C++, a programming language that is used for static declaration and programming of classes in our object model.

4.13 Exercises

4.1   For the diagram below, give the value of the class object Z. That is, give the values of the instance variables parents, ivdefs, mdefs, ivs, and mtab of the class object Z.

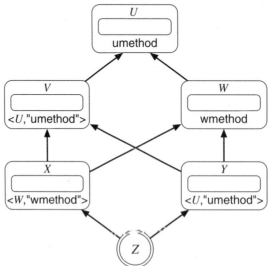

4.2   Write an iterative algorithm for computing method resolution order based on our conservative merge algorithm (page 65).

4.3   *MRO(Z)* is defined in terms of the MRO algorithm. This is not quite proper, because *MRO(Z)* should have a definition and the MRO algorithm should be shown to be an implementation of that definition. In terms of two predicates *cooperative* and *highlyCooperative*, write a definition of *MRO(Z)*.

4.4   Below is an algorithm that appears quite similar to conservativeMerge. Show that Theorem 5 does not hold for this algorithm.

```
list rlMerge ( list leftList, list rightList )
{
    list resultList = <>;
    int l = 0;
    int r = 0;
    int i,j;

    for ( i=l; i < #leftList; i++ )
        for ( j=r; j < #rightList; j++ )
            if ( leftList.i == rightList.j ) { // found a merge point
                for (; l<j; l++ )
                    if ( leftList.l ∉ resultList )
                        resultList = resultList ◁ <leftList.l>;
                for (; r <= i; r++ )
                    resultList = resultList ◁ <rightList.r>;
            }

    for (; l < #leftList; l++ )
        if ( leftList.l ∉ resultList )
            resultList = resultList ◁ <leftList.l>;

    for (; r < #rightList; r++ )
        resultList = resultList ◁ <rightList.r>;

    return resultList;
}
```

4.5   For the diagram below, if W_1 and W_3 define the same cooperative method, does a serious order disagreement arise when attempting to construct Z?

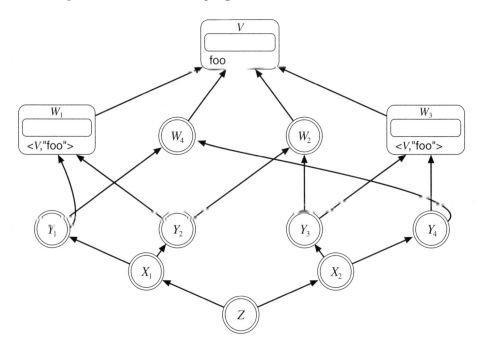

Chapter 5
DTS C++

One goal of this book is to demonstrate that our monotonic reflective class-based model has wide applicability. Toward this end, we have thus far presented our model in a manner independent of any particular programming language. We cannot, however, put off discussion of programming languages any further, for the following reasons.

- In subsequent chapters, we will present a metaobject protocol and a set of useful metaclasses. This presentation will be facilitated by a programming language with static class definitions and method invocations that are mapped to our model. The alternative would be to use the language in which we have expressed the model itself, without any of the syntactic conveniences afforded by a programming language. This would result in a tedious presentation, a point reinforced in Section 6.9, where we exhibit two versions of a metaclass: one expressed in terms of our model, and the other coded with the syntactic conveniences of a programming language.

- Our model has implications for typechecking. Because this chapter introduces a programming language based on our object model, this chapter is the appropriate place to discuss these implications.

We have chosen **DTS C++** to communicate our metaobject protocol and the corresponding approach to metaclass programming because it provides a familiar C++ syntax for defining classes and invoking methods. With a few important exceptions, DTS C++ programs appear and execute exactly as do C++ programs.

Our primary objective in this chapter is to provide enough information about DTS C++ to enable the reader to feel comfortable reading the code examples presented in the following chapters. Examples in this chapter are not intended to illustrate the scope of C++ or current practice with respect to its use. Our objective here is a clear presentation of the distinguishing aspects of DTS C++ required for understanding examples presented in subsequent chapters. In the process, we show how typechecking in C++ is extended to deal with the enhanced capabilities enabled by our model. We start with a quick review of C++ essentials, and then we discuss DTS C++ specifics.[1]

5.1 C++ Basics

As do many programming languages, C++ combines **statements** and **data expressions.** The execution of statements determines which data expressions to evaluate and where to store the resulting values. For example, execution of the assignment statement

```
z = x + y;
```

evaluates the data expression

```
x + y
```

to compute the sum of the values stored in the variables x and y, and stores the result in the variable named z.

Statements and the variables to which they refer are located within lexically scoped **blocks.** For example, here is a block that contains some simple variable declarations and assignment statements.

```
{
    int x, y, z;
    x = 1;
    y = 2;
    z = x + y;
}
```

A function can be thought of as a block that receives arguments and returns a result. For example, here is a simple function definition.

```
int sumOfSquares( int x, int y )
{
    return x*x + y*y;
}
```

---

1. The "DTS" stands for DirectToSOM, a term introduced by Tom Pennello of MetaWare. There are three dialects of DTS C++. Version 3.0 of the IBM Visual C++ compiler supports one dialect of DTS C++ and the MetaWare HighC/C++ compiler supports a similar one. Both compilers generate code that uses the metaobject protocol supported by IBM SOMobjects Toolkit versions 2.1 and higher. The third dialect is the one that is described in this chapter. Our dialect of DTS C++ is too close to the others to be given a new name, so we use this name despite the fact that our object model and metaobject protocol are somewhat different from those of the IBM SOMobjects Toolkit.

There are two different kinds of data in C++:

- Primitive data defined by the language (for example, integers, floating point numbers, and so on)
- Structured data defined by programmers (for example, objects)

Types are used by C++ programmers, as illustrated above, to indicate the kind of data that a variable or function argument contains. The fundamental purpose of types is to describe how data can be used. C++ provides a fixed set of type names for describing primitive data, and uses type expressions to describe nonprimitive data.

Type expressions are somewhat complicated in C++, because

- Different syntactic forms are used for describing different kinds of structured data
- A variety of different forms are used for giving names to types (again, depending on the kind of data being described)

Furthermore, with respect to objects, C++ makes it difficult to express only type (that is, usage) information. This is a result of how struct in the C language was generalized to provide classes in C++. In particular, a C++ class definition not only defines an object type and gives the type a name, but also provides information concerning the private instance variables and methods used to implement objects of the indicated class. Consequently, it is easy to confuse types (whose purpose is to provide usage information) with implementation information.

For example, the following C++ class definitions partially specify the classes named Part and Assembly (in terms of their instance data and method table layout) and completely specify corresponding object types of the same names (which determine how instances of these classes can be used).

```
class Part{
    private:
        float baseWeight;
    public:
        Part(); // a constructor, used for initialization
        virtual void setBaseWeight(float w);
        virtual float getTotalWeight();
};

class Assembly : public virtual Part{
    protected:
        Part **contained; // an array of references to subParts
    public:
        Assembly(); // a constructor, used for initialization
        virtual void setContainedParts(Part **cps);
        virtual float getTotalWeight();
};
```

The Part class introduces the baseWeight field as instance data. The Part constructor is executed when a new instance of the Part class (or one of its subclasses) is created, and is used to initialize this field. In general, when an instance of a C++ class is created, a constructor for that class and for every ancestor of that class is executed. In addition to instance data and a constructor, the Part class also introduces methods for setting the base weight of a Part and accessing its total weight. What we have called methods in our model are called virtual functions in C++, and thus the keyword virtual is used here. The class Assembly inherits Part's instance data and methods, introduces an instance variable and method for setting the parts contained by an assembly, and overrides the inherited method getTotalWeight.

By default, the instance variables and methods in an object are private, and cannot be accessed except by code defined by their introducing class. This aspect of object use, called **access control,** is an important part of object types in C++. Thus, in this example, code used to implement the Assembly class cannot access the inherited instance data baseWeight. In contrast (by way of illustration), the keyword protected indicates that descendant classes of Assembly (of which there are none in this example) may access the inherited contained field from within their method implementations.

Also, by default, the parents of a C++ class are private. Because the keyword public is used when declaring Part as the parent of Assembly, however, it is possible to pass an object of type Assembly to functions expecting a Part argument, and it is possible to invoke public methods of Part on variables of type Assembly. The meaning of the virtual keyword in the parent declaration is described in Section 5.3.

This example represents a situation in which the objects of interest either are atomic (modeled by objects of class Part) or are composed by including one or more parts into an overall assembly (modeled by objects of class Assembly). The total weight of an atomic part is determined as its base weight. The total weight of an assembly is determined as its weight without consideration of its contained subparts plus the sum of the total weights of its subparts. To complete a specification of the Part and Assembly classes that satisfies these intuitions, we can define their constructors and methods as follows, separately from the class definitions that declared them.

```
Part::Part() { baseWeight = 0.0; }
void Part :: setBaseWeight(float w) { baseWeight = w; }
float Part :: getTotalWeight() { return baseWeight; }
```

```
Assembly :: Assembly() { contained = 0; };
void Assembly :: setContainedParts(Parts **cps) { contained = cps; }
float Assembly :: getTotalWeight ()
{
    // initialize result with the total weight ignoring subParts
    float result = Part::getTotalWeight();
    if (contained) {
        // add the subPart weights to the result
        for (Part **cpp = contained; *cpp; cpp++)
            result += (*cpp)->getTotalWeight();
    }
    return result;
}
```

The implementation of getTotalWeight by the Assembly class is interesting. To determine the weight of an assembly without consideration of its contained parts, we use a non-virtual method call that explicitly invokes the implementation of getTotalWeight defined by Part. This simulates the semantics of a parent method call in our model.[2] If the assembly contains parts, their total weights are then added to produce the final result.

The example above illustrates C++ syntax for defining classes and illustrates the difference between object types (which determine how objects are used) and classes (which determine how objects are implemented). Normally, a definition is expected to specify completely the thing that it defines. As illustrated here, the syntactic unit called a class definition in C++ may not completely specify a class (it may leave method implementations undefined). It does, however, completely specify an object type.

To avoid confusion, we uniformly (throughout the entire book) use the word "type" to indicate object usage information and reserve the word "class" for indicating an object's implementation. This distinction is especially important in models where classes are themselves objects and types are not. Thus, when we refer to an object of class X, we mean that the object was constructed as an instance of class X. When we refer to an object of type X, we mean that the object can be used as if it were an object of class X. This does not necessarily mean that the object is an instance of X, because an instance of any descendant of the class X can also be so used.

---

2. Our model provides a very specific semantics for parent method calls. Among the properties guaranteed by what we call parent method calls are the following: the implementation defined by an ancestor is entered after that of a descendant, and each implementation for the method is executed exactly once (assuming that each descendant makes a single parent call). In general, nonvirtual method calls in C++ provide neither of these guarantees (nor do any other primitive mechanisms of the C++ language). In this particular example, a nonvirtual method call happens to produce these results, which is why we use the word "simulate."

Unless otherwise noted, we use the word "type" in its static (compile-time) sense, to represent information available at compile time based on the use of typed variables and method arguments.[3] Not all programming languages use static types (for example, Smalltalk does not). Two reasons are often cited for using static types:

- They allow a compiler to verify that the statements and data expressions in a program make sense.

- They provide information that aids in the efficient evaluation of expressions.

In C++, types are important for an additional reason. Recall from Section 4.1 that method invocation in our model requires the introducing class of the method. This is also necessary in C++. However, instead of requiring (or even allowing) a programmer to indicate this information explicitly, the C++ compiler uses type information to determine the introducing class. Thus, when a variable contains or points to an object, its type provides the compiler with the information necessary to determine the introducing class of the methods that are invoked on the object.

In particular, when a method with a given name is invoked on a data expression with an object type, the C++ compiler searches for a class that introduces a method with this name, starting with the class that corresponds to the type of the data expression and proceeding upward to its ancestors in the class hierarchy. If an introducing class is found, the compiler knows what method to invoke. Otherwise, a compile-time error is signaled.[4]

Here is an example that illustrates the use of object types to support method invocation.

```
Part* heavier(Part *c1, Part *c2)
{
    if ( c1->getTotalWeight() > c2->getTotalWeight() )
        return c1;
    else
        return c2;
}
```

In this example, the parameters of heavier are pointers to objects of type Part, so the compiler determines that the getTotalWeight method being invoked on these arguments is the one introduced by Part. Because Assembly is derived (publicly) from Part, either argu-

---

3. Dynamic "typechecking" in our model is done using data that is available at runtime. This data includes classes, but not types. The C++ standard now includes runtime type information (RTTI) [111]. This is metadata. Our feeling is that RTTI is not an essential component of DTS C++, however, because other mechanisms that provide the same capabilities are already available.

4. If different ancestors introduce methods of the same name, the rules become more complicated. Also, method argument types are taken into account during the search process, as necessary to support overloading in C++. There is no need to discuss these details, because they are not important for the code in this book.

ment might actually address an object of class Assembly. If so, the getTotalWeight implementation defined by Assembly is used for such arguments. In other words, C++ determines what virtual function is being invoked on an object at compile time (by using the target object's type) and then, given this information, performs runtime method resolution according to the target object's class.

The heavier function above is **polymorphic,** which simply means that its code is appropriate for use on different classes of objects. There are various ways of implementing polymorphic functions, but in object-oriented programming this is normally achieved as it is here, by using virtual functions when manipulating objects. Here is an example code block that illustrates the use of heavier on different classes of objects.

```
{
    Part cp1, cp2;
    Assembly assm1, assm2;

    cp1.setBaseWeight(1.0);
    cp2.setBaseWeight(2.0);

    assm1.setBaseWeight(1.0);
    Part *contained1[] = {&cp1, &cp2, 0};
    assm1.setContainedParts(contained1);

    assm2.setBaseWeight(1.0);
    Part *contained2[] = {&cp1, &assm1, 0};
    assm2.setContainedPart(contained2);

    Part *heavier1 = heavier(&cp1, &cp2); // returns a pointer to cp2
    Part *heavier2 = heavier(&assm1, &cp1); // returns a pointer to assm1
    Part *heavier3 = heavier(&assm1, &assm2); // returns a pointer to assm2
}
```

Virtual function implementations can themselves be polymorphic. For example, the implementation of getTotalWeight by Assembly is polymorphic. This is what allows correct computation of total weight for assemblies whose subparts are themselves assemblies. The word "polymorphic" has been used in various ways. For example, we have encountered the phrases "polymorphic object" and even "polymorphic class." In this book, we use this adjective to describe code, not data.

5.1.1 Program Initialization

The entry point for a C++ program is a function named main that is defined by the programmer. Before main is entered, however, various initialization activities are performed. These activities include execution of code that initializes the C++ runtime library, followed by execution of code that initializes any global variables that are used by the program. When global variables contain objects, their constructors are executed to perform the necessary initializations. Thus, by the time that main is actually entered, quite a lot of code may have been executed as part of program initialization. In DTS C++, statically defined classes are also global objects, so the program initialization phase is extended to include their construction as well, as discussed in the following section.

5.2 DTS C++ Basics

Although there is no compiler for the exact dialect of DTS C++ presented here, we write as if there were one. The job of this compiler is to translate DTS C++ into code that uses our metaobject protocol when appropriate. For example, the generated code that builds classes simply calls methods of the class construction protocol with the appropriate information. DTS C++ classes with static definitions (that is, classes defined using DTS C++ syntax) are constructed during the program initialization phase.

Recall that class construction begins by invoking makeInstance on a metaclass determined dynamically from the parent classes and the explicit metaclass. The default parent for a class is *Object* if no parent is specified. This is a difference between DTS C++ and C++, for which the inheritance hierarchy has no top. Similarly, *Class* is the default explicit metaclass when one is not indicated.

5.2.1 Class Definitions in DTS C++

The syntax of C++ already provides for specification of the parents of a class, but additional provision must be made for declaration of the explicit metaclass. DTS C++ therefore provides a special syntax for this purpose.[5]

```
class <class-name> : <parent-list> : <explicit-metaclass>
{
    <class-body>
};
```

The following example illustrates the use of this DTS C++ syntax to define a class whose explicit metaclass is *Class*. As illustrated by this example, the values for *Class* and *Object* are denoted in DTS C++ by the names Class and Object.[6] These two primitive classes are created during initialization of the DTS C++ runtime so that they are subsequently available during program initialization and execution.

---

5. This notation was introduced by Tom Pennello of MetaWare during the design of DTS C++.

6. In general, when used as a data expression in DTS C++, the name of a statically defined class denotes a pointer to that class at runtime.

Example.

```
class Example {
    ...
};
```

has the same meaning as

```
class Example : public virtual Object : Class {
    ...
};
```

☐

This example illustrates the fact that DTS C++ syntax retains the ability to indicate virtual bases explicitly, but use of this syntax is not necessary. Parent classes in DTS C++ are always treated as are virtual base classes in C++, whether or not the keyword virtual is used. (Details concerning inheritance are discussed in Section 5.3.) Once a class is created, the call to initializeClass informs the nascent class object of its parents and introduced instance variables.

5.2.2   Introducing Instance Variables in DTS C++

Here is an example that illustrates instance variable introduction in DTS C++, which is written exactly as in normal C++.

Example.

```
class Book {
      char* title;
      char* authors;
};
class InventoryItem : {
      long number;
      long cost;
};
class StockedBook : Book, InventoryItem {
      long price
      char* location;
};
```

The DTS C++ class definitions above are illustrated in Figure 5-1, where all the class objects are instances of *Class*.

☐

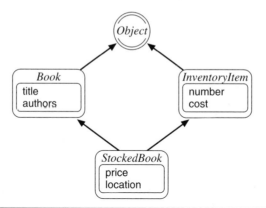

Figure 5-1. Graphical representation of ancestors of StockedBook.

5.2.3   Introducing Methods in DTS C++

In our object model, method implementations are defined when methods are introduced or when they are overridden. When constructing a class X, addMethod adds each newly introduced method <X,"mname"> and its corresponding code pointer to X's mdefs instance variable and to X's mtab instance variable. In DTS C++, the code pointers address member functions defined by the programmer, exactly as in normal C++. Here is an example that illustrates this.

Example.

```
class Book {
      string title;
      string authors;
      // declare and introduce the method <Book,"isAuthor">
      virtual boolean isAuthor( char* surName );
};

// define the code that implements the method <Book,"isAuthor">
boolean Book :: isAuthor(char* surName)
{
    return (strstr(authors, surName) != 0);
}
```

This class definition is depicted in Figure 5-2, where all the class objects are instances of Class.

□

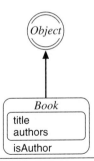

Figure 5-2. Graphical representation of Book.

5.2.4 Method Overrides and Parent Method Calls in DTS C++

For each inherited method <*Y*,"mname"> that is overridden by *X*, overrideMethod adds <*Y*,"mname"> and its corresponding code pointer to *X*'s mdefs instance variable and replaces the inherited code pointer associated with this method in *X*'s mtab instance variable. An example that illustrates this is presented below. Also, the override of <*InventoryItem*,"value"> in this example illustrates the DTS C++ syntax for parent method calls (see Section 4.7).

Example.

```
class Book : {
        string title;
        string authors;
        // Introduce <Book, "isAuthor">
        virtual boolean isAuthor( string surName )
};
class InventoryItem : {
        long number;
        long cost;
        // Introduce <InventoryItem,"value">
        virtual long value() { return number * cost; }
};
class StockedBook : Book, InventoryItem {
        long markup;
        string location;
        // Override <InventoryItem,"value">
        virtual long value()
        {
            return number * markup + __parent->value();
        }
};
```

This example is depicted in Figure 5-3, where all the class objects are instances of Class.

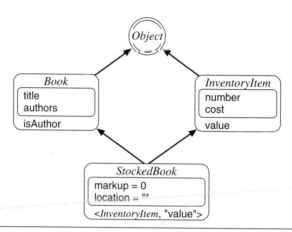

Figure 5-3. Graphical representation (including method definitions) of ancestors of StockedBook.

As illustrated by the examples above, DTS C++ uses C++ syntax to make our object model easy to use. To a large extent, DTS C++ code looks and executes exactly as would be expected by a C++ programmer. Aside from explicit metaclasses and parent method calls, the most important distinction between C++ and DTS C++ concerns the semantics of inheritance.

5.3 Graph Versus Tree Inheritance

C++ actually supports two different kinds of inheritance. The default can be termed **tree inheritance** for reasons explained below. Among object-oriented programming languages, this kind of inheritance is unique to C++. The other kind, called **graph inheritance,** is provided by our model as well as by all other multiple-inheritance object-oriented programming languages.[7]

---

7. The terms "tree inheritance" and "graph inheritance" were introduced by Alan Snyder early in the history of object-oriented programming [109]. In C++ terminology, tree inheritance is called simply "inheritance," and graph inheritance is called "virtual inheritance." We prefer Snyder's terminology because (as will be seen) it is motivated by a graphical representation that distinguishes between the semantics of these two different kinds of inheritance.

Graph inheritance is indicated in C++ by consistent use of the virtual keyword during declaration of parent classes (official C++ terminology for a parent class is "direct base class"). But virtual base classes in C++ are somewhat problematic. For example, avoiding multiple executions of operations in virtual bases during simulation of parent method calls in multiple-inheritance C++ hierarchies is quite awkward, nor is it easy to arrange for descendant classes' implementations to be entered before their ancestors' implementations. Monotonic linearization[8] and parent method calls (both explained in Chapter 4) solve these problems for DTS C++, which is good because both of these properties are important for reliable metaclass composition via multiple inheritance. We believe that they are useful properties in general.

In this section, we compare tree inheritance and graph inheritance, and explain why our model (and therefore DTS C++) omits support for tree inheritance. As a first step, we focus on the essential characteristic of tree inheritance. A C++ class that relies on tree inheritance inherits multiple copies of "the same" instance variables from some ancestor class through more than one inheritance path. Let us look at what this means, using a simple C++ example to illustrate the essential ideas.

Example.

Student employees have two names.

```
class Person {
  public:
    char name[100];
    Person() { strcpy(name, "unknown"); }
};
class Student : public Person { };
class Employee : public Person { };
class StudentEmployee : public Student, public Employee { };
```

□

In this example, the StudentEmployee class inherits from Person through two different inheritance paths (one through Student and one through Employee). The result, because of tree inheritance, is that a StudentEmployee object contains two copies of the Person instance variables — one copy within an Employee portion and the other copy within a Student portion. Figure 5-4 illustrates two graphical ways of viewing this situation. The inheritance hierarchy view explains the origin of the term "tree inheritance." The structural view illustrates the typical layout of a StudentEmployee object. Note the hierarchical containment relationships illustrated by the structural view.

---

8. As we explained in Chapter 4, monotonic linearization refers to the fact that the implementation chains of a class hierarchy (and not the method resolution order) are monotonically increasing.

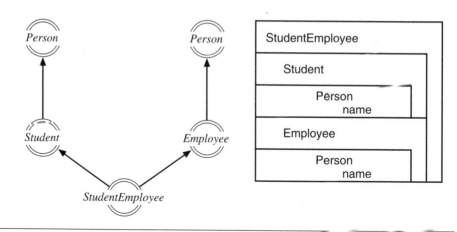

Figure 5-4. Tree inheritance: student employees have two names.

Thus, the following expression is ambiguous (and illegal) in C++.

(new StudentEmployee)->name; // Error. There are two different name fields in the object.

To access the name of a StudentEmployee it is necessary to select which Person's name is desired — the name in the Person in the Student in the StudentEmployee or the name in the Person in the Employee in the StudentEmployee. In general, these names can have different values. For example, we can rewrite the expression above to select the name in the Person in the new StudentEmployee by using typecasting as follows:

((Person*)(new StudentEmployee))->name;

In contrast, Figure 5-5 provides the corresponding graph inheritance illustrations. The class hierarchy view illustrates the reason for the term "graph inheritance," and the structural view is also important. One can interpret this structure as indicating that each ancestor of a class appears at the same level within an instance of the class. There are no inner containment relationships within the object. All methods and instance data relate to the object as a whole — not to different parts of the object.

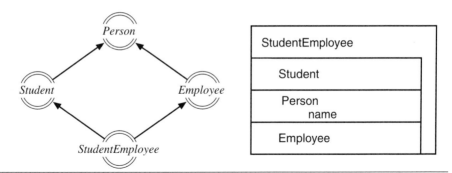

Figure 5-5. Graph inheritance: student employees have one name.

Example.

Student employees have one name.

```
class Person {
    public:
        char name[100];
        Person() { strcpy(name, "unknown"); }
};
class Employee : public virtual Person { };
class Student : public virtual Person { };
class StudentEmployee : public virtual Student, public virtual Employee { };
```

Assuming that we believe student employees should have only one name, the example above illustrates the fact that tree inheritance is not always the most appropriate model. So when is tree inheritance needed? Let us consider the motivating example for tree inheritance provided in Section 10.1 in *The Annotated C++ Reference Manual* [38]. This example should be more representative of situations in which tree inheritance is useful to C++ programmers. The example provided in [38] is not complete, but we believe that the following example represents a faithful rendering of its intention. The class hierarchy is basically identical to that of the previous example.

Example.

An example in which tree inheritance is relied on (part 1 of 2).

```
class Link {
    public:
        Link *next;
        Link() { next = 0; }
};
class X: public Link {
    public:
        void addX(X*);
        void processX();
};
class Y: public Link {
    public:
        void addY(Y*);
        void processY ();
};
class Z: public X, public Y {

// ...

};
```

□

The following code represents the use to which *The Annotated C++ Reference Manual* [38] suggests that tree inheritance can be put. The basic idea is that, because the X and Y portions of a Z object contain different Links, a Z object can be contained in two different (perhaps X and Y) lists.

Example.

An example in which tree inheritance is relied on (part 2 of 2).

```
void X :: addX( X* nextX ) { next = nextX; } // Add an X to the Link in an X

void X :: processX()  // process an X list starting with the target object
{   X *elem = this;
    do {
        // ...; // process a list element
        elem = (X*) (elem->next); // select next X from the Link in the target
    } while ( elem );
}
```

```
// similarly for Y

main() // Put Z objects on X and Y lists, and then process them
{
    typedef Z* pZ;
    pZ z1 = new Z, z2 = new Z, z3 = new Z, z4 = new Z, z5 = new Z;
    z1->addX(z2); z2->addX(z3);
    z1->addY(z2); z2->addY(z4); z4->addY(z5);
    z1->processX();
    z2->processY();
}
```

☐

Thus, tree inheritance in this case can be considered "useful."

What is different about the two examples above? One way of looking at this question is to suggest that tree inheritance confuses specialization by subclassing (the "is a" relationship) with aggregation by introduction of instance variables (the "has a" relationship). A simple linguistic test can be used to distinguish these two things. For example, it makes sense to say "A Student *is a* Person, and an Employee *is a* Person" but it does not make much sense to say that "A Student *has a* Person." As we have seen, graph inheritance is appropriate for implementing such class relationships. On the other hand, in the tree inheritance example above, the situation is exactly reversed. The statements "An X *has a* Link" and "A Y *has a* Link" seem to represent fairly well the underlying usage semantics that tree inheritance supports.

We believe that when tree inheritance is actually required by a C++ class hierarchy (as opposed to simply being used because it is the convenient default provided by the language), this represents a misuse of inheritance to achieve a result that should instead be arranged by using aggregation. For example, the classes X and Y above can each introduce a separate Link instance variable to support their respective lists.

The implication is that there is no fundamental need for tree inheritance, and that the default inheritance model of C++ supports (and, to some extent, represents) a confusion between aggregation and inheritance. This is why neither our object model nor our dialect of DTS C++ supports tree inheritance. Instead of using tree inheritance, DTS C++ programmers use design patterns based on aggregation and graph inheritance.[9] This is always possible, and although we do not elaborate on it here, it is always possible to convert C++ class hierarchies that rely on tree inheritance to DTS C++ hierarchies.[10]

---

9. Useful design patterns based on aggregation are presented in [47]. For an insightful discussion of fundamental principles (metapatterns) underlying these patterns, we recommend [107].

10. See Exercise 5.6. For those interested in exploring the issues of inheritance in object-oriented programming, an excellent tutorial can be found in [111].

This section has explained why tree inheritance is not needed in an object model. Because tree inheritance is most easily distinguished from graph inheritance in the case of multiple inheritance, we have used multiple-inheritance examples in our discussion. We have chosen these examples to focus as simply as possible on the difference between tree and graph inheritance, not to address the question of when single or multiple inheritance should be used in class frameworks. By their very nature, aggregation-based design patterns avoid the need for inheritance and specifically allow class designers to avoid design mistakes supported by tree inheritance. However, inheritance is still important because it provides the basis for polymorphic code, which supports reuse. In particular, multiple inheritance is essential to automatic composition of metaclasses, which allows reuse of metaclass code that implements object properties. This topic is addressed in subsequent chapters. Our purpose here remains an explanation of the distinguishing features of DTS C++.

5.4 Typechecking

Typechecking ensures that the values assigned to variables and formal parameters at runtime conform to their declared types and that, in the case of objects, the methods invoked on objects and the instance variables accessed in objects are supported by their classes. The set of types that are available and the rules for verifying conformance constitute the type system of a language.[11] Our object model has interesting implications with respect to the type system of DTS C++. This section addresses these issues.

Let us start with a quick review of typechecking in C++ before we consider typechecking in DTS C++. As part of typechecking, C++ compilers determine an "expected" type for all data expressions.[12] This is done using the statically declared types of variables and the signatures of the operations used in data expressions. It is a simple process to understand. For example, if add has the signature (int,int)->int, and the variables x and y are of type int, what do you think is the expected type of the data expression add(x,y)?

Given the ability to determine expected types, for each statement that assigns data to a variable the C++ compiler performs one of the following verifications.

* If nonobject data is being assigned, typechecking verifies that the expected type of the data is the same as the statically declared type of the variable.

* If an object is being assigned, typechecking verifies that the expected type of the object descends from the statically declared type of the variable.

---

11. Two excellent tutorials on the issues of type systems can be found in [19] and [28].

12. In our terminology, the terms "type," "static type," and "expected type" all mean the same thing. We use the term "expected type" to highlight the fact that a C++ compiler in general determines a type for all expressions, even when a programmer does not explicitly provide a type.

In short, typechecking for object assignment is based on the class hierarchy. Similar rules are followed for checking the arguments that are passed to operations. Additionally, for method invocation and instance variable access, the compiler verifies that the expected type of the target object supports the indicated method or instance variable. A combined result of all of the verifications above is a guarantee that the methods invoked on objects and the instance variables that are accessed in objects are always supported by their classes. Put simply, static typechecking in C++ prevents runtime method resolution errors.

There is an escape clause, however. Dynamic cast operations allow a programmer to convert a pointer to an expected object type into a pointer for a more special (that is, descendant) object type. This can be very useful because it extends the available behaviors of the object, but it delegates responsibility for type safety to the programmer, who is assumed to have knowledge of a wider context than that employed by static typechecking. Although this is an important facility, programmers have been known to err in their reasoning. Therefore, such dynamic cast operations are verified at runtime. This does not prevent runtime type errors caused by faulty reasoning on the part of a programmer, but it guarantees that type errors will be recognized immediately at their source – an invalid cast operation.[13]

5.4.1   Typechecking and Metaclasses in DTS C++

Our object model has important implications for the expected types of class objects in DTS C++. This can be seen most clearly by considering the signature of getClass, a primitive function of our metaobject protocol that returns the value of the class slot.

The argument type for getClass is Object*. In other words, getClass can be applied to all objects. This should come as no surprise, because all objects have a class slot. In contrast, the expected type of the result returned by getClass is a matter of some interest. Let us begin understanding this type by considering the result of getClass more closely.

The result of getClass is an object reference, and thus one possible expected type for this result would be Object*. But we can be more exact than this. The result is also a class reference, and so a better expected type would be Class*. But even this can be improved. Consider the following code fragment. Note that ordinary objects are typed with ordinary classes whereas ordinary classes are typed with metaclasses.

```
X aVar;
Class* aClass = getClass( &aVar );
```

In this example, the result of the call to getClass must be an instance of X's metaclass. How can we use this fact to improve the expected type of the getClass result? The answer is provided by the explicit metaclass for X.

---

13. See Exercise 5.7. Also, as suggested by Exercise 5.8, static typechecking can prevent runtime dynamic cast errors for an important special case of metaclasses.

A class object responds to all methods supported by its explicit metaclass. Thus, in the case in which getClass is invoked on an instance of a class whose declaration includes an explicit metaclass, an even better result type for getClass is the explicitly indicated metaclass (where the expected type of the object being passed to getClass is what we look at to find an explicit metaclass declaration).

Notice how the expected type of the result returned from getClass now depends on the expected type of its argument. Such a function is said to have a **dependent type.** C++ provides no direct way of specifying the signature of such a function, but full knowledge of this aspect of getClass can and should be included in how DTS C++ does typechecking.[14] The reason is that the more precisely we approximate the actual class of the result returned from getClass, the more useful this result becomes — because it can be passed to more operations and therefore can be used in more ways.

And we are not finished. Just as a class must respond to the methods supported by its explicit metaclass, we know that all of its descendants must likewise respond to these methods (owing to our model's use of derived metaclasses to guarantee inheritance of metaclass constraints). So, finally, the expected type of the result returned from getClass can be represented as a metaclass derived from all of the metaclass constraints of the argument object's expected type.

In summary, when a class X is defined by subclassing, typechecking in DTS C++ uses a derived metaclass (in general) to represent the expected type of the subclass. This metaclass is derived from the expected types of the parents of the new class, which is justified by the use of derived metaclasses to satisfy inheritance of metaclass constraints at runtime. Then, when getClass is executed on an object whose expected type is the class X, the expected type of the result is the metaclass that was derived as the expected type of X when X was defined. This is the only change to the normal computation of expected types in C++ that is required for incorporation of our object model.

---

14. C++ already includes limited support for dependent types. A C++ virtual function is allowed to specialize the type of its result in comparison with the result types declared for the method by its ancestors. Thus, the expected type for the result of a method invocation can depend on the expected type of the target object on which the method is invoked. Unfortunately, the ability to specify such methods (which are said to be covariant with respect to their return types) cannot be used to provide a C++ declaration for the getClass function. First, the capability just described relates to the expected type of the method target, not of a method argument. Second, the textual specification of such a virtual function is distributed throughout separate class definitions as method overrides. Even if getClass were modeled as a method (instead of a primitive function), no such overrides for getClass would appear. A general discussion of covariance (and contravariance) for methods in object-oriented programming can be found in [28].

5.4.2   Expected Types and Method Resolution

As we have mentioned, C++ (and also DTS C++, of course) uses the expected type of an object at compile time to determine an introducing class when a method is invoked on the object. This is necessary because C++ syntax does not allow a programmer to indicate this information explicitly.[15] Here is a DTS C++ example that illustrates how all this plays out when derived metaclasses are used to represent the expected type returned by getClass.

```
class MX : public Class {
    public:
    void foo() { printf("1"); }
}
class MY : public Class {
    public:
    void foo() { printf("2"); }
}
class X : public Object : MX{
    public:
    void test() { getClass(this)->foo(); } // OK
}
class Y : public X : MY{
    void test1() {getClass(this)->foo();} //Error: which foo should be used (MX's or MY's)?
}

void bar(X* x)
{
    x->test(); // OK.
}

main()
{
    Y *y = new Y;
    bar(y); // OK
}
```

Figure 5-6 is an illustration to help readers understand the example above. Note that *MY* is the explicitly declared metaclass for *Y*, but the actual metaclass for *Y* is *DMC*, a derived metaclass. Further note that *Y* is the first parent of *DMC*.

---

15. C++ allows "nonvirtual" method invocations, using syntax such as X::foo(), but this requests X's implementation of foo, thus ignoring the contents of the actual target object's method table, and it still leaves the introducing class for foo up to the compiler.

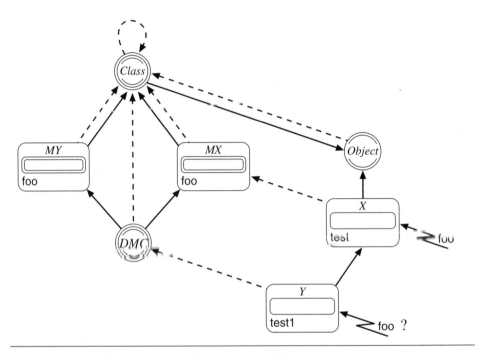

Figure 5-6. Example of a problem in C++ method resolution.

In Figure 5-6, by following the rules for typechecking mentioned above, it can be seen that *MX* is the expected type used by DTS C++ typechecking for the class of an object whose expected type is *X* (for example, *MX* is the expected type of the value returned by executing getClass on an instance of *X*). Likewise, *DMC* is the derived metaclass used by DTS C++ typechecking as the expected type of the class of an object whose expected type is *Y* (for example, *DMC* is the expected type of the value returned by executing getClass on an instance of *Y*). Note that there are two different foo methods inherited by *DMC* — that is, <*MX*,"foo"> and <*MY*,"foo"> are different methods (not overrides of the same method). The reason for the error in the code above is that the programmer has not provided the compiler with enough information to determine which of these methods is to be invoked by test1.

There is absolutely nothing wrong with the classes in this example, nor is there any fundamental reason for considering the methods supported by *DMC* to be in any way ambiguous. Of course, the programmer of test1 needs to decide what method is to be invoked, but programmers should always know what methods they intend their code to invoke. The only problem in this case is how to communicate a decision using C++ syntax, which does not allow the programmer to indicate an introducing class for a method when invoking it.

There is a simple way around this problem, which is hinted at by the signature of the function bar in this example. Notice that its argument is typed as an *X*, so even if a *Y* is passed to it, *MX*'s foo is executed. Similarly, to avoid a typechecking error and arrange for *MY*'s foo to be executed by test1 (assuming that this is what is desired), the programmer of *Y* can simply cast the result of getClass in test1 to MY* when invoking foo, as follows:

```
void Y :: test1()
{
    ((MY*)getClass(this))->foo();
}
```

In other words, because C++ uses static types to determine introducing classes, one can guide this determination by using typecasting on method targets. Use of typecasting for this purpose honors the semantics of the target object, and only affects the choice of introducing class. In contrast, nonvirtual method invocation in C++ requests a specific class's implementation, and therefore does not necessarily honor the true semantics of the target object.

With the above version of test1, invocations of test on objects of type *X* (or below) use *MX*'s foo, and invocations of test1 on objects of type *Y* (or below) use *MY*'s foo. Based on this example, you should now understand the important interaction between typechecking and method resolution in DTS C++, including the use of derived metaclasses as expected types in the case of getClass.

5.4.3 Dominance Violations

In addition to ensuring type conformance, and thus an absence of runtime method resolution errors, C++ typechecking is also responsible for preventing a particular misuse of graph inheritance. Because our model is based on graph inheritance, it is easy to see why this additional aspect of C++ typechecking is also important for DTS C++.

To explain the problem being checked, Figure 5-7 depicts a situation in which the class *Z* does not override <*W*,"foo">, although both of its two parents do. If the method <*W*,"foo"> in Figure 5-7 is a cooperative-override method, then, as discussed in the previous chapter, when it is invoked on an instance of *Z* (or some descendant of *Z*), both *X* and *Y* are able to enact the characteristic "behavior" of their objects. In general, because all overrides of a cooperative-override method make a parent method call, all classes that define an implementation participate in its overall execution. As a result, for cooperative-override methods, the semantics of subclassing that suggests in this case that a *Z* "is a" *X* and also "is a" *Y* is easily and naturally obtained.

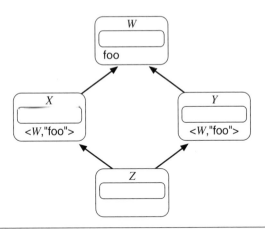

Figure 5-7. A C++ dominance violation.

However, C++ does not have cooperative-override methods, and if <*W*,"foo"> is not a cooperative-override method, there is no guarantee that both the *X* and *Y* implementations will get to execute when <*W*,"foo"> is invoked on a *Z* object (assuming that the class *Z* is allowed to exist). There is no reason whatsoever to believe that the behavioral requirements of both *X* and *Y* will be met in such a case, and C++ typechecking therefore prevents the creation of such classes by issuing a fatal error if they are defined. The typechecking rule used for this purpose can be understood as follows.

In Figure 5-7, because *X* and *Y* are unrelated by inheritance, neither *X*'s implementation nor *Y*'s implementation of <*W*, "foo"> "dominates" the other (or even necessarily knows about the other), so there is no good choice for which implementation should be inherited by *Z*. This is termed a **dominance violation** by *Z* with respect to the method <*W*, "foo">. If *Z* were to override <*W*,"foo"> in this example, there would be no dominance violation.

Of course, there are special cases of graph inheritance in which there can be no dominance violations. For example, if all classes that inherit a method override it, there can be no dominance violations on that method. Also, dominance violations cannot arise in purely single-inheritance hierarchies. However, multiple inheritance is an important capability that enables enhanced reuse of implementation, and requiring classes to override all methods prevents reuse.

Thus, it is crucially important that dominance is not necessary in the case of cooperative-override methods, which are designed to work with multiple inheritance and require only the absence of serious ordering disagreements among parents' method resolution orders. This suggests that methods supported by metaclasses should be cooperative-override methods — otherwise, derived metaclasses might have dominance violations — and it also underscores the importance of being able to declare cooperative-override methods explicitly. This is what allows the compiler to give special treatment to cooperative-override methods, ensuring that overrides perform parent method calls and checking for serious ordering violations rather than dominance violations.[16]

The keyword cooperative is used to declare a cooperative-override method, and it implies virtual. The following code fragment illustrates the syntax.

```
Class Example
{
    public:
        cooperative void exampleMethod();
};
```

So, when a class is defined, our DTS C++ compiler (which does not exist) statically verifies that

- There are no serious order disagreements among the ancestors of the class.
- Each override of a cooperative method makes a parent method call on all execution paths.
- For all other virtual methods, there are no dominance violations.

Let us review the two important results of this section. We have shown how to determine the expected type of the result returned by getClass, and we have shown that cooperative methods do not require the restrictive typechecking normally provided by C++ in the case of graph inheritance (although it is still required in the case of noncooperative methods). These are the only enhancements of the C++ static typechecking system required for typechecking DTS C++.

5.4.4 Cooperative Methods and Parent Calls

This subsection presents an example of the capabilities of cooperative methods and parent method calls. This example is similar to the situation depicted in Figure 5-7, where either of two different method implementations (neither of which dominates the other) could potentially be inherited into the method table of a subclass. The example is based on the Part/Assembly classes presented at the beginning of this chapter.

---

16. DTS C++ programmers normally use parent calls in cooperative methods to create implementations for which dominance violations can be ignored. To remind programmers of their responsibility to achieve this result, the compiler provides a warning for overrides of cooperative methods that do not make parent calls on all execution paths. It is therefore expected that programmers of cooperative methods will satisfy this responsibility. For noncooperative methods, there is no such expectation, and so the compiler issues errors when encountering dominance violations on such methods.

Example.

```
class Part{ // as it appeared in C++, but getTotalWeight is now cooperative
    private:
        float baseWeight;
    public:
        Part() { baseWeight = 0.0; }
        virtual void setBaseWeight(float w) { baseWeight = w; };
        cooperative float getTotalWeight() { return baseWeight; };
};
class Assembly : public virtual Part{ // note: cooperative override of getTotalWeight
    protected:
        Part **contained; // an array of references to subParts
    public:
        Assembly() { contained = 0; }
        virtual void setContainedParts(Part **cps) { contained = cps; }
        cooperative float getTotalWeight()
        {
            float result = __parent->getTotalWeight();
            if (contained) {
                // add the subPart weights to the result
                for (Part **cpp = contained; *cpp; cpp++)
                    result += (*cpp)->getTotalWeight();
            }
            return result;
        }
};
class PackagedPart : public virtual Part { // cooperative override of getTotalWeight
    private:
        float packageWeight;
    public:
        PackagedPart(); // a constructor used for initialization
        virtual void setPackageWeight(float w) { packageWeight = w; }
        virtual float getPostage(float rate) { return rate * getTotalWeight(); }
        cooperative float getTotalWeight()
        {
            return packageWeight + __parent->getTotalWeight();
        }
};
class Z1 : public virtual PackagedPart, public virtual Assembly { };
class Z2 : public virtual Assembly, public virtual PackagedPart { };
```

□

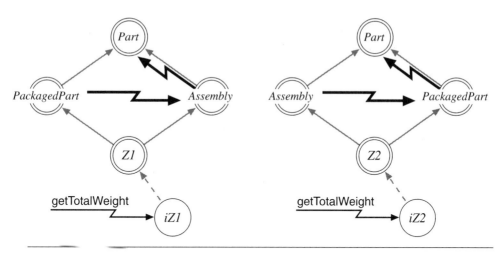

Figure 5-8. Composition of PackagedPart and Assembly using multiple inheritance.

Figure 5-8 provides diagrams that illustrate the execution of getTotalWeight when getPostage is invoked on either a Z1 or a Z2 object. The resulting execution path for getTotalWeight is highlighted using bold lightning. Remember that both PackagedPart and Assembly are independently derived from Part. These classes have no reason to expect (or not to expect) the existence of a future subclass that decides to inherit from both of them.

The classes Z1 and Z2 in Figure 5-8 represent two different ways of defining a packaged assembly. Note that it does not matter which implementation is inherited into the new subclass (that is, the ordering of parents does not matter). In either case, getTotalWeight is computed correctly by visiting each ancestor that defines it. More to the point, however, is the fact that neither the designer of PackagedPart nor the designer of Assembly would ever make a nonvirtual call to the implementation provided by the other. Only for instances of Z1 or Z2 is this even appropriate. Yet, this is exactly what is accomplished by parent method calls when they are based on monotonically linearized implementation chains.

Remember that the C++ implementation of Assembly (on page 89) made a nonvirtual method call to Part to "simulate" a parent call. This is the best that a C++ programmer can do, and, if no descendants of Assembly use multiple inheritance, it works fine. But if this had been done in the example above, neither Z1 nor Z2 would have operated correctly. Parent method calls in our model are guided by the class of the target object, just as normal method resolution is so guided.

With the right support from language primitives (namely, parent method calls based on a monotonically linearized implementation chain), it is possible to design and implement cooperative methods for which dominance violations are not a problem. Such methods are useful in multiple-inheritance languages because their executions can successfully compose implementations inherited from different parents. Without strong semantic support from language primitives, it is very hard to arrange for method executions with this property.

5.5 Summary

This chapter has provided an overview of DTS C++. Significant differences between C++ and DTS C++ are summarized in Table 5-1. After taking a language-independent approach for the first four chapters of this book, our reasons for introducing a language at this point were to:

- Provide a convenient syntax for class definition and method invocation. Without such a syntax, the examples we present in succeeding chapters would appear very awkward.

- Show how our metaobject protocol can be effectively used with a programming language. This chapter provides an example of a C++-based programming language that employs our metaobject protocol, and summarizes the enhancements required for extending C++ typechecking to handle our model.

DTS C++ differs from C++ in many ways. Most importantly (aside from the important capabilities that it adds to C++), DTS C++ does not support tree inheritance. We believe that this corrects a problem of C++, in which multiple inheritance allows the mixing of "has a" with "is a" relationships. Because most programmers have only seen the C++ version of multiple inheritance, multiple inheritance in general has been given an unwarranted bad reputation. Cooperative methods and parent calls in DTS C++ offer improved support for multiple inheritance, which becomes exceptionally valuable in the context of metaclass programming, as we shall see.

5.6 Exercises

5.1   Consider the following DTS C++ class declarations. Which are the metaclasses? (Hint: use Theorem 4.)

```
class X : Class { }
class Y : Object : X { }
class Z : X, Y { }
```

5.2   Section 4.2 describes the metaobject protocol methods getIV and setIV. As described in that section, these methods could be used to circumvent the access protection of DTS C++. This is not an issue that this book addresses. How should our object model be changed to allow enforcement of DTS C++ access control?

Table 5-1. Summary of Differences between DTS C++ and C++

Feature	DTS C++	C++
inheritance	all classes are descended from *Object*	it is not necessary for a class to have any parents
multiple inheritance	only graph inheritance	both graph and tree inheritance
cooperative methods	indicated by the keyword **cooperative** and facilitated by monotonic linearization	no distinction made between cooperative and noncooperative methods
parent method calls	expressed with syntax: __parent -> *<method-name>* (*<actual-parameters>*)	no such concept
metaclasses	expressed with syntax: class *<class-name>* : *<parent-list>* : *<explicit-metaclass>*	no such concept

5.3   Consider the following data model, which is expressed in C++ with tree inheritance:

```
class Tire {
        int pressure;
}
class LeftFrontTire : Tire {}
class RightFrontTire : Tire {}
class LeftRearTire : Tire {}
class RightRearTire : Tire {}
class Car : LeftFrontTire, RightFrontTire, LeftRearTire, RightRearTire { }
```

How many <Tire,"pressure"> instance variables does an instance of Car have? Does it seem reasonable to say that a Car is a special kind of LeftFrontTire (and so on)? What advice would you give the programmer of this code?

5.4   Consider the use of a cooperative-override method to determine which descendants of its introducing class view an object as containing data or functionality "matching" a search criterion. (a) If a cooperative-override method is used to implement a search in which there are multiple potential respondents, list different alternatives for collecting responses. (b) How could one collect a set of so-called dominant responses? (c) Identify a typical use for such patterns in class frameworks.

5.5   Based on the cooperative-override search patterns of Exercise 5.4, (a) suggest a general pattern for transforming C++ tree inheritance to graph inheritance. (b) Is there any need to consider multiple search responses?

5.6   Consider the general question of allowing a class to prescribe certain aspects of how subclasses should implement a method. (a) Why is this useful? (b) Can you think of useful examples other than cooperative overrides?

5.7   Refer to the example diagramed in Figure 3-17 on page 54. If DTS C++ is used to program these metaclasses and the cast operation includes dynamic verification, what can one conclude about invocation of hook on an instance *iY* of class *Y*?

5.8   Figure 3-17 on page 54 represents a situation typical of "implicit metaclasses" as provided by Smalltalk. As explained in [31], implicit metaclasses are type safe when programmed in this way because their instances are guaranteed to be of a specific class or of a descendant of that class, and the object involved in the cast operation (such as required for use of hook in the example) is an instance of the metaclass instance. Although implicit metaclasses are type safe, they cannot be reused, as can explicit metaclasses in our model. Suggest an enhancement of static typechecking in DTS C++ that allows explicit metaclasses to be programmed in this way while avoiding the need for dynamic verification during class construction (and the possibility of runtime type errors). Specifically, what additional static information about a metaclass is required at compile time for this purpose, and how would it be used by typechecking?

Chapter 6
Our Metaobject Protocol

A metaobject protocol is an interface to the implementation of a reflective class-based model that allows one to query information about the model and manipulate the model [69]. In the preceding chapters, some functions and methods of our metaobject protocol have been informally introduced to motivate the rationale for some aspects of the protocol. This chapter provides the entire rationale of our metaobject protocol, its interface (described in DTS C++), and its specification.

6.1 Interface to Our Metaobject Protocol

Let us begin our metaobject protocol specification with DTS C++ declarations for *Class* and *Object*. As preparation for this, we first define a few useful types and declare four primitive functions.

- string — This type is used to represent strings.

  typedef char* **string**;

- ObjectList — This type is used to represent lists of objects (often classes) that are passed to metaclass methods. This type has the definition

  class Object; // forward declare the Object type
  typedef Object** **ObjectList**;

  which is an array of pointers terminated by a NULL pointer.

- DataSegment — This type is used for describing instance variables in the interface to initializeClass. This type has the definition

```
typedef struct {
    string    name;
    long      size;
    void*     initialValue;
} DataSlot;
typedef DataSlot** DataSegment;
```

Note that this type emulates the inner dictionary needed to construct the data table for a class (see Definition 7).

- CodePtr — This type is used to represent the function pointers that access method implementations. This type has the definition
    ```
    typedef void* (*CodePtr)();
    ```
  For the sake of simplicity, we avoid the complexities of dealing with signature information here. This simplification eliminates what would be a large digression from our goal of showing how to put metaclasses to work. See Appendix B for details concerning this topic.

- MethodList — This type is used for retrieving the set of methods from a class. It has the definition
    ```
    class Class; // forward declare the Class type
    typedef struct {
        Class*   introducingClass;
        string   methodName;
    } Method;
    typedef Method** MethodList;
    ```

Our metaobject protocol includes four primitive operations that are represented as functions (not methods). These operations are declared as follows.

```
Class* getClass( Object* );
```

```
CodePtr parentResolve(   Object* target,
                         Class* overridingClass,
                         Class* introducingClass,
                         string methodName );
```

```
void apply( Object* target, CodePtr methodImpl, va_list paramList, void** result );
```

```
Class* solveMetaclassConstraints( ObjectList aMetaclassList, ObjectList aParentList );
```

The rationale for representing these primitives as functions rather than methods is our belief that their implementation should not be determined by programmers. Making them methods would require us to add the concept of a method that cannot be overridden, such as that provided by Java's final attribute. This is a useful concept, but not adding this complexity allows us to focus on putting metaclasses to work.

With the abovelisted type definitions and functions in mind, the DTS C++ declaration for *Object* is

```
class Object :  : Class{
    friend Class;
    public:
        cooperative boolean free();
        cooperative void* getIV( Class* aClass, string ivName );
        cooperative void setIV( Class* aClass, string ivName, void* value );
    protected:
        cooperative void initialize();
        cooperative void destroy();
        virtual void dispatch( Class* introducingClass,
                            string methodName,
                            va_list aParameterList,
                            void** result );
}
```

Note that with this declaration, the literal Object inside a fragment of DTS C++ has the same meaning as *Object* (the former, written in Helvetica, is a symbol declared to the C++ compiler, whereas the latter, written in italics, is our modeling notation that denotes the object reference to a particular class object).

Next we have the DTS C++ declaration for *Class*.

```
class Class : public virtual Object : Class {
    friend Object;
    protected:
        cooperative void deleteInstance( Object* anObject );
    public:
        cooperative Object* makeInstance( );

        cooperative boolean initializeClass(    ObjectList aParentList,
                                            DataSegment aDataSegment );
        cooperative void addMethod( Class* introducingClass,
                                string aMethodName,
                                CodePtr methodImpl );
        cooperative void overrideMethod(   Class* introducingClass,
                                        string aMethodName,
                                        CodePtr methodImpl );
        cooperative void readyClass();
```

```
        cooperative ObjectList getParents();
        cooperative ObjectList getMRO();
        cooperative boolean isSubclassOf( Class* anotherClass );
        cooperative boolean isDescendantOf( Class* anotherClass );
        cooperative boolean isAncestorOf( Class* anotherClass );

        cooperative boolean definesMethod( Class* aClass, string aMethodName );
        cooperative boolean supportsMethod( Class* aClass, string aMethodName );
        cooperative boolean introducesMethod( Class* aClass, string aMethodName );
        cooperative MethodList getSupportedMethods( );
        cooperative boolean supportsIV( Class* aClass, string anIVName );

        cooperative CodePtr resolveMethod( Class* introducingClass,
                                              string methodName);
        virtual CodePtr resolveTerminal( Class* introducingClass,
                                              string methodName);
        cooperative void putRDStub( Class* introducingClass, string methodName );
}
```

In the class declarations above, DTS C++ scope modifiers (public, private, and protected) are used to emphasize and enforce the usage rules for the methods. For example, initialize is declared protected because it can be invoked by makeInstance only. The DTS C++ declaration of various primitive functions indicates our belief that these may not be overridden (otherwise they would be methods of the appropriate class). Over the remainder of this chapter, all of these functions and methods are explained in a rational order, and a specification is given for each.

6.2 Object Creation

All classes respond to the method named makeInstance with the following specification.

```
Object* Class :: makeInstance( )
{ /* Specification */
```
Precondition:
        this->readyClass() *has been executed (that is, the class is usable)*
Action:
        Object* anInstance = {"class" = this} ◁ this.*Class*."ivs";
        // The above assignment sets anInstance to point to a dictionary that has the form
        // of an object. A heap memory allocation must be done for this new dictionary.
        anInstance->initialize( );
        return anInstance;
}

Let us take a moment to review our specification technique that was introduced in Section 1.3. A specification is divided into a precondition (a statement that must be true for the method to successfully execute) and an action (a small piece of procedural code that shows what the method does). The next thing to notice is that our specifications are not formal ("formal" means that there is a fixed syntax).

- Preconditions: The precondition for makeInstance is a statement about an event that must have occurred prior to the method executing.[1] In addition, if the method has appeared in any path expression, the path expression becomes part of the precondition (that is, the method can be invoked only under conditions that do not violate the path expression).

- Actions: An action is a procedural specification using C++ syntax as the outer syntax. The inner syntax uses the notation we developed for describing our object model. For example, the first line of the action for makeInstance indicates that the variable anInstance is set to an object reference to a new object (which must implicitly be created in the heap). The second line of the action expresses that makeInstance is obligated to invoke initialize. The third line is the specification of the return value. In addition, note that the methods invoked during an action are part of the specification (that is, any adherent implementation must call the methods indicated by the action, and only those methods).

The method makeInstance creates objects. This specification of makeInstance implies that there is a method named initialize to which all objects respond (that is, initialize is introduced by *Object*). initialize is a hook method[2]; it is made to be overridden by subclasses of *Object* so that the subclasses can initialize the instance variables of new objects. *Object*'s implementation of initialize does nothing because *Object* defines no instance variables.

```
void Object :: initialize()
{ /* Specification */
Action:
    // The default implementation of this method does nothing.
}
```

When *Object* was introduced in Section 2.6, we commented that it was convenient but not essential that all classes are descendants of *Object*. The combination of makeInstance and

---

1. There are formal languages called temporal logics that express such ideas, but to use them would be a digression from our objective of showing how to put metaclasses to work. Alternatively, historical data could be added to class objects to substitute for temporal predicates, but this would only obscure our concepts.

2. A hook method is one that is meant to be overridden [107]. It is a mechanism with which descendants can provide information to methods introduced by ancestors.

initialize reveals one aspect of the convenience. Because initialize is a method of *Object*, all objects respond to it. Therefore, our metaobject protocol can be designed to invoke it during object creation (execution of makeInstance). Without this convenience, object initialization is a notion separate from the metaobject protocol, and an important conceptual unification is lost.

6.3   Retrieving the Class of an Object

Once one has created an object, it is essential (for reflection) to allow the class of the object to be discovered at runtime. The function getClass has the following specification.

```
Class* getClass( Object* anObject )
{ /* Specification */
Action:
      return anObject."class";
}
```

This function returns the class reference of the class of the target object. Note that the C++ type of the returned value is declared here as Class*. As explained in Chapter 5, DTS C++ provides special typechecking support for getClass, a language primitive whose expected result type depends on the expected type of the argument. Owing to the limitations of DTS C++, it is not possible to specify more precisely the result type for getClass here.

One might consider an alternative approach, in which getClass is specified as a method (it would be introduced by *Object*). But, as mentioned above, getClass is given special support by DTS C++ typechecking, and it seems natural to associate such support with a primitive function instead of a method. Also, we wish to guarantee that an object cannot lie about its class, which could happen if getClass were a method that could be overridden. This could be prevented with a special case precondition in the specification of overrideMethod, but using a primitive function seems more natural.

This raises the question of what one can and cannot change with a metaobject protocol, which depends directly on the objective of the metaobject protocol. Our metaobject protocol is not intended to enable changes in our object model, which we carefully constructed from first principles. The objective of our metaobject protocol is to program metaclasses, which are to be class transformations. We want metaclasses viewed as transformations to be composable. This focuses the capabilities of the metaobject protocol and allows us to put metaclasses to work.

6.4 Freeing Objects

Because makeInstance dynamically allocates space for an object, our metaobject protocol must have a way to free the space when the object is no longer needed.

free is the name of the method to which all objects respond and that commands the object to release its storage. Symmetry might seem to indicate that free should be a method to which the class responds, because makeInstance is a method to which class objects respond. But usually the programmer has an object reference and is forced to write

    getClass(anObject)->free(anObject)

This is too distasteful when

    anObject->free( )

gets the job done. On the other hand, it might be better to have a class method. For example, an override of makeInstance would have a corresponding override of free, which would make metaclass programming simpler. The way out of this conundrum is to have two methods: free on all objects, which invokes the class method deleteInstance to actually free the storage.

```
boolean Object :: free()
{ /* Specification */
```
Precondition:
    this $\in$ *C implies* (*extentOf*(this) $==$ $\varnothing$ *and strictDescendants*(this) $==$ $\varnothing$)
Action:
    this."class"->deleteInstance(this);
    return TRUE;
```
}
```

The consequent of the precondition of free uses primitives that are defined in Chapter 2 (in this case, Definitions 4 and 15). One reason for introducing such primitives is to ease the writing of our specifications. More importantly, note that neither term is an intrinsic property of our object model. Because a class object does not contain information about its instances or its subclasses, there is no way to compute the predicate. This could be remedied by two additional instance variables in *Class*, extentCount and subclassCount, in each class object. These instance variables would be incremented by makeInstance and readyClass (respectively) and would be decremented by deleteInstance. Not deleting a class object that has instances or subclasses is an example of an obligation that our model places on the programmer, but does not enforce.

```
void Class :: deleteInstance( Object* anObject )
{ /* Specification */
```
Precondition:
>   this ∈ *C implies* (*extentOf*(this) == ∅ *and strictDescendants*(this) == ∅)

Action:
>   anObject->destroy();

```
}
```

Note the call to destroy. This is another hook method that allows the class programmer to free any storage or undo any operation that occurred during the object's existence (including actions taken by initialize).

```
void Object :: destroy()
{ /* Specification */
```
Precondition:
>   this ∈ *C implies* (*extentOf*(this) == ∅ *and strictDescendants*(this) —— ∅)

Action:
>   this."class" = NULL;
>   // The above assignment makes the space a nonobject, because every object
>   // must have a class. After this, the memory space allocated for the object is released.

```
}
```

One aspect of the design of our metaobject protocol should be apparent now. The pair of methods initialize/destroy exists for class programmers to initialize and deinitialize an object. The corresponding pair of methods makeInstance/deleteInstance may be overridden by metaclass programmers to initialize and deinitialize an object. This helps make metaclass programming as easy as class programming.

Another aspect of the design is the Boolean return of free. Once deleteInstance is invoked (by <*Object*,"free">), it is clear that the object must be deleted. However, an override of free may choose not to invoke its parent method — thus, deleteInstance is not executed and the object is not deleted. In this case, the override of free must return FALSE (to indicate that the object has not been deleted). Therefore, our metaobject protocol embodies the convention that free is for deciding whether to delete an object, while deleteInstance and destroy are part of the deletion process. An implication of this convention is that it is a programming mistake to release resources in an override of free.

We conclude with an obvious but important theorem.

Theorem 8. Neither *Class* nor *Object* can be deleted.

Proof.
>   The extent of *Class* is never empty, because *Object* is an instance of *Class*. The set of strict descendants of *Object* is never empty, because *Class* is a subclass of *Object*. The precondition of free can never be true for either of these classes. $\square$

The presence of the free method in our metaobject protocol is not intended to convey the idea that garbage collection is precluded. In a system with garbage collection, free is called by the garbage collection algorithm. This ensures that the finalization protocol of this section is enacted.

6.5 Initializing Classes

The next group of methods of our metaobject protocol deal with the construction of class objects. These methods (initializeClass, addMethod, overrideMethod, and readyClass) were introduced in Chapter 4. Invoking makeInstance on a metaclass (including *Class*) creates a nascent class object that is readied (that is, made usable) by the protocol given by the path expression in Figure 4-3 on page 71. The first step in the initialization is the execution of initializeClass, which adds the data segment for the introduced instance variables and performs the inheritance computation based on a parent list.

```
boolean Class :: initializeClass( ObjectList aParentList, DataSegment aDataSegment )
{ /* Specification */
```
Precondition:
> *Path expression of Figure 4-3 is obeyed and*
> aParentList ≠ <> *and*
> *for all X ∈* aParentList, X->readyClass() *has been executed*

Action:
```
    Class* X;
    for ( X=aParentList; X != NULL; X++)
        if ( !(this."class" isDescendantOf X."class") ) {
            return FALSE; }
    this.Class."parents" = aParentList ;
    if ( MRO(this) == NULL ) {
        this.Class."parents" = <>;
        return FALSE; }
    this.Class."ivdefs" = {this = aDataSegment} ⊲ this.Class."ivdefs";
                        // reminder: "{this = aDataSegment}" is a dictionary with one slot
```

$$\text{this.}Class.\text{"ivs"} = \bigtriangleup_{W \in MRO(\text{this})} W.Class.\text{"ivdefs"};$$

$$\text{this.}Class.\text{"mtab"} = \bigtriangleup_{W \in MRO(\text{this})} W.Class.\text{"mdefs"};$$

```
    return TRUE;
}
```

The for loop at the beginning of the action enforces the invariant implied by inheritance of metaclass constraints (see Section 3.3). Note that initializeClass returns FALSE if given a list of parent classes that could cause a metaclass incompatibility.

The action of initializeClass essentially adheres to Definition 16. Note that the method resolution order can be meaningfully computed because the parent list is set first. The specification of initializeClass is expressed in terms of the *MRO* function; this means that other metaclasses are not allowed to change the method resolution order computation.

Theorem 9. The inheritance graph must be acyclic.

Proof.

> Only readied classes (ones for which readyClass has been executed) may be used in the parent list of initializeClass because the precondition requires it.

$\square$

Below are the specifications of five methods for answering common questions about the inheritance hierarchy.

ObjectList Class :: **getParents**()
{ /* Specification */
Action:
    return this.*Class*."parents";
}

ObjectList Class :: **getMRO**()
{ /* Specification */
Action:
    return *MRO*(this);
}

boolean Class :: **isSubclassOf**(Class* anotherClass)
{ /* Specification */
Action:
    return (anotherClass $\in$ this.*Class*."parents");
}

boolean Class :: **isDescendantOf**(Class* anotherClass)
{ /* Specification */
Action:
    return (anotherClass $\in$ *ancestors*(this));
}

boolean Class :: **isAncestorOf**(Class* anotherClass)
{ /* Specification */
Action:
    return (this $\in$ *ancestors*(anotherClass));
}

These methods are nearly identical to primitives that we introduced to specify our object model. This is to be expected, because the object model is the subject of both the specification language and the metaobject protocol. One could propose the following as a guideline for designing metaobject protocols: start with an object model specification and reflect its primitives in the metaobject protocol.

6.6   Solving a Set of Metaclass Constraints

Our metaobject protocol obeys Postulate 10:

> The metaclass for a class must be a descendant of the metaclass for each of its parents

and the specification of initializeClass ensures that this postulate is never violated (because initializeClass returns FALSE rather than violate it). This leaves the programmer with the problem of creating a class object with makeInstance that is compatible with the parents of the class object that are set with initializeClass. To remedy this problem, the following primitive function is provided. solveMetaclassConstraints receives lists of metaclasses and parent classes and provides a metaclass that solves all the constraints. The algorithm essentially does the computation that is depicted in Figure 3-8 on page 45. Note that the algorithm calls itself recursively and uses our metaobject protocol to create new metaclasses if required to do so.

Class* **solveMetaclassConstraints**(ObjectList aMetaclassList, ObjectList aParentList)
{ /* Specification */
Precondition:
    readyClass *has been executed for all entries of* aMetaclassList
    and readyClass *has been executed for all entries of* aParentList
Action:
    Class* M;
    Class* P;
    Class* metaclassForSolution;
    Class* solution;
    ObjectList aMetaclassConstraintList = <>;
    // Reduce aMetaclassList into the solution being constructed
    for (M=aMetaclassList; M != NULL; M++)
      if (isNotAncestorOfAnyOf(*M, aMetaclassConstraintList)) {
        aMetaclassConstraintList = aMetaclassConstraintList ◁ <*M>;
      }
    // Add parent metaclasses to produce a solution
    for (P=aParentList; P != NULL; P++)
      if (isNotAncestorOfAnyOf(*P."class", aMetaclassConstraintList) {
        aMetaclassConstraintList = aMetaclassConstraintList ◁ <*P."class">;
      }
    {
      // See Exercise 6.7 to improve the above solution
    }
    if (*aMetaclassConstraintList++ == NULL) { // Is there one element in the list?
      // If list has just one element, it is the solution
      solution = *aMetaclassConstraintList; }
    else {
      // Derive a new metaclass from all the constraints
      metaclassForSolution = solveMetaclassConstraints(<>, aMetaclassConstraintList);
      solution = metaclassForSolution->makeInstance();
      solution->initializeClass(aMetaclassConstraintList, {});
               // reminder: "{}" is the empty dictionary
      solution->readyClass(); }
    return solution;
}

where the helper function isNotAncestorOfAnyOf is defined as follows.

```
boolean isNotAncestorOfAnyOf( Class* aClass, ObjectList aClassList )
{ /* Specification */
Action:
    Class* X;
    for ( X=aClassList; X !=NULL; X++) {
        if ( aClass isAncestorOf X )
            return FALSE;
    }
    return TRUE;
}
```

One might think that the call to solveMetaclassConstraints can be avoided in some cases, if one has sufficient knowledge about the metaclass and the parents. Actually, the invocation of solveMetaclassConstraints may be avoided only in the case when one is constructing a class that is an instance of *Class* and whose only parent is *Object* or *Class*. This is the result of the desire for evolvability and is explained fully in Chapter 11.

Despite the indispensability of solveMetaclassConstraints, a superficial analysis of our metaobject protocol might judge it awkward. For example, one might think that if the parent list is provided as a parameter to makeInstance, then it is unnecessary to have solveMetaclassConstraints as a separate procedure (its function would be incorporated into makeInstance). This change by itself is not complete in the context of good metaobject protocol design. Consider the following use of our metaobject protocol. Metaclasses (which are used to create classes) tend to impart properties (as we argued in Chapter 3). A language designer might wish to allow multiple metaclasses to be used in a class declaration. For example, using our object model, the class declaration of C++ might be extended as follows.

```
class <name> : <parent-list> : <metaclass-list> {
    <class-body>
}
```

This language design has the virtue of succinctness when there are many useful properties captured by metaclasses. In this case, the procedure solveMetaclassConstraints seems more natural than overloading makeInstance with a form that has a second parameter.

In any case, for pedagogical reasons that relate to demonstrating the importance of inheritance of metaclass constraints, we choose to emphasize the solution process rather than hide it.

6.7 Defining Methods of a Class

Let us specify addMethod for adding methods to a class and overrideMethod for overriding inherited methods.

```
void Class :: addMethod( Class* introducingClass,
                         string aMethodName,
                         CodePtr methodImpl )
```
{ /* Specification */

Precondition:

   Path expression of Figure 4-3 is obeyed and
   <introducingClass,aMethodName> $\notin$ *supportedMethods*(this)

Action:

   this.*Class*."mdefs" = {introducingClass={aMethodName=methodImpl}}
                                          $\lhd$ this.*Class*."mdefs";
   this.*Class*."mtab" = {introducingClass={aMethodName=methodImpl}}
                                          $\lhd$ this.*Class*."mtab";

}


```
void Class :: overrideMethod( Class* introducingClass,
                              string aMethodName,
                              CodePtr methodImpl )
```
{ /* Specification */

Precondition:

   Path expression of Figure 4-3 is obeyed and
   <introducingClass,aMethodName> $\subset$ *supportedMethods*(this)

Action:

   this.*Class*."mdefs" = {introducingClass={aMethodName=methodImpl}}
                                          $\lhd$ this.*Class*."mdefs";
   this.*Class*."mtab" = {introducingClass={aMethodName=methodImpl}}
                                          $\lhd$ this.*Class*."mtab";

}

Both of these methods update the mdefs instance variable to ensure that Definition 16 remains true. It is curious to have two methods that have identical actions when one method might do (the precondition would be the disjunction of the two preconditions). Our experience is that having this separation makes the writing of metaclasses easier. That is, metaclasses that would override either addMethod or overrideMethod know the intention of the method, whereas if there were one method the intention would have to be ascertained dynamically.

Below are four methods that answer questions about the interface of a class.

boolean Class :: **supportsMethod**(Class* aClass, string aMethodName)
{ /* Specification */
Action:
    return <aClass,aMethodName> $\in$ *supportedMethods*(this);
}

boolean Class :: **definesMethod**(Class* aClass, string aMethodName)
{ /* Specification */
Action:
    return <aClass,aMethodName> $\in$ *definedMethods*(this);
}

boolean Class :: **introducesMethod**(Class* aClass, string aMethodName)
{ /* Specification */
Action:
    return <aClass,aMethodName> $\in$ *introducedMethods*(this);
}

MethodList Class :: **getSupportedMethods**( )
{ /* Specification */
Action:
    return *supportedMethods*(this);
}

Now we introduce several methods that tell us about the implementation of methods (in that these methods return code pointers). The first method returns method table content. This method can be used to implement method invocations.[3]

CodePtr Class :: **resolveMethod**(Class* introducingClass, string methodName)
{ /* Specification */
Action:
    if (<introducingClass,aMethodName> $\in$ *supportedMethods*(this))
      return this.*Class*."mtab".introducingClass.aMethodName;
    else
      return NULL;
}

---

3. Section 4.1 describes the meaning of method invocation in terms of direct access to the method table. However, one purpose of our metaobject protocol is to encapsulate the object model. Tools (such as the DTS C++ compiler) do not have access to the method table and other structures of the object model. Instead, they must use our metaobject protocol.

Parent method calls are more complex, as we saw in Section 4.7. Below is the function that does resolution for parent method calls. parentResolve is invoked with the class whose implementation is currently being executed (which is named overridingClass); the other parameters of parentResolve are the target object and the method; parentResolve returns the next implementation in the classes of the method resolution order (beyond the class whose implementation is currently executing) that defines the method.

```
CodePtr parentResolve( Object* target,
                       Class* overridingClass,
                       Class* introducingClass,
                       string methodName )
{ /* Specification */
```

Precondition:
    target."class" *isDescendantOf* overridingClass *and*
    <introducingClass,aMethodName> $\in$ *supportedMethods*(target."class")

Action:

```
    boolean foundClass = FALSE;
    for ( int i = 0; #MRO(target."class"); i++ ) {
      if ( !foundClass ) {
        if ( MRO(target."class").i == overridingClass ) {
          foundClass = TRUE; } }
      else {
        if ( <introducingClass,aMethodName> ∈ definedMethods(MRO(target.class).i) ){
          return MRO(target."class").i->resolveTerminal(  introducingClass,
                                                           methodName ); } } }
      return NULL;
}
```

The action above is a bit tricky. The loop first searches *MRO*(target."class") for the overriding class. After the iteration finds the overriding class in the method resolution order, the iteration does not stop; it continues until the next class that defines the method is found.

Note that the introducing class does not have to be an ancestor of the class of the target because *definedMethods* is used in the specification of the action. As a result, NULL is returned if a parent method call is made from an implementation defined by a class but there is no other definition for that method among the successors in the method resolution order of the target class. Obviously, this cannot happen within an override. But addMethod can be used to define an implementation that uses parentResolve, and it can be useful to do this. For example, this approach can be used to construct a "mixin" that is useful to classes that do inherit the method.

Note also that parentResolve uses the method resolveTerminal (rather than resolveMethod) to access the method table entry. Initially, resolveTerminal and resolveMethod are identical, but the next chapter shows a case in which only one of these needs to be changed.

CodePtr Class :: **resolveTerminal**(Class* introducingClass, string methodName)
{ /* Specification */
Precondition:
      <introducingClass,aMethodName> ∈ *supportedMethods*(this)
Action:
      return this.*Class*."mtab".introducingClass.aMethodName;
}

6.8 Readying a Class

The class construction protocol ends with the execution of readyClass. This method is not required to do anything (although if the path expression is to be enforced, one might expect readyClass to set some indicator in the class object). The method does provide a convenient hook in which to place some last-minute changes in any class object being constructed.

void Class :: **readyClass**()
{ /* Specification */
Precondition:
      Path expression of Figure 4-3 is obeyed
Action:
      // The default implementation of this method does nothing.
}

Let us review the class construction process. Figure 6-1 shows a timeline of class construction starting with a nascent class, which is created on the left with an invocation of makeInstance on some metaclass and is completed on the right when the invocation of readyClass completes. In between there is exactly one invocation of initializeClass that returns true. We do not preclude the possibility that during the class construction process, initializeClass could be invoked multiple times if all but the last return false. The timeline indicates that initializeClass begins before *Class*'s implementation of initializeClass begins and ends afterwards. The invocations of makeInstance and readyClass are similarly depicted. This accounts for the possibility of overriding initializeClass in the metaclass that is used for creating the nascent class. Another implication of Figure 6-1 is that if a metaclass overrides initializeClass or readyClass, the override is required to make a parent method call. This ensures that the implementations provided by *Class* are executed.

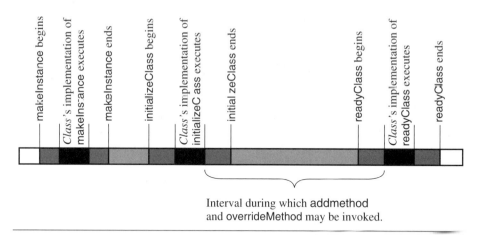

Interval during which **addmethod**
and **overrideMethod** may be invoked.

Figure 6-1   A timeline for class construction.

6.9   Example: A Metaclass for Managing the Extent of a Class

ExtentManaged is a metaclass that implements the property of extent management. That
is, instances of this metaclass are classes for which the extent is kept in an instance variable named extent. The design concept is given in Figure 6-2, which indicates that
makeInstance and deleteInstance are overridden and the method getExtent is introduced.

We present two implementations for *ExtentManaged*. The first implementation uses
our metaobject protocol to create this metaclass dynamically. The second implementation
illustrates a static declaration in DTS C++. The first implementation illustrates the kind of
code generated by a DTS C++ compiler for the second implementation.

In the implementation below, the procedure ExtentManagedNewClass dynamically
creates the metaclass for extent management, which is saved in the static (global) variable
ExtentManagedClassObject. The signatures of the procedures ExtentManaged_New,
ExtentManaged_Delete, and ExtentManaged_getExtent are method-like — that is, they
have an explicit first parameter that is an *Object*.

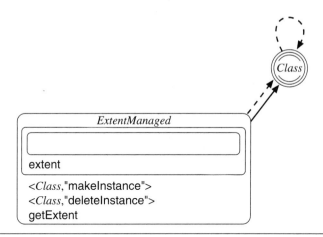

Figure 6-2. Design concept of the *ExtentManaged* metaclass.

static Class* ExtentManagedClassObject;

Class* **ExtentManagedNewClass**()
{ /* Specification */
Action:
  ObjectList metaclassList = <Class>;
  ObjectList parentList = <Class>;
  Class* aMetaclass = solveMetaclassConstraints(metaclassList, parentList)
  ExtentManagedClassObject = aMetaclass->makeInstance();
  dictionary emIVDefs = {"extent"=<>};
  ExtentManagedClassObject->initializeClass(parentList, emIVDefs);
  ExtentManagedClassObject->addMethod(ExtentManagedClassObject,
             "getExtent",
             ExtentManaged_getExtent);
  ExtentManagedClassObject->overrideMethod(Class,
              "makeInstance",
              ExtentManaged_New);
  ExtentManagedClassObject->overrideMethod(Class,
              "deleteInstance",
              ExtentManaged_Delete);
  ExtentManagedClassObject->readyClass();
  return ExtentManagedClassObject;}
}

where the method implementations for getExtent and the two overrides are as follows.

```
Object* ExtentManaged_New( Class* this )
{ /* Specification */
Action:
    CodePtr fp;
    fp = ExtentManagedClassObject->parentResolve( this, Class, makeInstance );
    Object* instanceOfAnEMClass = tp( this );
    this.ExtentManagedClassObject."extent" =
                this.ExtentManagedClassObject.extent◁ <anInstanceOfAnEMClass>;
    return anInstanceOfAnEMClass;
}
```

```
void ExtentManaged_Delete( Class* this, Object* target )
{ /* Specification */
Action:
    this.ExtentManagedClassObject.extent :=
                    this.ExtentManagedClassObject."extent" − <target>;
    CodePtr fp = ExtentManagedClassObject->parentResolve( this,
                                                    Class,
                                                    deleteInstance );
    fp( this, target );
}
```

```
ObjectList ExtentManaged_getExtent( Class* this )
{ /* Specification */
Action:
    return this.ExtentManagedClassObject."extent";
}
```

The implementation of *ExtentManaged* above is the dynamic equivalent of declaring the following in DTS C++.

```
class ExtentManaged : public virtual Class {
    private:
        list extent = <>;
    public:
        Class* makeInstance();
        void deleteInstance();
        cooperative ObjectList getExtent();
}
```

```
Object* ExtentManaged :: makeInstance( Class* this )
{ /* Specification */
```
Action:
```
    Object* instanceOfAnEMClass = __parent->makeInstance();
    extent = extent ◁ <anInstanceOfAnEMClass>;
    return anInstanceOfAnEMClass;
}
```

```
void ExtentManaged :: deleteInstance()
{ /* Specification */
```
Action:
```
    extent := extent − <this>;
    __parent->deleteInstance();
}
```

```
ObjectList ExtentManaged :: getExtent()
{ /* Specification */
```
Action:
```
    return extent;
}
```

In the DTS C++ version, the identifier ExtentManaged subsumes the introduction of the global variable ExtentManagedClassObject. The parent method calls are easy to write and read because the compiler provides a syntax for them. Similarly, instance variable access is also easy to write and read.

Now let us check to ensure that instances of *ExtentManaged* are proper classes; that is, let's look at the effect of the following program, where theEmptyDataSegment is a global variable that points to an empty data segment.

```
main( argc, argv ) {
```
Action:
```
    Class* M = solveMetaclassConstraints( <ExtentManaged>, <Object> )
    Class* X = new M;
    X->initializeClass( <Object>, theEmptyDataSegment );
    X->readyClass();
    Object* iX = new X;
}
```

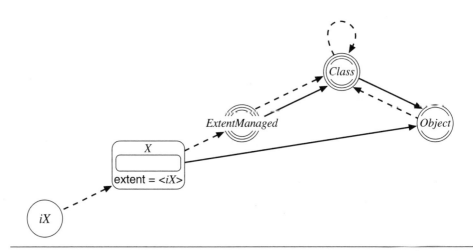

Figure 6-3. Class X is an instance of the metaclass *ExtentManaged*.

Figure 6-3 depicts the state of the environment just before this programs ends. Note that we have used the variable names (X and iX) as the symbols for the corresponding object references, too.

6.10 Invoking Methods from Interpreters

Section 4.1 specified method invocation. With resolveMethod and knowledge of parameter passing conventions (and other architecture-dependent considerations), a compiler designer can implement that specification. However, consider the plight of one who wishes to use our model to implement an architecture-independent interpreter for an object-oriented language. In this situation, one needs an abstraction to execute a method given its parameters. This can be accomplished with the function apply.

void apply(Object* target, CodePtr methodImpl, va_list args, void* *result)

The parameters are as follows.

- The target object on which the method implementation is to be invoked
- The method implementation, which is a code pointer returned by resolveMethod
- A va_list containing the method invocation parameters
- A pointer to a buffer to hold the result returned by the method invocation

    The specification of apply is as follows.

```
void apply(Object* target, CodePtr methodImpl, va_list arguments, void* *result)
{ /*Specification*/
```
Precondition:

       It is appropriate to invoke methodImpl *on the object target.*

Action:

       Follow the procedure linkage conventions so that the elements in the
       parameter va_list *are passed as arguments to the method*
       implementation designated by methodImpl.
       The result returned by methodImpl *is placed in the buffer pointed to by result.*
       We do not concern ourselves here with the details of how this is done.

```
}
```

Appendix B provides more details concerning how and why C/C++ va_lists are used in the DTS C++ implementation of apply. In general, an implementation of apply functionality requires knowledge of the procedure linkage conventions for the computer and operating system that one is using and additional information about the signature of the method implementation being invoked. One can see why most research in the area of metaobject protocols is done using Lisp or Smalltalk, both of which have the capability for easy implementation of apply.

In DTS C++, suppose one has a string specifying the name of a method and wishes to execute a method with this name on some target object. This can be done as follows.

```
Class* introducingClass = lookupIntroducingClass( getClass(anObject), methodName );
if ( introducingClass != NULL ) {
    CodePtr aCodePtr = aClass->resolveMethod( introducingClass, methodName );
    apply( anObject, aCodePtr, aParameterList, &result );
    }
else {
    // No introducing class -- report an error.
    ...
    }
```

where

Class* **lookupIntroducingClass**(Class* aClass, string methodName)
{ /* Specification */
Action:
    Class* introducingClass = NULL;
    for (ObjectList mro = aClass->getMRO(); mro != NULL; mro++)
      if ((*mro)->introducesMethod((*mro), methodName)) {
        if (introducingClass I– NULL)
          return NULL; // This means that the introducing class is not unique
        introducingClass = *mro;
      }
    return introducingClass;
}

Note that lookupIntroducingClass is not part of our metaobject protocol. The function lookupIntroducingClass is used here to illustrate how the primitive function apply in our metaobject protocol can be used to support interpretive method invocation when the introducing class of the method is not provided.[4] The example above is just one of many ways to associate an introducing class with a method name.

Our metaobject protocol takes no position with respect to how an introducing class is associated with a method name at the call site. This is a programming language issue. For example, C++ and DTS C++ use method target and argument types to determine an introducing class, and programmers use typecasting to guide this determination. One can also imagine a method invocation syntax in which programmers explicitly specify the method's introducing class.

In terms of our model, however, a programming language is inherently ambiguous if the introducing class used for a method call depends on the runtime class of the target object. This is because, in general, the programmer of a method call in such a language cannot know what specific method will actually be invoked. As demonstrated by Smalltalk (the classic example of such a language), ambiguity of this kind can be useful as long as methods with the same name receive the same arguments and are intended to implement the same semantics.

Interpretive method invocation with static knowledge of the introducing class is unambiguous, and is especially useful in our model when a metaclass adds a method to a class object. In such situations, the instance method is not statically declared by the class, and so a combination of resolveMethod and apply is the only way to invoke such a method. Section 6.12 gives an example of this situation.

---

4. A method name alone does not specify a method in our model. Therefore, to invoke a method given only a method name, an introducing class must first be determined.

6.11   Instance Variable Access

Our metaobject protocol requires two methods for instance variable access. The specification of each is given below.

void* Object :: **getIV**(Class* introducingClass, string anIVName)
{ /* Specification */
Precondition:
      <introducingClass,anIVName> ∈ *supportedIVs*(*class*(this))
         and introducingClass ≠ *Class*
Action:
    return this.anIVName;
}

void Object :: **setIV**(Class* introducingClass, string anIVName, void* value)
{ /* Specification */
Precondition:
      <introducingClass,anIVName> ∈ *supportedIVs*(*class*(this))
         and introducingClass ≠ *Class*
Action:
    this.anIVName = value;
}

We defer an example of the use of these methods to the next section.

The preconditions for these methods require that the introducing class of the instance variable not be *Class*. This is done to enforce the encapsulation of the object model by our metaobject protocol. Without this precondition, arbitrary changes could be made in class objects. If *Object* introduced instance variables, another conjunct would be necessary in the precondition to prevent their access with getIV and setIV.

For the sake of simplicity, the declarations of getIV and setIV assume that the value of an instance variable can be stored in a C++ void* type. A further implication of these declarations is that it is the obligation of the caller to know the C++ type of the instance variable. When our metaobject protocol is being used by a compiler (such as the DTS C++ compiler), this is not a significant issue, because one expects the compiler to know such things. However, when our metaobject protocol is used directly, this additional obligation is awkward, but necessary.

Finally, we need a method that enables testing the precondition of getIV and setIV. Note that supportsIV is a method that is invoked on classes — ordinary objects.

boolean Class :: **supportsIV**(Class* aClass, string anIVName)
{ /* Specification */
Action:
    return <aClass,anIVName> ∈ *supportedIVs*(this);
}

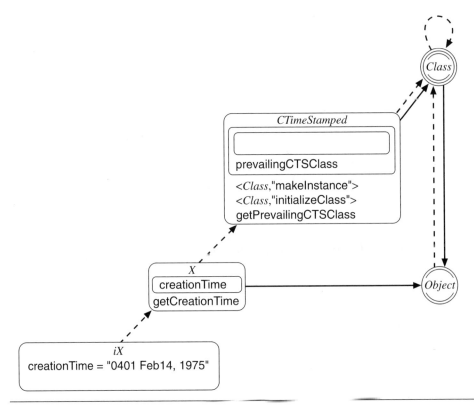

Figure 6-4. The design concept for *CTimeStamped* using an instance method.

6.12 Example: Creation Time Stamps

There are two kinds of properties that can be endowed by metaclasses. In the case of *ExtentManaged*, the property is endowed to the class. This section introduces the metaclass *CTimeStamped,* which endows the property that ordinary objects (which are instances of the class that is the instance of the metaclass) are stamped with their creation times. *CTimeStamped* is a much more interesting metaclass in that there are two levels of indirection to be considered. That is, the metaclass transforms each of its instances (which are classes) so that they endow the property to their instances.

We exhibit two alternative designs that have the same purpose. Figure 6-4 shows the first design concept for *CTimeStamped* and a sample instance (class *X* with instance *iX*). The creation time is the time at which makeInstance is invoked, and so a simple override can be used to change makeInstance. However, the design is somewhat complex because the instance variables that store the creation times are not statically introduced, but are dynamically added by classes with the property *CTimeStamped*. To do this, we must override initializeClass to add both a new instance variable and a new method during class construction.

Below is the specification for *CTimeStamped* with a DTS C++ class declaration, where osCurrentTime is an operating system primitive that returns the current time as a string. Notice that initializeClass adds to the set of instance variables of its target (in Figure 6-4, creationTime is added to *X.X*.ivdefs) and adds to the methods of its target (in Figure 6-4, getCreationTime is added to *X.X*.mdefs).

```
class CTimeStamped : public virtual Class {
    private:
        Class* prevailingCTSClass = NULL;
    public:
        Class* makeInstance();
        void initializeClass( ObjectList aParentList, DataSegment aDataSegment ) ;
}


void CTimeStamped :: initializeClass( ObjectList aParentList,
                                      DataSegment aDataSegment )
{ /* Specification */
Action:
    boolean ctsDescendant = FALSE;
    int i;
    for( i = 0; i < #aParentList; i++ ) {
        if ( getClass(aParentList.i)->isDescendantOf( CTimeStamped ) {
            ctsDescendant = TRUE;
            prevailingCTSClass = (aParentList.i)->getPrevailingClass();
            break;
        }
    }
    if ( !ctsDescendant ) {
        aDataSegment = aDataSegment ◁ {"creationTime"=""};
        prevailingCTSClass = this;
    }
    __parent->initializeClass(aParentList,aDataSegment) ) {
    if ( !ctsDescendant )
        this->addMethod( CTimeStamped,
                        "getCreationTime",
                        CTimeStamped_getCreationTime );
}
```

```
Object* CTimeStamped :: makeInstance()
{ /* Specification */
Action:
     Object* iCTSClass = __parent->makeInstance();
     iCTSClass->setIV( prevailingCTSClass, "creationTime", osCurrentTime() );
     return iCTSClass;
}


Class* CTimeStamped :: getPrevailingCTSClass()
{ /* Specification */
Action:
     return prevailingCTSClass;
}


string CTimeStamped_getCreationTime( Object* this )
{ /* Specification */
Action:
     return (string)this->getIV( getClass(this)->getPrevailingCTSClass(), "creationTime" );
}
```

The override of *initializeClass* performs four tasks.

- It determines whether or not the creation-time-stamped property is already inherited. If the property is not inherited, the other three functions are performed.
- The class instance variable *prevailingCTSClass* is set, if NULL. This ensures that if the property is inherited from multiple parents, there is one prevailing creation time stamp (see Exercise 6.11).
- The override adds an additional instance variable to the data segment of the class being created.
- After the method table is created (that is, after the parent method call), a new method (for retrieving the creation time) is added to the method table.

Because the method for retrieving the creation time is added by the metaclass, calls to that method cannot be written without the use of *apply*. The reason for this is simple; there is no prototype for that method in the class declaration of any instance of *CTimeStamped*. This illustrates one of the uses of *apply*.

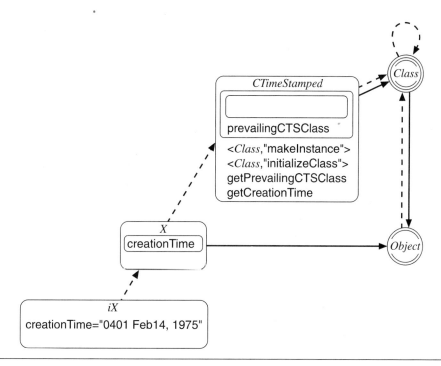

Figure 6-5. The design concept for *CTimeStamped* using a class method.

Now let us consider a second design, which is depicted in Figure 6-5. The only difference from the previous design is that the getCreationTime method is introduced by the metaclass *CTimeStamped* (rather than being dynamically introduced during class construction).

```
class CTimeStamped : public virtual Class {
    private:
        Class* prevailingCTSClass = NULL;
    public:
        Class* makeInstance();
        void initializeClass( ObjectList aParentList, DataSegment aDataSegment ) ;
        cooperative string getCreationTime( Object* this )
}
```

```
boolean CTimeStamped :: initializeClass( ObjectList aParentList,
                                          DataSegment aDataSegment )
{ /* Specification */
Action:
    boolean ctsDescendant = FALSE;
    int i;
    for( i = 0; i < #aParentList; i++ ) {
      If ( getClass(aParentList.i)->isDescendantOf( CTimeStamped ) {
         ctsDescendant = TRUE;
         break;
      }
    }
    if ( !ctsDescendant ) {
       aDataSegment = aDataSegment ◁ {"creationTime"=""};
       if ( prevailingCTSClass == NULL )
          prevailingCTSClass = this;
    }
    return __parent->initializeClass(aParentList,aDataSegment) );
}
Object* CTimeStamped :: makeInstance()
{ /* Specification */
Action:
    Object* iCTimeStamped = __parent->makeInstance();
    iCTimeStamped->setIV( prevailingCTSClass, "creationTime", osCurrentTime() );
    return iCTimeStamped;
}
string CTimeStamped :: getCreationTime( Object* anInstance )
{ /* Specification */
Precondition:
    anInstance ∈ extentOf(CTimeStamped)
Action:
    return (string)anInstance->getIV( prevailingCTSClass, "creationTime" );
}
```

The pragmatic difference between these two designs is realized in how one retrieves a time stamp. Below are written two functions (one corresponding to each design) that illustrate this difference. The functions retrieve the creation time stamp from an arbitrary object (or return NULL if the object is not time stamped). With the design in Figure 6-4, one retrieves the time stamp with:

```
string getCreationTimeStampIfApplicable( Object* anObject )
{ /* Specification */
Action:
    string timeStamp = NULL;
    aCodePtr = getClass(anObject)->resolveMethod( CTimeStamped,
                                                    "getCreationTime" );
    if ( aCodePtr != NULL )
      apply( anObject, aCodePtr, <>, &timeStamp );
    return timeStamp;
}
```

With the design in Figure 6-5, the time stamp is retrieved with:

```
string getCreationTimeStampIfApplicable( Object* anObject )
{
    if ( getClass(anObject)->supportsMethod( CTimeStamped, "getCreationTime" );
      return ((CTimeStamped*)getClass(anObject))->getCreationTime(anObject);
    else
      return NULL;
}
```

The main difference is that the second function has a static reference to the class *CTimeStamped* and the method getCreationTime, which can be resolved only by a compiler if there is a static class declaration. Clearly, the second design is easier to write in DTS C++. However, the first design may have advantages in other contexts (for example, when the application programs are written in a dynamic language that does not have static class declarations).

There is a third possible design: the time stamped property can be implemented with an ordinary class (without the use of a metaclass), because the initializer (initialize) can set the creation time stamp. The specification for such an ordinary class looks like this:

```
class CTimeStampedObject : public virtual Object {
      string creationTime;
    public:
      void initialize();
      public virtual string getCreationTime( ) ;
}
void CTimeStamped :: initialize( )
{ /* Specification */
Action:
    creationTime = osCurrentTime();
}
```

```
string CTimeStamped :: getCreationTime( )
{ /* Specification */
Action:
      return creationTime;
}
```

This class can be used as a **mixin.**[5] However, we are interested in putting metaclasses to work, and so we will continue to use the metaclass form for time stamping for illustrative purposes.

The metaclass *CTimeStamped* composes with the metaclass *ExtentManaged* in that any class that is an instance of both (which can happen with the use of multiple inheritance in the metaclass hierarchy) has the properties of both. This works neatly, because the parent call mechanism ensures that the makeInstance overrides of both metaclasses perform their actions (which do not interfere with each other). In the next chapter, we discuss and solve the general problem of composing metaclasses.

6.13   Redispatching a Method

Suppose one wishes to funnel all or a specific set of method invocations through a single piece of code; this can be done with a **redispatch stub.** A redispatch stub is a method implementation that converts any method invocation into a call to the method dispatch. A redispatch stub has the following schema.

```
void* <method-name>RedispatchStub( Object* anObject, <formal-parameter-list> )
{ /*Specification*/
Action:
      void* returnValue;
      convert-the-actual-parameters-into-a-list-for-the-next-step
      anObject->dispatch( introducingClass, <method-name>, aParameterList, returnValue);
      return returnValue;
}
```

This schema can be used to create a redispatch for each introduced method. That is, there is one redispatch stub for each introduced method, because a redispatch stub must have the same signature as the method. To implement redispatch stubs, one needs to know the signature of the method and how parameters are passed in order to package the actual

---

5.   A mixin is a class that is never intended to be instantiated, but implements a property that it conveys to other classes when joined with multiple inheritance. It is appropriate for the mixin class to make parent method calls to methods that its descendants must inherit from elsewhere in the hierarchy [15]. This is an example of a facility that requires the use of our metaobject protocol, because in DTS C++ a parent method call must be to a method introduced by an ancestor.

parameters in a list for dispatch.[6] dispatch is a hook method that must be overridden if one uses redispatch stubs. Note that the code pointer for the redispatch stub is placed in the method table.

```
void Object :: dispatch( Class* introducingClass,
                         string methodName,
                         ObjectList aParameterList,
                         void** returnValue)
{ /* Specification */
```
Precondition:
    The call to dispatch comes from a method that is invoked on this target object.
Action:
    // This is a hook method that does nothing.
}

Instead of the empty action for dispatch as a default, one might be tempted to specify an invocation of the code pointer in the method table. This is a mistake. If one replaces a method table entry with a redispatch stub, the redispatch stub is invoked (when the corresponding method is called), which in turn calls dispatch, which calls the redispatch stub, and so on. This causes a **redispatch loop.** Clearly, if one intends to use redispatch stubs, something else must be done. Our solution is discussed in Chapter 7.

One replaces the method table entry with a redispatch stub by using the following method.

```
void Class :: putRDStub( Class* introducingClass, string methodName )
{ /*Specification*/
```
Precondition:
    <introducingClass,aMethodName> $\in$ *supportedMethods*(this)
    and <introducingClass,aMethodName> $\neq$ <*Object*,"dispatch">
Action:
        Replace the method table entry for the method
            <introducingClass,methodName>
        with the corresponding redispatch stub.
        We do not concern ourselves with the details of
        how a redispatch stub is created.
}

The implementation of putRDStub is programming system dependent, because it depends on the following factors.

• The signature of the method that is being redispatched

---

6. See Appendix B for additional details concerning the topic of redispatch stubs.

- What types of data can be passed in method invocations
- How each type of datum is passed (call-by-value, call-by-reference, and so on)
- How each formal parameter is stored in the call stack

This is an important issue, but it is beyond the scope of this book. We obviously need a simplifying assumption here. We assume that enough information exists in the call stack so that a single generic redispatch stub can work for all methods.[7]

If a redispatch stub is placed in the method table with putRDStub (in place of the method for which it has been created), all method invocations to the replaced method are routed through dispatch. Now you have probably noticed a little problem here. If the redispatch stub routes the invocation to dispatch and <*Object*,dispatch> has no implementation, how does any meaningful action take place? Our metaobject protocol does not take a position on this issue; dispatch is a hook method that must be overridden. However, Chapter 7 describes metaclasses that address this issue, and Chapter 8 describes a metaclass that uses redispatch stubs.

6.14 Summary

This chapter has introduced our metaobject protocol (summarized in Figure 6-6), and now we are ready to put metaclasses to work. Most of the remainder of this book deals with examples of useful metaclasses that are designed with our metaobject protocol. Many examples are still expressed with the specification technique introduced in this chapter, because we wish to avoid the tedium of exception handling. However, beyond this point, the specification primitives introduced in Chapter 2 (for example, *this.class, extentOf, supportedMethods,* and so on) are no longer used. Instead, all specifications are expressed in terms of methods and functions of our metaobject protocol.

---

7. Making such a powerful assumption is not satisfying. However, you must take our word that there are no hidden unsolved problems here, just many tedious details. In the IBM SOMObjects Toolkit, method signature information was stored in class objects (after all, it was metadata). Subsequently, there was enough information to generate a redispatch stub. Appendix B describes how redispatch stubs can be implemented in C/C++ based on the functions with a variable number of arguments.

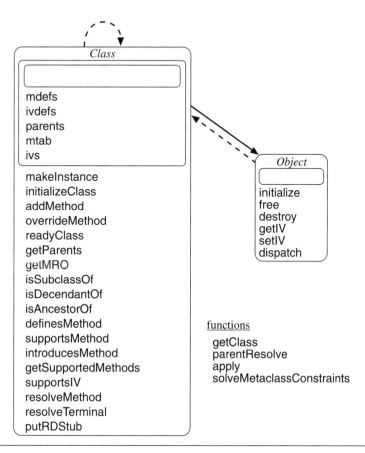

Figure 6-6. Summary of our metaobject protocol.

6.15 Exercises

6.1   An invariant is a statement that is true of the environment when control is not inside of any
        method of our metaobject protocol. List all of the invariants of our object model.

6.2   Our metaobject protocol provides the methods supportsMethod and definesMethod. Use
        these methods to program the Boolean methods inheritsMethod, introducesMethod, and
        overridesMethod. The specification for each should be based on Definition 18.

6.3   Implement CTimeStamped as an ordinary class.

6.4   Write the code that dynamically creates CTimeStamped. (This is similar to the dynamic creation of ExtentManaged.)

6.5   In Section 6.10, the procedure lookupIntroducingClass is used to implement a language semantics in which a method name denotes the closest method of this name that is introduced by an ancestor of the target object's class (where "closest" is defined using the target object class's method resolution order). Write a Boolean procedure that responds TRUE if and only if there is exactly one method with a given name introduced among the ancestors of a given class.

6.6   Show that solveMetaclassConstraints($<X>$, $<Object>$) returns X for any metaclass X.

6.7   Our algorithm for calculating the proper metaclass, solveMetaclassConstraints in Section 6.6, does not remove a metaclass from aMetaclassConstraintList if it is followed by a descendant. Modify solveMetaclassConstraints to fix this inadequacy.

6.8   Two possible convenience methods for *Class* are join and endow. They have the following signatures:

    Class* join(Class* aClass);
    Class* endow(Class* aMetaclass);

join returns the pure multiple inheritance joining of the target class with the first parameter. endow returns the class whose parent is the target and whose metaclass is the first parameter (think of this as endowing the target with the property of the metaclass). Write specifications for these two methods for addition to *Class*.

6.9   Our metaobject protocol lacks introspective iterators for instance variables. That is, one cannot list the instance variables that a class supports. Augment the protocol to do this.

6.10   Invent a new class construction protocol that hides solveMetaclassConstraints.

6.11   It is possible for a class Z to inherit the CTimeStamped property from multiple parents X and Y. (a) Examine this situation and convince yourself that there is but one creation time stamp that is associated with each instance of Z. (b) Despite the fact that there is only one time associated with each instance of Z, there are multiple instance variables. Analyze our metaobject protocol and suggest an improvement that eliminates the unneeded instance variables.

6.12   Our object model does not make provision for classes to have programmer-supplied printable names, because this is not essential to our presentation. (A class reference is not such a name.) Printable names are essential to any practical programming environment. Modify our metaobject protocol so that it has printable names.

Chapter 7
Cooperation among Metaclasses

As we are about to see, the actions of one metaclass at class construction time can interfere with the ability of another metaclass to impart its property. Now let us give our metaobject protocol a real test by writing a metaclass that enables metaclasses to cooperate instead of interfere with each other. One should bear in mind that this is both an exercise in using our metaobject protocol and the development of a fundamental concept (metaclass cooperation) that is required to put metaclasses to work effectively. This is the beginning of a **metaclass framework** that enhances the facilities of our metaobject protocol and makes writing new metaclasses easier.

7.1 Requirements for Cooperative Metaclasses

Consider the following class declarations.

```
class ExtentManagedX : public virtual X : ExtentManaged {
    }
class CTimeStampedX : public virtual X : CTimeStamped {
    }
class ExtentManagedCTimeStampedX :    public virtual ExtentManagedX,
                                      public virtual CTimeStampedX { }
```

where ExtentManaged and CTimeStamped are the metaclasses introduced in Chapter 6. Chapter 3 established and justified that a derived metaclass must be created for ExtentManagedCTimeStampedX, as shown in Figure 7-1; Chapter 6 showed how this is done using solveMetaclassConstraints. Both of the metaclasses ExtentManaged and

CTimeStamped require that particular actions take place when makeInstance is invoked on any of its instances (these actions are, of course, those specified by the overrides of makeInstance). Fortunately, because of the semantics of parent method calls, although the derived metaclass in Figure 7-1 inherits the override specified by ExtentManaged, the successor to that override is the one specified by CTimeStamped (which in turn invokes the implementation introduced by *Class*). Because neither override interferes with the other, the creation of the derived metaclass composes the properties that are embodied in the two metaclasses, ExtentManaged and CTimeStamped.

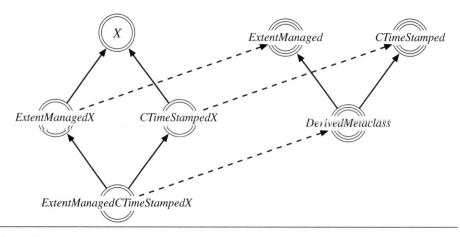

Figure 7-1. Example of two composed metaclasses.

The felicitous composition of the metaclasses in Figure 7-1 is the result of each metaclass overriding its own inherited methods in a cooperative manner. A problem can arise if a metaclass attempts to override the methods of its instances during the class construction process. The override (based on the meaning of <*Class*,"overrideMethod">) replaces the content of the method table entry. If multiple metaclasses (participating in the construction of a class) override the same method, the last one to execute overrideMethod determines the content of the method table, and all previous overrides are lost. This is clearly not cooperative and an impediment to composition of classes (and, ultimately, reusability). The next section introduces a metaclass that implements the ability of metaclasses to cooperate when overriding methods in their instances.

7.2 A Metaclass for Cooperation

Subclassing allows a descendant of a class to add to the implementation of an inherited method by replacing the method table entry with a new implementation that at some point invokes the original functionality with a parent method call. When many subclasses do this for a method, the result is an implementation chain. Metaclass programmers require the same capability. That is, metaclass programmers must be able to add to the chain of implementations of an instance method. overrideMethod does not satisfy this requirement; it merely replaces the implementation in a method table entry.

Let us be a bit more concrete. Figure 7-2 is a repeat of a diagram used in Section 4.6 to explain parent method calls. Let us further assume that *ACooperativeMetaclass* adds an implementation that has a code pointer coopFoo to be executed whenever the method <*U*,"foo"> is invoked (on an instance of an instance of *ACooperativeMetaclass*). We have drawn coopFoo as a black box because this implementation belongs to the metaclass but does not reside in the method table of *ACooperativeMetaclass*. The figure shows that the added cooperative method executes prior to the sequence of overrides that ultimately calls the introduced method. Thus, we may understand cooperative methods as the means by which a metaclass adds to the sequence of method implementations formed by parentResolve. Now, to get coopFoo into the act, its code pointer must be placed in the method table of Z. Also note that the call from coopFoo to the next implementation cannot be performed with a parent method call.

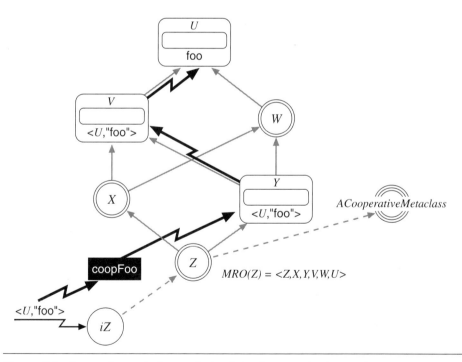

Figure 7-2. Cooperative methods precede the chain of ancestor implementations.

To solve these two problems, a new facility is provided; this facility is the *Cooperative* metaclass that is shown in Figure 7-3. This metaclass uses our metaobject protocol to provide facilities that ease the burden of writing cooperative metaclasses. The main function of the class is implemented in addCooperativeMethod, which adds an implementation to a chain of implementations. The prefix of an implementation chain that is added by cooperating metaclasses is called the **cooperation chain.** The method getNextCooperative is used to retrieve the next cooperative implementation (similar in concept to parentResolve). The other two methods (requestFirstCooperativeMethodCall and satisfyRequests) are used when the metaclass requires its implementation to be the first one called. The methods of *Cooperative* are designed to be used in an override of initializeClass; that is, after *Class*'s implementation of initializeClass, these methods can be used to add implementations to methods.

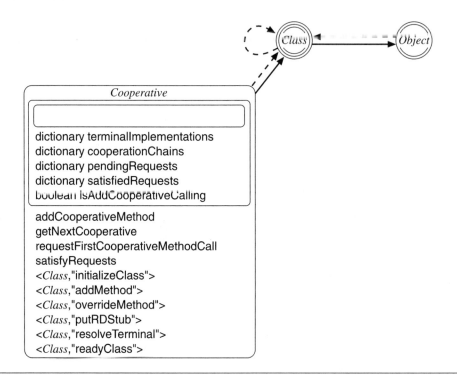

Figure 7-3. *Cooperative* metaclass.

The use of addCooperativeMethod, which has the signature

```
void* addCooperativeMethod(  Class* introducingClass,
                             string methodName,
                             CodePtr cooperativeImpl );
```

is based on the programming model depicted in Figure 7-4. Suppose the metaclass programmer wishes to cooperate on instance method foo (this is a method supported by a class that is an instance of a metaclass that is a descendant of *Cooperative*). The metaclass programmer writes a procedure coopFoo that has the same signature as the foo method. (Note that the name coopFoo is arbitrary.) The idea is that addCooperativeMethod stores the content of the method table entry for foo in a representation of the cooperation chain and puts a code pointer for coopFoo in the method table entry. In the implementation of coopFoo, the metaclass programmer can use getNextCooperative to retrieve the code pointer to the next implementation on the cooperation chain, which is the implementation that was in the method table before addCooperativeMethod was called. This transformation to the class object (Z) can be done in an override of initializeClass (as depicted in Figure 7-4) or in an override of readyClass. Note that coopFoo is not a method, but a function that has a method-like signature.

The DTS C++ declaration for *Cooperative* is as follows.

```
class Cooperative : public virtual Class : Class {
    private:
        dictionary cooperationChains = {};
        dictionary terminalImplementations = {};
        dictionary pendingRequests = {};
        dictionary satisfiedRequests = {};
        boolean isAddCooperativeCalling = FALSE;
    public:
        cooperative void addCooperativeMethod(  Class* introducingClass,
                                                string methodName,
                                                CodePtr cooperativeImpl );
        CodePtr getNextCooperative( Class* introducingClass,
                                    string methodName,
                                    CodePtr cooperativeImpl );
        cooperative boolean requestFirstCooperativeMethodCall(
                                                Class* introducingClass,
                                                string methodName,
                                                CodePtr cooperativeImpl );
        cooperative void satisfyRequests( );
```

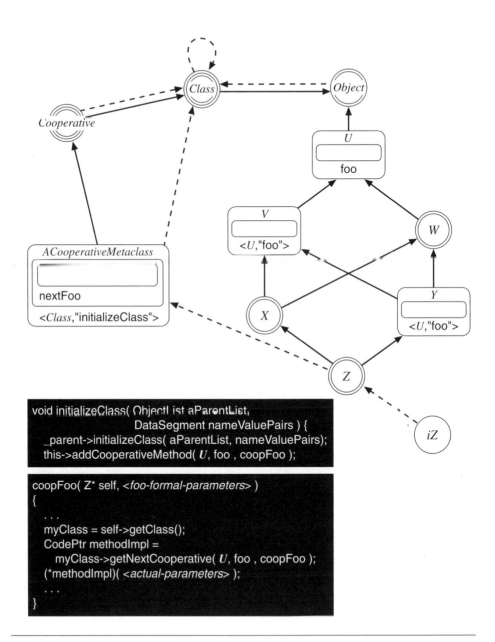

Figure 7-4. Programming model for *Cooperative*.

```
      boolean initializeClass( ObjectList aParentList, DataSegment nameValuePairs );
      void addMethod(   Class* introducingClass,
                        string aMethodName,
                        CodePtr methodImpl );
      void overrideMethod( Class* introducingClass,
                        string aMethodName,
                        CodePtr methodImpl );
      void putRDStub( Class* introducingClass, string methodName );
      CodePtr resolveTerminal( Class* introducingClass, string methodName );
      void readyClass();
}
```

Figure 7-5 shows the path expression for *Cooperative*; it is also part of the specification. The path expression requires that all requests for the first cooperative method occur prior to any calls to addCooperativeMethod and, furthermore, that the set of calls to requestFirstCooperativeMethodCall be terminated with a call to satisfyRequests.

```
      ( addCooperativeMethod*
        |
        (requestFirstCooperativeMethodCall*
        satisfyRequests
        addCooperativeMethod*)
      )
      getNextCooperativeMethod*
```

Figure 7-5. Path expression for *Cooperative*.

As before, the specification of *Cooperative* (below) does not enforce the path expression in Figure 7-5. The explanation of *Cooperative* is divided into two parts. First, we explain the specification for adding a cooperative method. Once this has been accomplished, we explain how one ensures that a cooperative method is the first to be called. Please bear in mind that this is both an exercise in using our metaobject protocol and the development of a fundamental concept (cooperation) that is required to put metaclasses to work effectively.

The basic idea underlying cooperation, as depicted in Figure 7-2, seems quite simple. However, making it work correctly is complicated by the following factors.

- One should be able to add a cooperative method in an override of either initializeClass or readyClass. The path expression for class creation (see Figure 4-3 on page 71) implies that adding a cooperative method may precede or succeed the addition of new methods and the overriding of inherited methods.

- Adding a cooperative method changes the method table. This should not adversely impact the parent method call semantics.

Fundamentally, any solution for the conflict among metaclasses over the one resource (the method table entry) involves creation of more resources (that is, more places to put cooperative method implementations). Correct implementation of cooperation in the presence of these complicating factors requires two of the data structures declared in Cooperative: terminalImplementations and cooperationChains. Let us start with an explanation of terminalImplementations. In the presence of cooperation, in order for a method invocation to begin with the cooperative method, we know that there is a cooperative method in the method table. Therefore, if a parent method call is to be properly effected from a descendant of a cooperative class, the content of the method table before cooperation must be saved. This, then, is the purpose of terminalImplementations: whenever a cooperative method is first added, the content of the method table must be saved, which is done in the definition of addCooperativeMethod below. But first let us recognize that the terminalImplementations must be inherited, because once a cooperative method has been placed in the mdefs of a class, it is the cooperative method that is inherited. This means that initializeClass must be overridden as follows.

```
boolean Cooperative :: initializeClass( ObjectList aParentList,
                                        DataSegment nameValuePairs )
{/* Specification */
Action:
    if ( __parent->initializeClass( aParentList, aDataSegment ) ) {
        // The line below does inheritance of terminal implementations.
        this.Cooperative."terminalImplementations" =
```

$$\triangleleft W.Cooperative."terminalImplementations";$$
$$W \in this\text{->}gotMBO()$$
$$and$$
$$getClass(W)\text{->}isDescendantOf(Cooperative)$$

```
        boolean doOverride = TRUE;
        for ( int i = 0; #aParentList; i++ ) {
            if ( getClass( aParentList[i] )->isDescendantOf( Cooperative ) )
                doOverride = FALSE;
        }
        if ( doOverride )
            this->overrideMethod( Object, "dispatch", coopDispatch );
        return TRUE;
    }
    else
        return FALSE;
}
```

The recursive merge above is over all cooperative classes, because classes that are not cooperative do not have a terminalImplementations instance variable (in which case, the expression is not defined). Note that, because we have saved the terminal implementation, a useful implementation of dispatch can now be effected. This is done at the end of initializeClass with the override that uses the following implementation.

```
void coopDispatch( Object* target,
                   Class* introducingClass,
                   string methodName,
                   ObjectList aParameterList,
                   void** returnValue )
{
    apply(  target,
            getClass(target)->
                    getIV(Cooperative, "terminalImplementations")
                            .introducingClass.methodName,
            aParameterList,
            &returnValue );
}
```

The override of dispatch may seem a bit odd in this context, where we are emphasizing being cooperative, but dispatch is not required to be cooperative. To bootstrap cooperative classes, dispatch must be overridden. Because dispatch is declared to be noncooperative, a metaclass can override it with an implementation that does not make a parent method call. The override of dispatch is performed only for the maximal classes that are instances of *Cooperative*. After this override, ordinary inheritance rules are in effect. In addition, other metaclasses may add cooperative implementations to dispatch. Further note that if an ordinary class overrides dispatch, that override is saved in the terminalImplementations structure and invoked by coopDispatch.

Next, resolveTerminal must be overridden so that parent method calls invoke what would be the content of the method table if there were no cooperation. An appropriate override is

```
CodePtr Cooperative :: resolveTerminal( Class* introducingClass, string methodName )
{ /* Specification */
```
Action:
```
    if ( methodName ∈ terminalImplementations.introducingClass )
        return terminalImplementations.introducingClass.methodName;
    else
        return this->resolveMethod( introducingClass, methodName );
}
```

Now that inheritance of terminal implementations and proper invocation of parent method calls have been established, we can move on to the addition of cooperative methods. This requires the instance variable cooperationChains, which is structured as a method table — that is, it is a dictionary of dictionaries in which the first-level key is a class reference and the second-level key is a method name. The values (at the bottom of this nesting of dictionaries) are a list of code pointers that contains the cooperation chain followed by an additional element, as shown in Figure 7-6. The additional entry is a code pointer to the terminal implementation or a redispatch stub. The preceding entries are pointers to the cooperative implementations that have been added to the methods. getNextCooperative retrieves the code pointer for the next entry in the cooperation chain when given the pointer to the preceding entry.

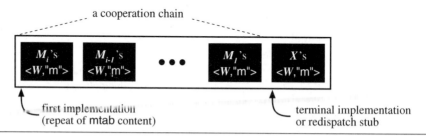

Figure 7-6. Example of a list in the cooperationChains structure.

A procedural specification for addCooperativeMethod is as follows.

```
void Cooperative :: addCooperativeMethod(Class* introducingClass,
                                          string aMethodName,
                                          CodePtr cooperativeMethod )
{ /* Specification */
Precondition:
      Path expression of Figure 7-5 is obeyed and
      this->supportsMethod( introducingClass, aMethodName )
Action:
      CodePtr mtabEntry = this->resolveMethod( introducingClass, aMethodName );
            // If the method has not yet been added, the above call returns NULL;  this is
            // okay and is corrected when addMethod is invoked.

      if ( aMethodName ∉ cooperationChains.introducingClass ) {
        if ( aMethodName ∉ terminalImplementations.introducingClass ) {
          terminalImplementations = terminalImplementations
                          ◁ {introducingClass={aMethodName=mtabEntry}};
        }
```

```
        CodePtr aTerminalImplementation =
                terminalImplementations.introducingClass.aMethodName;
        cooperationChains = cooperationChains
                ◁ {introducingClass={aMethodName=<aTerminalImplementation>}};
    }
    list chain = cooperationChains.introducingClass.aMethodName;
    chain = <cooperativeMethod> ◁ chain;
    cooperationChains = {introducingClass={aMethodName=chain}}◁cooperationChains;
    if ( mtabEntry != NULL ) {
        isAddCooperativeCalling = TRUE;
        this->overrideMethod( introducingClass, aMethodName, cooperativeMethod );
        isAddCooperativeCalling = FALSE;
        }
}
```

Given the specification above for addCooperativeMethod, the procedural specification for getNextCooperative is quite simply a search to find the cooperative method being executed and return the next entry of the appropriate list in cooperationChains.

```
CodePtr Cooperative :: getNextCooperative(Class* introducingClass,
                                          string aMethodName,
                                          CodePtr cooperativeMethod )
```

{ /* Specification */
Precondition:
        let coopList == cooperationChains.introducingClass.aMethodName
            cooperativeMethod ∈ coopList[0,#coopList-2]
        // In other words, cooperative method must be in the cooperation chain for the
        // method <introducingClass,aMethodName>
Action:
        for (int i = 0; i < #cooperationChains.introducingClass.aMethodName; i++) {
            if (cooperationChains.introducingClass.aMethodName[i] == cooperativeMethod)
                return cooperationChains.introducingClass.aMethodName[i+1]
        }
}

To complete this first part of the description of *Cooperative*, the overrides of addMethod, overrideMethod, and putRDStub must be specified. If there is cooperation on the method being added, then addMethod must place the new method implementation in the last entry of the cooperation chain, insert the new implementation into terminalImplementations, and add the first entry of the cooperation chain to the method table.

```
void Cooperative :: addMethod(Class* introducingClass,
                              string aMethodName,
                              CodePtr methodImpl )
{ /* Specification */
Action:
    if ( aMethodName ∈ cooperationChains.introducingClass ) {
        terminalImplementations
            = {introducingClass={aMethodName=methodImpl}} ◁ terminalImplementations;
        long indexOfLastImpl = #cooperationChains.introducingClass.aMethodName-1;
        cooperationChains.introducingClass.aMethodName[indexOfLastImpl]
            = methodImpl;
        methodImpl = cooperationChains.introducingClass.aMethodName[0]
    }
    __parent->addMethod( introducingClass, aMethodName, methodImpl );
}
```

If there is cooperation on the method, then the override for overrideMethod replaces the terminal implementation in the cooperation chain and in terminalImplementations; otherwise, there is just a normal override. In addition, if the call is from addCooperativeMethod, a normal override is also executed. Note that this form of communication between overrideMethod and addCooperativeMethod is problematic if concurrency is introduced into the class construction process.

```
void Cooperative :: overrideMethod(Class* introducingClass,
                                   string aMethodName,
                                   CodePtr methodImpl )
{ /* Specification */
Action:
    if ( !isAddCooperativeCalling &&
            ( aMethodName ∈ cooperationChains.introducingClass ) ) {
        CodePtr tempImpl = this->resolveMethod( introducingClass, aMethodName );
        // Make call to overrideMethod that changes nothing.
        // This ensures that the override being implemented is cooperative.
        __parent->overrideMethod( introducingClass, aMethodName, tempImpl );
        terminalImplementations = {introducingClass={aMethodName=methodImpl}}
                        ◁ terminalImplementations;
        long indexOfLastImpl = #cooperationChains.introducingClass.aMethodName-1;
        cooperationChains.introducingClass.aMethodName[indexOfLastImpl]
            = methodImpl;
    }
    else
        __parent->overrideMethod( introducingClass, aMethodName, methodImpl );
}
```

In addition, it is necessary to override putRDStub in case it is executed before addCooperativeMethod. The override ensures that the terminal method is saved.

```
void Cooperative :: putRDStub( Class* introducingClass, string methodName )
{/*Specification*/
```
Action:
```
    if ( aMethodName ∉ cooperationChains.introducingClass ) {
        if ( aMethodName ∉ terminalImplementations.introducingClass ) {
            CodePtr mtabEntry = this->resolveMethod( introducingClass, aMethodName );
            // If the method has not yet been added, the above call returns NULL;
            // this is okay and is corrected when addMethod is invoked.
            terminalImplementations = terminalImplementations
                        ◁ {introducingClass={aMethodName=mtabEntry}};
        }
        CodePtr aTerminalImplementation
                    = terminalImplementations.introducingClass.aMethodName;
        cooperationChains = cooperationChains
                    ◁ {introducingClass={aMethodName=<aTerminalImplementation>}};
    }
    __parent->putRDStub( introducingClass, aMethodName );
}
```

It is now time to explain the rest of the interface to *Cooperative*. There are times when a metaclass insists that a cooperative method be first on the chain. The metaclass may make such a request with requestFirstCooperativeMethodCall. Requesting the first cooperative method is in effect requesting the method table entry. Of course, that position on the chain is now a resource over which metaclasses can conflict, and requests for it may be denied.

Understanding the purpose of each of the two dictionary instance variables is the key to understanding *Cooperative*.

- The satisfiedRequests dictionary contains all the requests (for the first chain position) that have been satisfied.

- New requests (made by calls to requestFirstCooperativeMethodCall) are checked against the satisfied requests for conflicts. If there is no conflict, the request is inserted into the pendingRequests dictionary.

After all the requests have been made by a particular metaclass (in its override of initializeClass), the requests are moved from the pendingRequests dictionary to the satisfiedRequests dictionary by invocation of satisfyRequests. The pendingRequests dictionary is needed so that all the requests of a metaclass must be satisfied or none are. Note that if any call to requestFirstCooperativeMethodCall fails (returns FALSE), then the pendingRequests dictionary is cleared. This gives the metaclass programmer the opportunity to try another approach to cooperation (that is, requestFirstCooperativeMethodCall makes no permanent changes if it fails).

boolean Cooperative :: **requestFirstCooperativeMethodCall**(Class* introducingClass,
                                                                        string aMethodName,
                                                                        CodePtr cooperativeMethod)

{ /* Specification */
Precondition:
    Path expression of Figure 7-5 is obeyed and
    this->supportsMethod(introducingClass,aMethodName)
Action:
    if (<introducingClass,aMethodName> ∈ satisfiedRequests ◁ pendingRequests) {
      pendingRequests = {}; // Note that a failed request clears all pending requests
      return FALSE; // There is a conflicting request (made by another metaclass)
      }
    pendingRequests = pendingRequests ◁
        {introducingClass={aMethodName=cooperativeMethod}};
    return TRUE;
}

void Cooperative :: **satisfyRequests**( )
{ /* Specification */
Action:
    satisfiedRequests = satisfiedRequests ◁ pendingRequests;
}

    In satisfyRequests, the pending requests are copied to satisfiedRequests but the pending requests are not cleared. In the code fragment below (in the override of readyClass), the pending requests are used to make calls to addCooperativeMethod and then the pending requests are cleared.

void Cooperative :: **readyClass**( )
{ /* Specification */
Action:
    MethodList icList = α(pendingRequests);
    for (int i = 0; i < #icList; i++) {
      Class* introducingClass = icList[i];
      List nmList = α(pendingRequests.icList[i]);
      for (int j= 0; j< #nmList; j++) {
        string   aMethodName = nmList[j];
        CodePtr   methodPtr = pendingRequests.introducingClass.aMethodName;
        this->addCooperativeMethod(introducingClass, aMethodName, methodPtr);
      }
    }
    __parent->readyClass( );
    pendingRequests = {};
}

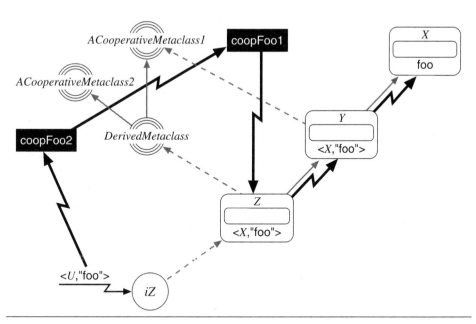

Figure 7-7. Overrides are nested inside cooperative implementations.

7.3 Notes on the Design of Cooperation

At this point, one might raise the question of whether the functionality of *Cooperative* should be made a separate facility (as we have done here) or an alternative design should be used in which the functionality is incorporated into the object model (that is, made part of *Class*). The design described here reflects the evolution of the IBM SOMobjects Toolkit and illustrates the efficacy of a good metaobject protocol in adding new abstractions to an object model. There are advantages and disadvantages of the alternative (incorporating the functionality of *Cooperative* into *Class*). The main advantage is that all metaclasses are cooperative and the parent method call mechanism can be reused. Our decision to present cooperation separately is motivated mainly by pedagogical concerns. We leave the design of the alternative object model as an exercise for the reader (see Exercise 7.3). The disadvantage of the alternative is performance: every entry in a method table must reserve space for a metaclass to add a cooperative method. As hardware evolves, object model designers may choose the simplicity of the alternative design over the performance of the one presented here.

A second point to note is the order in which cooperative implementations and overrides are executed. As Figure 7-7 shows, all overrides are nested inside cooperative implementations. That is, although the order of execution of implementations of foo on an instance of *Y* is

coopFoo1 ⟶ Y's override of foo ⟶ X's implementation

the order of execution for an instance of *Z* is as shown in Figure 7-7. This may seem counterintuitive, but it follows our philosophy that the metaclass provides a property for the whole object.

Next, because overrideMethod is used to implement addCooperativeMethod, which is used to implement requestCooperativeFirstMethodCall, the path expression of the class construction protocol (see Figure 4-3 on page 71) constrains these methods to the time of class construction. Figure 7-8 depicts the time interval of class construction. The class construction protocol in Figure 4-3 constrains all executions of overrideMethod to the interval between the two black regions in Figure 7-8.

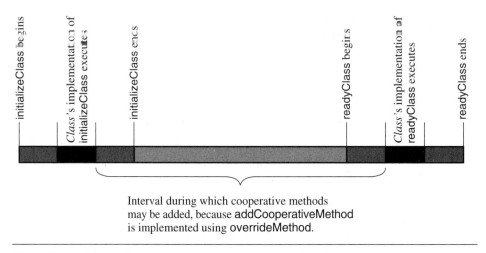

Interval during which cooperative methods
may be added, because addCooperativeMethod
is implemented using overrideMethod.

Figure 7-8. Addition of cooperative methods must occur during class construction.

Finally, our approach to putting metaclasses to work has the pleasant property that composition is associative in the following sense. Figure 7-9 shows three metaclasses, *X1*, *X2*, and *X3*, with a common parent *X*. Pure subclassing (that is, subclassing with no method changes or additions) is used to form the metaclasses *Y1*, *Y2*, *Z1*, and *Z2*, as indicated in the figure. *Z1* and *Z2* are equivalent, because *X1*, *X2*, and *X3* appear in the same sequence in the method resolution order of *Z1* and *Z2*, which implies that they (*Z1* and *Z2*) are identically initialized. Of course, composition is not commutative: reversing the order of execution of addCooperativeMethod reverses the order in which the cooperative methods are executed.

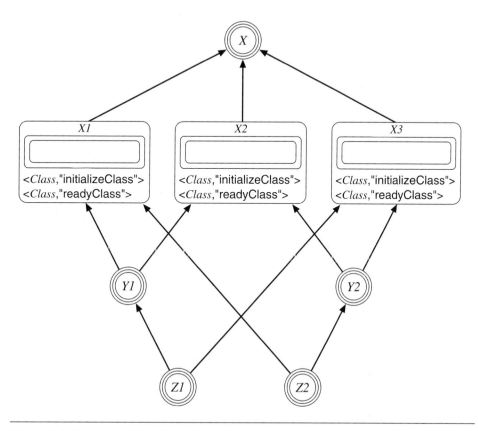

Figure 7-9. The composition of metaclasses is associative.

7.4 Conflicts and Library Design

A metaclass endows a class with a property by transforming the class object during the execution of initializeClass and readyClass. When each of a set of metaclasses attempts to endow a class with a distinct property, their composition is accomplished successfully if the transformations enacted by the several metaclasses do not conflict with one another. The main source of conflict involves the definition of method table entries. The *Cooperative* metaclass mitigates this problem by changing the granularity of that resource (the method table entry).

Among instances of *Cooperative*, conflicts occur only between the metaclasses that demand the first method call for the same method. For any class library, such demands should be an advertised constraint on the use of the library.

Among the set of cooperative implementations for a method, there are other factors that can affect the composability of a metaclass.

The first factor is whether or not an implementation calls the next implementation on the cooperation chain. Not calling the next implementation could mean that vital actions are not taken. This is analogous to an override not doing a parent method call. Therefore, a truly cooperative method must ensure that the cooperation chain is followed, because no programmer of any class (including, of course, metaclass programmers) can know what implementations follow any override on the class cooperation chain.

7.5 A Discussion of Parameter Passing

The second factor (that affects the composability of a metaclass) is the handling of the actual parameters and the return value. A change in an input parameter is harmless if done in a monotonic manner. For example, a metaclass can add instance variables to its instances by modifying an input parameter of initializeClass; this does not conflict with any other metaclass contributing to the creation of the instance as long as the name of the instance variable is unique (which can be handled by a naming convention based on the address of the metaclass, which is unique).

Now, for a cooperative method implementation to modify parameters in a nonmonotonic manner, it is required that the metaclass request the first cooperative method call. Such a method implementation modifies input parameters before calling the next cooperative method implementation and modifies output parameters just before returning. In this way, no other method implementation on the cooperation chain can change the return value, and all other method implementations receive the modified input parameters. Note that a cooperative method implementation could change an input parameter noncooperatively without it being the first on the cooperation chain; this, however, would be a programming mistake.

7.6 A Metaclass for Redispatching All Methods

The metaclass *Redispatched* (Figure 7-10) is a convenience that places a redispatch stub in each method table entry except dispatch. Below is the DTS C++ class declaration and the override for readyClass.

```
class Redispatched : public virtual Cooperative : Class {
    public:
        void readyClass();
}


void Redispatched :: readyClass()
{/* Specification */
Action:
    MethodList methods = this->getSupportedMethods();
    Method* mp;
    for ( mp= methods; mp != NULL; mp++ )
        if ( mp->introducingClass != Object || mp->methodName != "dispatch" )
            this->putRDStub( mp->introducingClass, mp->methodName );
    }
    __parent->readyClass();
}
```

This metaclass may seem trivial, but it is an important part of our plan to create a metaclass framework that is highly usable yet relieves the programmer of the burden of knowing all of the intricacies of the metaobject protocol.

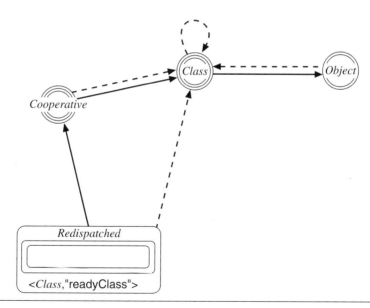

Figure 7-10. *Redispatched* metaclass.

7.7 Example: A Simple Trace Facility

Before ending this chapter, let us look at an example of the use of *Redispatched*. Suppose one wants to create a metaclass that simply traces all method invocations (that is, prints just the name of the method when it is called and when it returns). This can be accomplished by subclassing *Redispatched* and adding a cooperative method to dispatch.

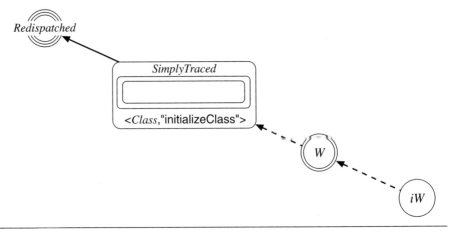

Figure 7-11. A simple metaclass for tracing method invocations.

Figure 7-11 depicts the basic design. If class *W* is an instance of the metaclass *SimplyTraced*, then for instances of *W* (for example, *iW*), each method invocation prints a message before the method executes and another message when the method terminates. The DTS C++ code that implements this class is given below.

```
class SimplyTraced : cooperative Redispatched {
      public:
          CodePtr nextDispatch;
          boolean initializeClass( ObjectList aParentList, DataSegment nameValuePairs );
}
```

```
void* simplyTracedDispatch( Object* self,
                            string aMethodName,
                            ObjectList aParameterList )
{/* Specification */
Action:
    printf( "%s invoked\n", aMethodName );
    Class* myClass = self->getClass();
    // Use the handle to get the code pointer
    // to the next cooperative method implementation.
    CodePtr nextImpl
            = myClass->getNextCooperative( Object, "dispatch", simplyTracedDispatch );
    (*nextImpl)( self, aMethodName, aParameterList );
    printf( "%s returned\n", aMethodName );
}


boolean SimplyTraced :: initializeClass(ObjectList aParentList,
                                        DataSegment nameValuePairs )
{/* Specification */
Action:
    if ( __parent->initializeClass( aParentList, nameValuePairs ) ) {
        this->addCooperativeMethod( Class, "dispatch", simplyTracedDispatch );
        return TRUE;
    }
    else
        return FALSE;
}
```

A good metaclass for tracing should print values of the actual parameters and the return value of the method. This is beyond the scope of this book, because our metaobject protocol does not have the metadata that would allow one to parse the parameter list (that is, the second parameter to dispatch). In the IBM SOMobjects Toolkit, there is such a metaclass; if the class object is registered in a CORBA Interface Repository, that metaclass can access this additional source of metadata so as to print the parameters and the return value. This leads one to an obvious but important point:

The utility of a metaobject protocol is limited by the availability of metadata.

7.8 Summary

This chapter has introduced the concept of cooperation, which allows a metaclass to add an implementation to a method in much the same way that an override adds to the implementation of a method. This turns out to be a very valuable concept, because in the creation of reusable metaclasses, the capability of adding methods and overriding methods is useful, but the capability of cooperating with an existing method is of the utmost importance.

7.9 Exercises

7.1   The last implementation added by addCooperativeMethod is the first one invoked. Reimplement *Cooperative* so that the first implementation added by addCooperativeMethod (for a particular method) is first. Evaluate the differences between the specification in the text and the one proposed in this exercise.

7.2   In the definition of the override of initializeClass for Cooperative (on page 158), we used "this->getMRO() and getClass(W)->isDescendantOf(*Cooperative*)" as the index set for the recursive merge. Write a function that computes this index set.

7.3   Design the alternative object model in which the functionality of *Cooperative* is part of *Class*. In this design, the parent method call mechanism should be used in cooperative methods added by a metaclass (that is, there should be no need for a separate programming convention for cooperative methods such as the one we introduced in Figure 7-4).

7.4   Formalize the notion of a monotonic change in an input parameter. (This is a hard problem.)

7.5   Show that, despite the power of CLOS, there is no direct analog of our notion of a cooperative method in CLOS (see [69] or [104]).

Chapter 8
Before/After Metaclasses

To this point, our metaclasses have either extended our metaobject protocol (in particular, *Cooperative*) or implemented class properties (for example, *CTimeStamped*). Between these two notions is that of a metaclass that facilitates the composition of classes. This chapter presents one such metaclass. It is a metaclass that wraps all methods of a class with before/after methods.

A **before method** is a behavior that precedes the action of some method. An **after method** is a behavior that succeeds the action of some method. Before and after methods are familiar to users of CLOS in which the granularity of application is the individual method. In a class-based object model, the more natural granularity for before/after methods is the class, because there are many applications that fit this granularity (see Section 8.5). This chapter presents *BeforeAfter* with two methods beforeMethod and afterMethod such that the instances (classes) of this new metaclass have these methods run, respectively, before and after each instance method. By default, these two methods do nothing: to define a specialized before/after behavior, one creates a subclass and overrides the beforeMethod and the afterMethod with the desired behavior.

For example, consider the arrangement in Figure 8-1. The *Barking* metaclass overrides beforeMethod and afterMethod with a method that makes a "woof" sound when executed. As a result, all methods supported by the class *BarkingDog* (an instance of *Barking*) exhibit this before/after behavior. That is, the object *Lassie* goes "woof" before and after the execution of each basc implementation, because it is an instance of *BarkingDog*.

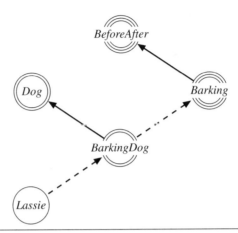

Figure 8-1. Example of wrapping the methods of a class with before/after methods.

8.1 The Composition Problem

It is not enough to wrap one pair of before/after methods around all of the methods of a class. Consider Figure 8-2, in which there are Before/After Metaclasses *Barking* (as in Figure 8-1) and *Fierce*, which has a beforeMethod and an afterMethod that both growl. That is, both make a "grrr" sound when executed. It should be clear that we can now create a *FierceDog* class or a *BarkingDog* class, but we have not yet addressed the question of how to compose the properties of *Fierce* and *Barking*. Composability means the ability to create easily a fierce barking dog class whose instances go "grrr woof woof grrr" when responding to a method call, or a barking fierce dog class whose instances go "woof grrr grrr woof" when responding to a method call.

The problem of composing the properties of *Fierce* and *Barking* is complicated by the fact that there are several ways in which one might express such compositions. Figure 8-3 depicts three techniques in which such a composition might naturally be indicated by a programmer. These techniques, labeled Technique 1, Technique 2, and Technique 3, create the fierce barking dog classes named *FB-1*, *FB-2*, and *FB-3*, respectively. The DTS C++ declaration for each of these classes is shown above a diagram that depicts the context in which the class description is given.

In Technique 1, a new metaclass (*FierceBarking*) is created with both *Fierce* and *Barking* as parents; an instance of this new metaclass (that is, *FB-1*) should be a fierce barking dog (if *Dog* is a parent).

In Technique 2, a new class is created that has parents that are instances of *Fierce* and *Barking*, respectively; that is, *FB-2* should be a fierce barking dog also (assuming that *FierceDog* and *BarkingDog* do not further specialize *Dog*).

In Technique 3, *FB-3*, which should also be a fierce barking dog, is created by declaring that its parent is a *BarkingDog* and that its explicitly declared metaclass is *Fierce*.

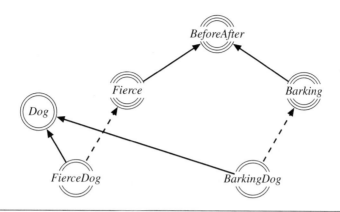

Figure 8-2. Composition of a Before/After Metaclass is required.

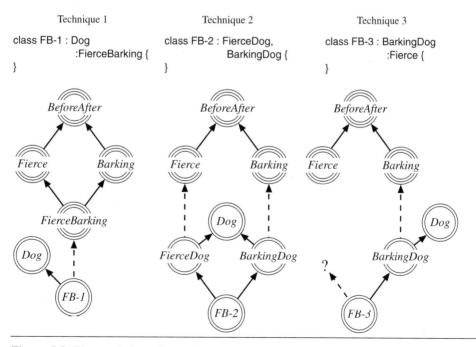

Figure 8-3. Three techniques for creating a fierce barking dog class.

Looking at Figure 8-3, we ask the question: "Should the three techniques produce the same result?" That is, should *FB-1*, *FB-2*, and *FB-3* be equivalent classes? The answer must be "YES," because composition of metaclasses must be easily understood by the programmer. Nonequivalence of these three techniques would certainly lead to a system in which programming would be complex and error-prone. This conclusion leads us to ask what common property these techniques have on which an equivalence can be based. As we know, there is such a property that is provided by the derived metaclass.

When one considers this situation, one obvious conclusion is unavoidable: Before/After Metaclasses are not useful unless they compose, because if they do not, the use of one Before/After Metaclass will preclude the use of others. We now return to an examination of the techniques in Figure 8-3. Here, the derived metaclass constructed for *FB-3* is equivalent to *FierceBarking*, not *Fierce*. Now look at the diagram for Technique 2 in Figure 8-3; here also, although the metaclass for *FB-2* is not explicitly declared, the derived metaclass for *FB-2* is equivalent to *FierceBarking*.

Figure 8-4 combines the diagrams in Figure 8-3 and shows a stylized form of the actual class relationships (which are established when the class objects are created). The solution of the composition problem jumps out at us. The common element among the three techniques for expressing before/after composition is the metaclass *FierceBarking* or an equivalent derived metaclass, which is the class of *FB-1*, *FB-2*, and *FB-3* (in the case of *FB-1* the relationship is explicit, and in the cases of *FB-2* and *FB-3* the relationship is derived). Therefore, composition can be based on the "completed" metaclass hierarchy that results from the use of derived metaclasses.

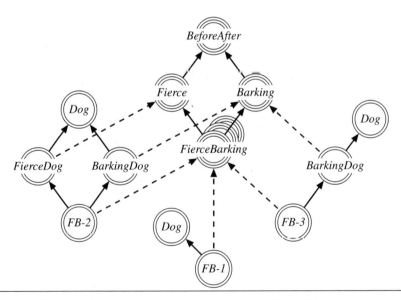

Figure 8-4. The equivalence of the three techniques shown in Figure 8-3.

8.2   Design of the Before/After Metaclass

BeforeAfter is a metaclass that is not meant to be directly instantiated. It introduces two methods: beforeMethod and afterMethod. A subclass of *BeforeAfter* overrides either of these methods to capture a property that the subclass imparts to its instances, which are classes whose instances have the property because each method invocation is preceded by the beforeMethod or succeeded by the afterMethod.

In addition to this basic requirement, there is also the requirement that beforeMethod return a code that indicates whether the rest of the implementation chain and the corresponding afterMethod should be skipped. This facility is intended for handling exception conditions. Clearly, skipping the execution of the rest of the implementation chain is not being very cooperative.

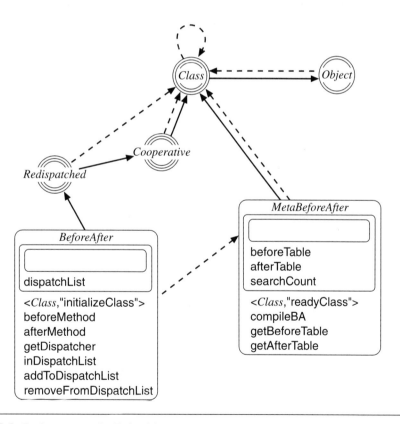

Figure 8-5. Design concept for *BeforeAfter*.

Figure 8-5 depicts the design concept for *BeforeAfter*. Note that redispatch stubs are used to invoke dispatch, because *BeforeAfter* is a subclass of *Redispatched*. Further, *BeforeAfter* is an instance of *MetaBeforeAfter*, which is the metametaclass used to initialize Before/After Metaclasses.

Each Before/After Metaclass contains two sequences of method pointers: beforeTable and afterTable. Our metaobject protocol is such that once a class has been created, the class hierarchy above it never changes (here "above" means all classes reachable by any combination of the parent and instance relations). Because of this property, the search can be made once at the time of the creation of a metaclass, which has the effect of compiling the sequences of before/after methods into the metaclass object.

Below are the DTS C++ class declarations for *BeforeAfter* and *MetaBeforeAfter*. In addition, there is a static variable (that is, a global) named globalSearchCount that is used for the marking algorithm that searches the metaclass hierarchy when the tables of before and after methods are constructed. Before a search of the metaclass hierarchy is performed, globalSearchCount is incremented; this number is used to mark metaclasses as having been visited (that is, any metaclass marked with a lower number has not been visited on this search). This technique trades space for time over the many searches that may be needed.

```
class MetaBeforeAfter : public virtual Class : Class {
    private:
        dictionary beforeTable = {};
        dictionary afterTable = {};
        long searchCount = 0;
    public:
        void readyClass( );
        cooperative ObjectList compileBA( string baMethodName, ObjectList anInList );
        cooperative ObjectList getBeforeTable( );
        cooperative ObjectList getAfterTable( );
}


static long globalSearchCount = 0;
```

```
class BeforeAfter : public virtual Redispatched : MetaBeforeAfter {
    private:
        ObjectList dispatchList = <>;
    public:
        boolean initializeClass( ObjectList aParentList, DataSegment nameValuePairs );
        cooperative CodePtr getDispatcher( );
        cooperative boolean inDispatchList( Object* target );
        cooperative void addToDispatchList( Object* target );
        cooperative void removeFromDispatchList( Object* target );
    protected:
        virtual long beforeMethod( Object* target,
                            Class* introducingClass,
                            string methodName,
                            va_list vaList );
        virtual void afterMethod( Object* target,
                            Class* introducingClass,
                            string methodName,
                            va_list vaList,
                            void** returnValue );
}
```

Now let us continue our explanation with the methods of *MetaBeforeAfter*. To compile properly the lists of before methods and after methods, readyClass must be overridden (because this is the method of class construction protocol that is called after all methods have been added and overridden). The precondition states that a Before/After Metaclass must define (provide an override for) both a before method and an after method, or neither. The reason for this precondition is explained in Section 8.3. In the override below, the method compileBA is called twice: once for the beforeTable and once for the afterTable. The method compileBA conducts a search of the metaclass hierarchy to find Before/After Metaclasses that define either a before method or an after method. When such a metaclass is found, the contents of its method table entries for beforeMethod and afterMethod are appended to the beforeTable and the afterTable, respectively.

```
void MetaBeforeAfter :: readyClass( )
{/* Specification */
```
Precondition:
```
        ( this->defines( BeforeAfter, "beforeMethod" )
            and this->defines( BeforeAfter, "afterMethod" ) )
        or
        ( not this->defines( BeforeAfter, "beforeMethod" )
            and not this->defines( BeforeAfter, "afterMethod" ) )
        // The rationale for this precondition is given in Subsection 8.3.2.
```
Action:
```
    globalSearchCount++;
    beforeTable = this->compileBA( "beforeMethod", beforeTable );
    globalSearchCount++;
    afterTable = this->compileBA( "afterMethod", afterTable );
    __parent->readyClass( );
}
```

We named the method compileBA because it does a compiler-like operation at class construction time (which, in the context of separately compiled and dynamically linked class libraries, is the time that this information is available — see Chapter 11). The algorithm for compileBA is a depth-first search, where the nodes (metaclass objects) are marked with the global search count. If the metaclass defines either a before method or an after method, the search halts. The code pointer of the implementation in the method table is placed in the list.

```
ObjectList MetaBeforeAfter :: compileBA( string baMethodName, ObjectList aList )
{/* Specification */
```
Action:
```
    if ( this->searchCount >= globalSearchCount )
        return aList;
    this->searchCount = globalSearchCount;
    if ( this->defines( BeforeAfter, "beforeMethod" )
          || this->defines( BeforeAfter, "afterMethod" ) )
        return aList ◁ <this->resolveMethod( BeforeAfter, baMethodName )>;
    else {
        ObjectList parents;
        for ( parents = this->getParents(); parents != NULL ; parents++ ) {
            if ( getClass(*parents)->supportsMethod( MetaBeforeAfter, "compileBA" ) )
                aList = (*parents)->compileBA( baMethodName, aList );
        }
        return aList;
    }
}
```

The following two methods enable the dispatcher to retrieve the compiled tables of before methods and after methods.

ObjectList MetaBeforeAfter :: **getBeforeTable**( ) { return this.beforeTable; }
ObjectList MetaBeforeAfter :: **getAfterTable**( ) { return this.afterTable; }

Now that we understand what the metametaclass does, we can move on to *BeforeAfter*. This metaclass installs the dispatcher in its instances. The override of initializeClass (below) requests the first cooperative method for dispatch. The dispatcher is retrieved with the method getDispatcher (which has the benefit of allowing subclasses of *BeforeAfter* to override the dispatcher).

```
boolean BeforeAfter :: initializeClass( ObjectList aParentList,
                                        DataSegment nameValuePairs)
{/* Specification */
Action:
    if ( __parent->initializeClass( aParentList, nameValuePairs ) &&
        this->requestFirstCooperativeMethodCall( Object,
                                                 "dispatch",
                                                 this->getDispatcher() ) ) {

        this->satisfyRequests();
        return TRUE;
        }
    else
        return FALSE;
}
```

```
CodePtr BeforeAfter :: getDispatcher( ) { return befaftDispatch; }
```

Next are default implementations for beforeMethod and afterMethod. The value returned by beforeMethod is used to control the dispatcher. There are three possible return values:

- 0 — The dispatcher should continue to the next before method or the rest of the implementation chain (whichever is appropriate).
- 1 — The dispatcher should continue with the after method of the previously executed before method (which means that the rest of the implementation chain is not executed).
- 2 — The dispatcher should continue with the after method corresponding to the before method that returned this value.

```
long BeforeAfter :: beforeMethod( Object*  target,
                                  Class* introducingClass,
                                  string methodName,
                                  va_list vaList )
{
     return 0;
}
void BeforeAfter :: afterMethod( Object* target,
                                 Class* introducingClass,
                                 string methodName,
                                 va_list vaList,
                                 void* returnValue )
{
}
```

It is easy to get into a redispatch loop with an improperly designed dispatcher; all one needs to do is invoke a method on the target object from a before method (or an after method). The dispatcher also has the obligation to protect against redispatch loops by invoking the before and after methods only if execution is not already in the dispatcher for the target object. This is determined by having the dispatcher keep a record of the target objects (for which it is executing) in a class variable (that is an instance variable of the metaclass *BeforeAfter*). The three methods inDispatchList, addToDispatchList, and removeFromDispatchList are introduced to manage this list.

- Prior to executing before methods, the dispatcher checks if the target object is already in dispatchList. If so, execution continues with the next cooperative method for dispatch. If not, the target object is added to dispatchList and normal before/after dispatching continues.

- Subsequent to executing after methods, the target object is removed from dispatch.

The rationale for this design is that a Before/After Metaclass is providing a service for the entire object. If the object is on the dispatch list, there is no need to perform the service again.

```
boolean BeforeAfter :: inDispatchList( Object*  target )
{ /* Specification */
```
Action:
```
     return  target ∈ dispatchList;
}
void BeforeAfter :: addToDispatchList( Object*  target )
{ /* Specification */
```
Action:
```
     dispatchList = dispatchList ◁ < target>;
}
```

```
void BeforeAfter :: removeFromDispatchList( Object*  target )
{ /* Specification */
Action:
      dispatchList = dispatchList − < target>;
}
```

Because we are using DTS C++ and are also using code pointer to invoke methods, the following three type definitions are required when executing the code pointers to beforeMethod, afterMethod, and dispatch. Remember that we are working under the assumption that method invocations are translated to function calls in which the first parameter is the target object of the method invocation. For example, the method beforeMethod is defined to have four parameters whereas in the type definition below there are five parameters.

```
typedef long (BeforeMethodType*)( BeforeAfter*,
                                  Object*,
                                  Class*,
                                  string,
                                  va_list ),

typedef void (AfterMethodType*)( BeforeAfter*,
                                 Object*,
                                 Class*,
                                 string,
                                 va_list,
                                 void**);

typedef void* (DispatchType*)( Object*,
                               Class*,
                               string,
                               va_list );
```

Below is the dispatcher for Before/After Metaclasses; that is, it is the method on the chain of cooperative methods that receives the first call. The design choice to make the dispatcher the first cooperative method on dispatch ensures that beforeMethod implementations are before all other implementations, including other cooperative methods. Now, because the before/after methods are introduced by the metaclass, they are executed with calls to the class object. The implementation of the dispatcher has three sections. First, the before methods are executed in the order of the beforeTable. Second, the rest of the implementation chain is executed. Third, the after methods are executed in the reverse order of the afterTable.

```
void befaftDispatch( Object* target,
                     Class* introducingClass,
                     string aMethodName,
                     va_list aParameterList,
                     void** returnValue)
{ /* Specification */
```
Action:

```
    long i = 0;
    long j = 0;
    long beforeReturnCode;

    Class* myMetaclass = getClass( getClass(target) );

    ObjectList beforeTable = myMetaclass->getBeforeTable();

    ObjectList afterTable = myMetaclass->getAfterTable();


    //-------------------------------------Section 0 -- protect against loop-----------------------------

    if ( getClass(target)->inDispatchList( target ) )
       CodePtr nextDispatch = getClass(target)->getNextCooperative(   Object,
                                                                      "dispatch",
                                                                      befaftDispatch );

       return (DispatchType)nextDispatch(   target,
                                            introducingClass,
                                            aMethodName,
                                            aParameterList);
    getClass(target)->addToDispatchList( target );


    //-------------------------------------Section 1 -- invoke before methods---------------------------

    for ( ; i < #beforeTable; i++ ) {
       beforeReturnCode = ((BeforeMethodType)beforeTable[i])(   getClass(target),
                                                                target,
                                                                introducingClass,
                                                                aMethodName,
                                                                aParameterList );
```

```
            if ( beforeReturnCode == 1)
                break;
            else if ( beforeReturnCode == 2 ) {
                // The corresponding After Method is to be executed, so by incrementing i
                // the after dispatch loop (below) starts in the correct place.
                i++;
                break;
                }
            }


//----------Section 2 -- invoke next implementation on the implementation chain----------

CodePtr nextDispatch = getClass(target)->getNextCooperative(  Object,
                                                             "dispatch",
                                                             befaftDispatch );
if ( beforeReturnCode == 0 )
    (*nextDispatch)(   target,
                       introducingClass,
                       aMethodName,
                       aParameterList,
                       returnValue );


//------------------------------------Section 3 -- invoke after methods----------------------------

for ( j = i-1; j>=0; j-- )
    ((AfterMethodType)afterTable[i])(   getClass(target),
                                        target,
                                        introducingClass,
                                        aMethodName,
                                        aParameterList,
                                        returnValue );


//------------------------------------Section 4 -- protect against loop----------------------------

getClass(target)->removeFromDispatchList( target );
}
```

Example.

The *Barking* metaclass is defined as follows.

```
class Barking : public virtual BeforeAfter {
    long beforeMethod(  Object*  target,
                        Class* introducingClass,
                        string methodName,
                        va_list vaList )
  {
      printf( "woof" );
      return 0;
  }
    void afterMethod(  Object*  target,
                       Class* introducingClass,
                       string methodName,
                       va_list vaList,
                       void** returnValue )
  {
      printf( "woof" );
  }
}
```

If a subclass of *Dog* is created from the metaclass *Barking* and subsequently an ordinary object is created, the result may look like the left side of Figure 8-6. The right portion of Figure 8-6 shows (in terms of how the dispatcher uses the code pointer) the values of the first two parameters to the before method. A similar situation occurs on call to the after method.   □

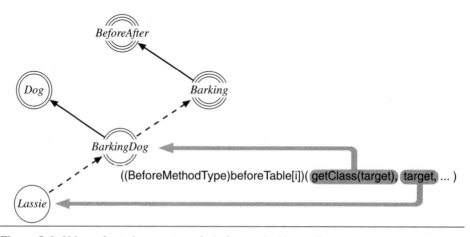

Figure 8-6. Values of actual parameters of a before method invocation.

8.3   Discussion

There are several issues about the design of *BeforeAfter* that need to be discussed.

- The difference between cooperation and Before/After Metaclasses
- The notion of correspondence between before and after methods in the dispatcher design
- The associativity of Before/After Metaclasses

8.3.1   Difference between Cooperation and Before/After Metaclasses

A cooperative method implementation has the property of executing both before and after the rest of the implementation chain. Further, Before/After Metaclasses are implemented by requesting the first cooperative method call for dispatch. One might be fooled into thinking that there is no value added by Before/After Metaclasses. However, this is not the case. Before/After Metaclasses place behavior around all methods, whereas cooperation places behavior around only a single method. This is more than simply providing an abstraction for iterating over the set of methods. Using cooperation requires the programmer to know the signature of the base implementation. Programmers of the Before/After Metaclasses do not necessarily need to know the signature of the base implementation being invoked. (For simplicity, we have eschewed the problem of how a metaclass programmer might acquire signature information.) Now, if sufficient signature information about a method invocation were available in the stack frame, a before/after property could be implemented as an iteration of addCooperativeMethod over all methods of the class being created. However, there is a slight difference in meaning. Because Before/After Metaclasses are implemented with requestFirstCooperativeMethodCall, all of the before/after methods execute around the cooperative method chain.

8.3.2   Correspondence between Before Methods and After Methods

The value returned by beforeMethod controls the continuation of the dispatcher. The value is given meaning in terms of the **corresponding after method.** The notion of correspondence is simple when both beforeMethod and afterMethod are always defined or neither is defined in each Before/After Metaclass. When this condition is relaxed so that either may be defined, the notion of correspondence is not self-evident.

The reason for this is illustrated in Figure 8-7, where the metaclass *MZ* must have the before behavior of both *MX*'s and *MY*'s overrides of beforeMethod. The after behavior of *MZ* might be defined to be simply *MW*'s override of afterMethod. A problem arises if *MY*'s override of beforeMethod returns a code that indicates that after behavior should be skipped; it is unclear whether or not *MY*'s override of beforeMethod should be executed.

Because of such situations, we have required that each Before/After Metaclass provides an override for both beforeMethod and afterMethod, or neither.

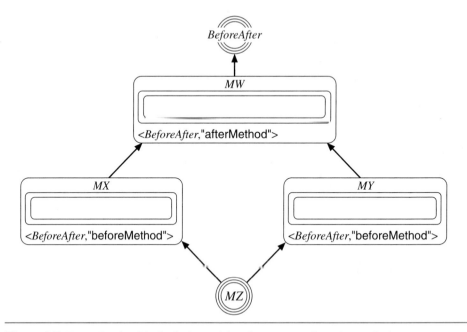

Figure 8-7. Example of ambiguity in determining the corresponding after method.

8.3.3   Associativity of Before/After Metaclasses

Our solution for the composition of Before/After Metaclasses has a pleasant property: composition is associative. Figure 8-8 (which is reminiscent of Figure 7-9) shows three Before/After Metaclasses that introduce three before methods, respectively. The derived Before/After Metaclasses *BAZ1* and *BAZ2* are equivalent. Of course, composition is not commutative. For example, a *FierceBarkingDog* is not the same as a *BarkingFierceDog* (which goes "woof grrr grrr woof"). The order of the metaclasses depends on the search order that is determined by the order of the parents.

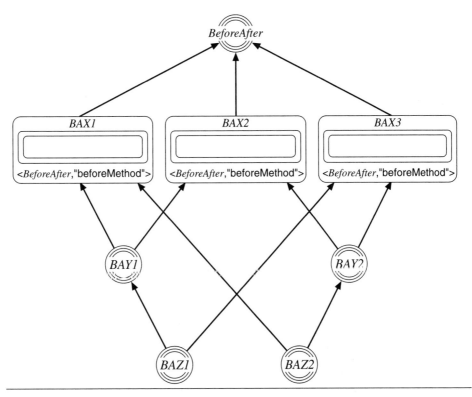

Figure 8-8. The composition of Before/After Metaclasses is associative.

8.4 Example: A Simple Metaclass for Thread Safety

Let us subclass *BeforeAfter* to create a simple metaclass for thread safety. Assume that our operating system offers semaphores. Semaphore handles are of type OSSemaphore, and the following four operations are available on that type.

```
OSSemaphore* osCreateSemaphore();
    // returns a handle to a newly created semaphore
void osAcquireSemaphore( OSSemaphore* );
    // acquires the semaphore -- other threads attempting this are blocked
void osReleaseSemaphore( OSSemaphore* );
    // releases an acquired semaphore
void osDestroySemaphore( OSSemaphore* );
    // destroys the semaphore
```

As usual, we have brushed aside all concerns about error handling in order to stay focused on putting metaclasses to work. The design concept for our simple metaclass is given in Figure 8-9.

The declaration and implementation of a simple metaclass for implementing thread safety are as follows.

```
class SimpleThreadSafe : public virtual BeforeAfter {
        OSSemaphore semaphoreForClass;
        long beforeMethod(   Object*  target,
                             Class* introducingClass,
                             string methodName,
                             va_list vaList );
        void afterMethod(  Object*  target,
                           Class* introducingClass,
                           string methodName,
                           va_list vaList,
                           void** returnValue );
        void initialize( );
        void destroy( );
}
void SimpleThreadSafe :: initialize( )
{
     __parent->initialize( );
     semaphoreForClass = osCreateSemaphore();
}
void SimpleThreadSafe :: destroy( )
{
     osDestroySemaphore( semaphoreForClass );
     __parent->destroy( );
}
long SimpleThreadSafe :: beforeMethod( Object*  target,
                                       Class* introducingClass,
                                       string methodName,
                                       va_list vaList )

{
     osAcquireSemaphore( semaphoreForClass );
     return 0;
}
```

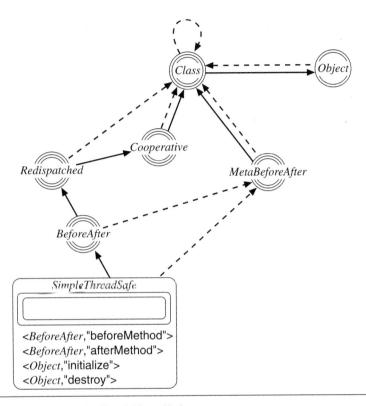

Figure 8-9. Design concept for *SimpleThreadSafe*.

```
void SimpleThreadSafe :: afterMethod( Object*  target,
                                      Class* introducingClass,
                                      string methodName,
                                      va_list vaList,
                                      void** returnValue )
{
     osReleaseSemaphore( semaphoreForClass );
}
```

This metaclass is called "simple," because there is only one semaphore for each class that is made thread safe. This means that if any method of an instance of *SimpleThreadSafe* is executing, all methods on any other instance are blocked. Clearly, this is not a desirable property; we have left the problem of improving this metaclass as an exercise (see Exercise 8.2).

8.5   Summary

As mentioned earlier, CLOS incorporates the notion of before/after methods, but our experience indicates that the more useful granularity for a class-based object model is the class. Foote and Johnson [41] advocate class-level granularity. So does Pascoe [106] (but his encapsulators apply to all method invocations on a class instance rather than a class). This is also the granularity used by the Demeter system [81] (which does the implementation by source code transformation).

Software engineering of classes has many examples of uses of before/after methods. Method tracing is a primary example of a useful software engineering tool that fits naturally into the before/after paradigm at the class granularity [77]. Another example is invariant checking; one can imagine a metaclass that checks the invariant supplied by the class programmer as a method on the class. In addition to its reusability, such a metaclass would have the advantage of ensuring that the invariant is checked when new methods are added to the class. Other types of verification and monitoring are also feasible (for example, path expressions [21] and behavioral expressions [4]).

Concurrency yields other opportunities to use Before/After Metaclasses. For example, one can factor thread safety into a metaclass; the before method acquires a semaphore and the after method releases the same semaphore. In addition, we have found that Before/After Metaclasses provide a convenient way to offer framework capabilities to customers. The IBM SOMobjects Toolkit 2.1 contains a framework for creating replicated objects [62]; this framework has a set of coding rules for conveying the replicated property to a class. Basically, the rules require the locking of a set of replicas prior to an update, followed by the propagation and unlocking after the update (the objective is to ensure one-copy serializability). The majority of the work required by this set of rules can be done by a Before/After Metaclass. We have used *BeforeAfter* to construct metaclasses for both tracing and replication. Transaction processing is another candidate application [95]. Elsewhere, a detailed example of how to use a metaclass in CLOS to make a class persistent is given in [103].

The Before/After Metaclass has been available inside IBM since August 1993; for example, the traced metaclass is used in parts of the SOMobjects Toolkit (version 2.0). The facility became generally available as part of SOMobjects Toolkit (version 2.1) in November 1994, where it aids in the use of a framework for creating replicated objects.

8.6 Exercises

8.1   The algorithm for compileBA uses a global variable; this implies a problem when multiple
        threads create Before/After Metaclasses. Assume your operating system offers the follow-
        ing operations:

> osCreateSemaphore
> osAcquireSemaphore
> osReleaseSemaphore
> osDestroySemaphore

Modify the algorithm for compileBA so that it is thread safe.

8.2   Now that you have had some practice with semaphores, create a Before/After Metaclass
        for the thread-safe property such that there is one semaphore per ordinary object. (Hint:
        review Section 6.12 for the technique of adding instance variables to ordinary objects
        from a metaclass.)

8.3   <*MetaBeforeAfter*,"readyClass"> makes two passes on the metaclass hierarchy by calling
        compileBA twice. Rewrite *MetaBeforeAfter* so that only one pass is made.

8.4   A Before/After Metaclass must provide an override for both beforeMethod and
        afterMethod. Relax this condition and rewrite *BeforeAfter*, *MetaBeforeAfter*, or both so
        that *BeforeAfter*'s implementations beforeMethod and afterMethod are not invoked.

8.5   In addition to the fact that it uses global memory, there is another reason why *BeforeAfter*
        is not suitable for use in a multithreaded environment. Explain why. Assume that the oper-
        ating system has a primitive:

> long osThreadId();

that returns the identifier of the current thread. Reprogram *BeforeAfter* so that it can be
used by multiple threads.

Chapter 9
Proxies

9.1 The Purpose of Proxies

As the name implies, a **proxy** object is one that can substitute for another object, as illustrated in Figure 9-1. If object *iX* has a proxy *proxyForIX*, then the proxy contains an instance variable that holds the object reference for *iX*, which is called the **target** object. Any method that is invoked on the proxy is forwarded to *iX*. This enables application programs to use *iX* without having the object reference for *iX*.

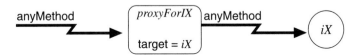

Figure 9-1. Proxy objects forward method invocations.

The main purpose of a proxy is to hide the object reference. A fundamental premise of all object-oriented programming systems is that to use an object, one must have the object reference for the object. With a proxy, even the object reference is hidden. This can be very useful. For example, if object references are implemented with the computer address of the object, then the object is not movable. However, if a class gives out only references to proxies, the object can be moved (concurrently with a change of the object reference in the proxy). Another example is remote method invocation, in which the object resides in another computer; this example is discussed in greater detail in Section 9.4. In addition, there is an excellent presentation of proxies in [47].

9.2 Design of a Proxy Metaclass

Creating a proxy is not quite the same as embodying a property in a metaclass. Consequently, an effective design requires a helper class — that is, a base class from which all
proxy classes are derived.

Figure 9-2 depicts the design concept, which is based on the following decisions.

- Method forwarding is accomplished by using redispatch stubs. Thus, the metaclass for
  proxies, which is named *ProxyFor*, must be a subclass of *Redispatched*.

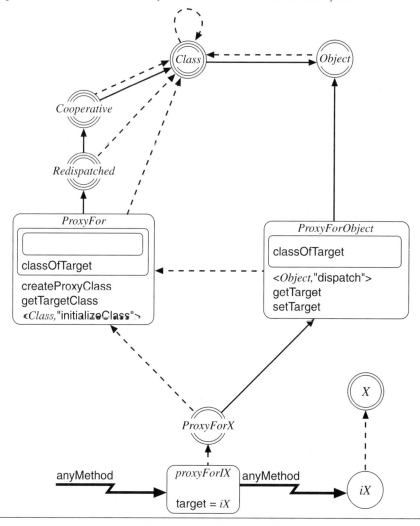

Figure 9-2. Design concept for *ProxyFor* and *ProxyForObject*.

- Because redispatch stubs are being used, dispatch must be overridden; this is done in the ordinary class, named *ProxyForObject*. A descendant of *ProxyForObject* is called a **base proxy class.**

- The metaclass *ProxyFor* contains the primary part of the interface, the method createProxyClass, which dynamically creates a **proxy class.** As a class method, createProxyClass is invoked on descendants of *ProxyForObject* (that is, on the class objects themselves). The basic idea is that descendants of *ProxyForObject* are the base classes from which one invokes createProxyClass to create a proxy class.

- A **proxy** is created by instantiating a proxy class.

These design decisions lead from Figure 9-1 to Figure 9-2, which illustrates our design concept. *ProxyForObject* is the only base proxy class; *ProxyForX* is the proxy class; and *proxyForIX* is the proxy. The difference between a base proxy class and a proxy class is as follows. A base proxy class is a subclass of *ProxyForObject* that does not have a target class. A proxy class is created only with createProxyClass and always has a target class.

Notice that class *X* is not a parent of *ProxyForX*; instead, *ProxyForX* merely supports the interface of *X*. Because the introducing class is a parameter of addMethod, a class may implement the interface of another class. That is, in all the previous uses of addMethod, the introducing class parameter has been the same as the target of the method call. Now we have a use of addMethod in which they are different. This capability is used in the implementation of createProxyClass to construct a proxy class that has the same interface as the target class.

The class declarations for *ProxyFor* and *ProxyForObject* are as follows.

```
class ProxyFor : public virtual Redispatched{
    private:
        Class* classOfTarget;
    public:
        cooperative Class* createProxyClass( Class* targetClass );
        cooperative Class* getTargetClass( );
        boolean initializeClass( ObjectList aParentList, DataSegment nameValuePairs );
}

class ProxyForObjoot : public virtual Object : ProxyFor {
    private:
        Object* target = NULL;
    public:
        cooperative Object* getTarget( );
        cooperative void setTarget( Object* targetObject );
        void dispatch(   string methodName,
                         va_list aParameterList,
                         void** result );
}
```

Presented below are the method specifications for the classes. Let us start with an explanation of the methods of *ProxyFor*. The implementation of createProxyClass uses the class construction protocol to create a proxy class. The interesting feature shown below is the use of addMethod to give the proxy class the interface of the target class. Note that the NULL code pointer is used in the implementation for these methods. This succeeds because these new method table entries are replaced with redispatch stubs and the override of dispatch (in *ProxyForObject*) forwards the invocation to the target object.

```
Class* ProxyFor .. createProxyClass( Class* targetClass )
{/* Specification */
Action:
    Class* metaclassForProxy ;
    metaclassForProxy = solveMetaclassConstraints( <getClass(this)>, <> );
    Class* proxyClass = metaclassForProxy->makeInstance();
    proxyClass->initializeClass( <this>, {} );
    //
    // Below, the interface of the target class is added to the proxy.
    MethodList methods = targetClass->getSupportedMethods();
    Method* mp;
    for ( mp= methods; mp != NULL; mp++ ) {
        if ( !this->supportsMethod( mp->introducingClass, mp->methodName ) )
            proxyClass->addMethod( mp->introducingClass, mp->methodName, NULL );
    }
    proxyClass->readyClass( );
    proxyClass->setIV( ProxyFor, "classOfTarget", targetClass );
    return proxyClass;
}
```

A proxy class should be able to divulge its target class (although it is not used in this book).

```
Class* ProxyFor :: getTargetClass( )
{/* Specification */
Action:
    return classOfTarget;
}
```

Let us move on to the methods of *ProxyForObject*, the most important of which is the override of dispatch. Recall from the design of *Redispatched* that its implementation of readyClass replaces all method table entries with redispatch stubs (except for dispatch). However, not all methods should be forwarded to the proxy object. There are several cases to consider.

- Certainly, the methods introduced by *ProxyForObject* should not be forwarded, because in general they are not supported by the target class. Such methods are, however, supported by the target class if it happens to be a proxy. But in this subcase, setTarget must be used on the proxy if it is to have a target in the first place.

- In the case of the methods introduced by *Object*, initialize, dispatch, and destroy are protected methods that are invoked in special ways, and consequently these methods should not be forwarded. getIV and setIV calls are forwarded only if the instance variable is not supported by the base proxy class. This leaves free, which requires a special implementation that is supplied by *ProxyForObject*.

- The last case is that of an unknown ancestor of the base proxy class (which can occur by subclassing *ProxyForObject*). In this case, the decision not to forward implies that the programmer of the base proxy class can exempt the methods of a class *Y* from being forwarded by simply subclassing *ProxyForObject* and using *Y* as a parent. In addition to being a convenient programming practice, this is also the most sensible rule for resolving the ambiguity when both the target class and the proxy class support the method being invoked on the proxy.

Therefore, the rule is that methods supported by the base proxy class are not forwarded. Equivalently, dispatch can determine whether or not the proxy class is a descendant of the introducing class and thus determine if the method is to be forwarded. This decision leads to one of two possible actions.

1. When methods are not forwarded, a combination of resolveTerminal (against the proxy class) and apply is used. Although the method table has redispatch stubs, this works because resolveTerminal returns the original method table entry by virtue of the fact that *Redispatched* is a descendant of *Cooperative*.

2. The alternative action of the dispatch override is to forward the method invocation to the target, which is accomplished by a combination of resolveMethod (against the class of the target object) and apply.

```
void ProxyForObject :: dispatch( Class* introducingClass,
                                 string methodName,
                                 va_list aParameterList,
                                 void** result )
{/* Specification */
Precondition.
    target != NULL
Action:
    CodePtr aCodePtr;
    if ( getClass(this)->isDescendantOf(introducingClass) ) {
        // The method is introduced by the base proxy class or one of its ancestors, and
        // consequently the method is not forwarded, that is, the method is invoked
        // on the proxy object itself.
        aCodePtr = getClass(this)->resolveTerminal(introducingClass,methodName);
        apply( this, aCodePtr, aParameterList, result );
```

```
    } else {
        // The method is introduced by the target class or one of its ancestors that is not
        // common to the ancestors of the base proxy class, and consequently the method
        // is forwarded to the target.
        aCodePtr = getClass(target)->resolveMethod(introducingClass,methodName);
        apply( target, aCodePtr, aParameterList, result );
    }
}
```

The override on initializeClass in *ProxyFor* has the purpose of requesting the first cooperative method call for free, getIV, and setIV. Each of these three methods is declared cooperative in the declaration of *Object*, but the implementations of each of these three overrides are not cooperative. Therefore, a normal override in *ProxyForObject* is not possible because a cooperative override is constrained to make a parent method call on every path. The solution to this dilemma is for the metaclass to request the first method call. When doing so, the metaclass does not have to be cooperative. In the override of initializeClass below, all three requests are made before the satisfyRequests command is issued. By inheritance of metaclass constraints, all descendants of *ProxyForObject* are also initialized with the override below.

```
boolean ProxyFor :: initializeClass( ObjectList aParentList,
                                      DataSegment nameValuePairs)
{/* Specification */
Action:
    if ( __parent->initializeClass( aParentList, nameValuePairs )
        && this->requestFirstCooperativeMethodCall( Object,
                                                    "free",
                                                    ProxyForObject__free )
        && this->requestFirstCooperativeMethodCall( Object,
                                                    "getIV",
                                                    ProxyForObject__getIV )
        && this->requestFirstCooperativeMethodCall( Object,
                                                    "setIV",
                                                    ProxyForObject__setIV ) ) {

        this->satisfyRequests();
        return TRUE;
        }
    else
        return FALSE;
}
```

As mentioned above, free has a special specification: it frees both the proxy and the target. Notice that it uses the same combination of resolveMethod and apply that dispatch uses to forward the call to the target. The call to apply (which attempts to free the target) can return FALSE, causing an immediate return without calling any of the other implementations in the cooperation chain (which is not a cooperative behavior).

```
boolean ProxyForObject__free( Object* proxyThis )
{/* Specification */
Action:
    boolean returnValue = TRUE;
    Object* target = proxyThis->getTarget();
    if ( target != NULL ) {
        CodePtr aCodePtr = getClass(target)->resolveMethod( Object, "free" );
        apply( target, aCodePtr, <>, &returnValue );
        if ( !returnValue )
            return FALSE;
    }
    proxyThis->setTarget( NULL );
    // Below, the cooperation chain is executed,
    // which is equivalent to a parent method call.
    CodePtr theNextFree
                = getClass(proxyThis)->getNextCooperative( Object,
                                                           "free",
                                                           ProxyForObject__free );
    return (*theNextFree)( proxyThis );
}
```

In addition, a call to deleteInstance on the class object only frees the proxy. This is perfect, because if one asks the class to do a delete, it is reasonable that the class should free only the proxy (which the class created).

The implementations for the overrides of getIV and setIV that begin the cooperation chain are presented below. On one path (the else path), no parent method call is made. But the case represented by this path has no meaning for a parent method call — that is, if the class of the object does not support the instance variable, then getIV and setIV for the instance variable must not be called. In spirit, these methods are cooperative. However, the cooperative declaration for DTS C++ is a structural test that these implementations do not pass. Therefore, these implementations cannot be simple overrides.

```
void* ProxyForObject__getIV( Object* proxyThis, Class* aClass, string ivName )
{/* Specification */
```

Precondition:

      <introducingClass,ivName> $\in$ *supportedIVs*(*class*(proxyThis))

      or <introducingClass,ivName> $\in$ *supportedIVs*(*class*(proxyThis->getTarget()))

Action:

```
    if ( getClass(proxyThis)->supportsIV(aClass,ivName) ) {
        // Below, the cooperation chain is executed,
        // which is equivalent to a parent method call
        CodePtr theNextGetIV
            = getClass(proxyThis)->getNextCooperative( Object,
                                                       "getIV",
                                                       ProxyForObject__getIV );
        return (*theNextGetIV)( proxyThis, aClass, ivName );
    }
    else {
        Object* target = proxyThis->getTarget();
        return target->getIV( aClass, ivName );
    }
}
void ProxyForObject__setIV( Object* proxyThis,
                            Class* aClass,
                            string ivName,
                            void* value )
{/* Specification */
```

Precondition:

      <IntroducingClass,ivName> $\in$ *supportedIVs*(*class*(proxyThis))

      or <introducingClass,ivName> $\in$ *supportedIVs*(*class*(proxyThis->getTarget()))

Action:

```
    if ( getClass(this)->supportsIV(aClass,ivName) ) {
        // Below, the cooperation chain is executed,
        // which is equivalent to a parent method call.
        CodePtr theNextSetIV = getNextCooperative( Object,
                                                   "setIV",
                                                   ProxyForObject__setIV );
        (*theNextSetIV)( proxyThis, aClass, ivName, value );
    }
    else {
        Object* target = proxyThis->getTarget();
        target->setIV( aClass, ivName, value );
    }
}
```

The methods getTarget and setTarget have simple specifications. Note that the precondition of setTarget requires that the class of the target be the same as the target class used to create the proxy class.

Object* ProxyForObject :: **getTarget**( )
{/* Specification */
Action:
    return target;
}

void ProxyForObject :: **setTarget**(Object* targetObject)
{/* Specification */
Precondition:
    targetObject.class = this.class.*ProxyFor.*classOfTarget
Action:
    target = targetObject;
}

This completes the description of the design of the proxy metaclass and its helper. Before we discuss deeper issues, we present a short example that shows how this system is to be used.

Example.
    Let *iX* be an instance of class *X*, which supports foo. In addition to invoking foo with
        iX->foo();
it can also be invoked by the sequence
        Class* proxyClass = ProxyForObject->createProxyClass(*X*);
        X* proxy = (X*)proxyClass->makeInstance();
        ((ProxyForObject*)proxy)->setTarget(*iX*);
        proxy->foo();
The first command creates the proxy class; the second creates the proxy itself; the third tells the proxy what object it is a proxy for; and the final command invokes the method on the proxy, which is forwarded to the target object. In DTS C++, the type of the variable proxy is X*, because there is no statically declared class for the proxy class. Because of this type declaration, the cast must be used in the third statement. As the fourth command indicates, code that uses the object is written the same regardless of whether the variable contains a reference to the object or a reference to a proxy.

                                                               □

9.3 Properties of Proxies

9.3.1 Subclasses of *ProxyForObject*

The base proxy class *ProxyForObject* can be subclassed to create a proxy class with special properties. This is the reason for our choice of names. *ProxyFor* may seem to be an odd name for a metaclass, but it is the most distinctive linguistic way to continue placing metaclass names (which generally are adjectives) in front of class names and still distinguish the properties of the proxy from those of the target.

Example.

The declaration

```
class TracedProxyForObject : public virtual ProxyForObject : Traced {
}
```

creates the structure shown in Figure 9-3, where a special proxy class that traces method invocations on the proxy is created.

☐

Now, when using proxy classes, one must remember a very important point:

A proxy class does not inherit the metaclass constraints of its target class.

This is implied by the fact that createProxyClass uses only the methods supported by the target class to create the proxy class. This means that properties that are imparted by metaclasses to the target class are not present in the proxy.

Example.

Continuing the previous example, consider the following fragment.

```
class X; // an arbitrary class
class ThreadSafeX : public virtual X : SimpleThreadSafe {
}
...
    ThreadSafeX* iX = ThreadSafeX->makeInstance();
    ProxyFor* proxyClass;
    proxyClass = TracedProxyForObject->createProxyClass(ThreadSafeX);
    X* proxy = (X*)proxyClass->makeInstance();
    ((ProxyForObject*)proxy)->setTarget( iX );
```

The result of executing this fragment is depicted in Figure 9-4. The proxy object is not thread safe but is traced. This is exactly the behavior we want. If the proxy were implicitly thread safe (because the target class is), the semaphore would be allocated twice. The behavior of *TracedProxyForThreadSafeX* is exactly what its name implies.

☐

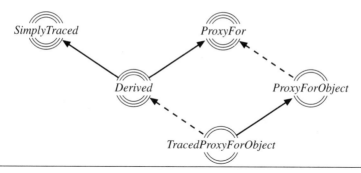

Figure 9-3. A proxy class that traces.

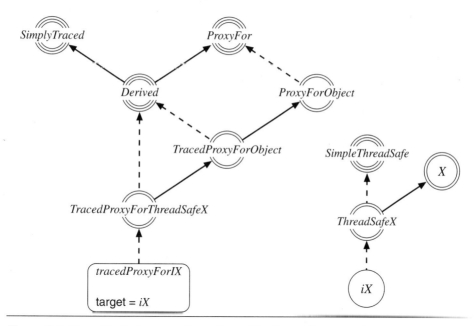

Figure 9-4. Example of why proxy classes do not inherit metaclass constraints.

Implicit in the example above is the fact that base proxy classes compose with Before/After Metaclasses. A base proxy class redefines dispatch, whereas *BeforeAfter* requests the first cooperative method for dispatch. When a Before/After Metaclass is used with a base proxy class, the redispatch stub invokes the before/after dispatcher, which invokes the before/after method for the proxy object. In the middle of its execution, the before/after dispatcher invokes the cooperation chain, during which the method invocation is forwarded to the target object.

9.3.2 Proxies for Class Objects

A proxy can also be created for a class object.

Example.

Figure 9-5 is constructed by the following fragment.

```
class X; // an arbitrary class that is an instance of Class
...
ProxyFor* proxyClass;
proxyClass = ProxyForObject->createProxyClass(Class);
Class* proxy = (Class*)proxyClass->makeInstance();
((ProxyForObject*)proxy)->setTarget( X );
X* iX = (X*)proxy->makeInstance();
```

The call to createProxyClass above creates a proxy class for creating proxies for class objects. Using *ProxyForObject* as the base proxy class is a natural decision that is based on Postulate 3 (every class is an object). The succeeding line makes such a proxy, which is targeted to the class *X*. In the last command, the call to makeInstance is forwarded to the class object, which creates an instance of class *X* and returns the object reference.

□

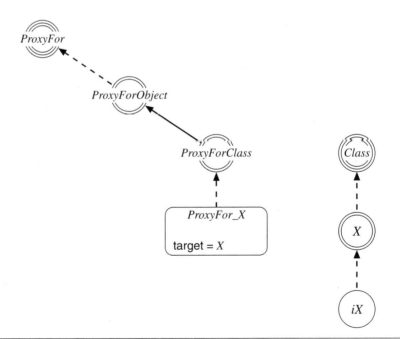

Figure 9-5. Example of a proxy for a class object.

9.3.3   Proxies for Proxies

A proxy object may also be a proxy for another proxy object. In this case, method invocations are passed from one proxy to another until the target is reached.

Example.

In the fragment below, a proxy object is created for a proxy object. Figure 9-6 depicts the objects that are created.

```
class X; // an arbitrary class
...
X* iX = X->makeInstance();
ProxyFor* proxyClass;
proxyClass = ProxyForObject->createProxyClass(X);
X* proxy = (X*)proxyClass->makeInstance();
((ProxyForObject*)proxy)->setTarget( iX );
ProxyFor* proxyClassOfProxyClass;
proxyClassOfProxyClass = ProxyForObject->createProxyClass(proxyClass);
X* proxyOfTheProxy = (X*)proxyClassOfProxyClass->makeInstance();
((ProxyForObject*)proxyOfTheProxy)->setTarget( proxy );
```

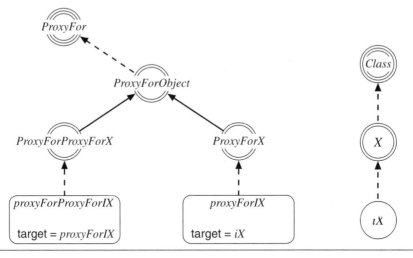

Figure 9-6. A proxy object may have a proxy.

9.4   Distributed Systems

An important function of proxies is to provide a natural interface for remote method invocation. **Remote method invocation** is the capability of invoking a method on an object that resides in another address space, usually in another computer. Figure 9-7 illustrates this concept: a process on one computer, called the **client,** invokes a method on an object in another computer, called the **server.** All of the details of an implementation of remote method invocation are well beyond the scope of this book. This section shows the feasibility of using the proxy metaclass to hide the details of remote method invocation.

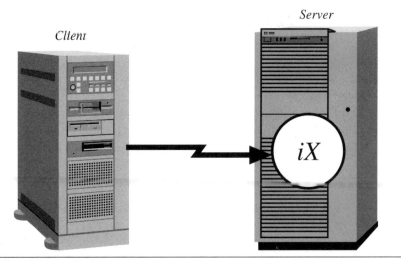

Figure 9-7. Remote method invocation.

A proxy hides the object reference. To this point, we have assumed that the target instance variable in a proxy contains the object reference being hidden,[1] but this is not necessarily so. The target instance variable may contain other information that is required in order for dispatch to transform the method invocation to one on a remote computer. The Object Management Group specifies an architecture, **CORBA** [99], on which we can build remote method invocation by means of proxies. This is done through a facility called the **ORB,** or Object Request Broker (Figure 9-8). The ORB must provide the following services: marshaling the actual parameters of the invocation, forwarding the invocation to the appropriate process, invoking the method at the server process, and finally returning any computed values. Figure 9-8 shows that the job of the proxy is to transform the method invocation, using the ORB facilities, into a remote method invocation.

---

1. We have also assumed that an object reference is an address in the local address space.

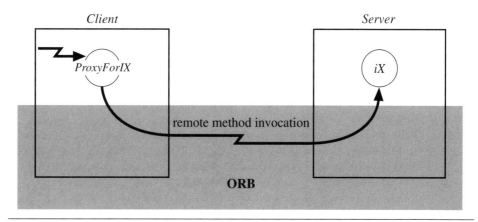

Figure 9-8. The job of the Object Request Broker.

In the remainder of this section, we concentrate on the problem of creating a proxy on the client with an appropriate interface.

As we have said, actually producing an ORB implementation is beyond the scope of this book. Such an implementation must solve many problems. Figure 9-9 shows that the basic concept for interfacing with an ORB can be based on subclasses of *ProxyForRemoteObject*. An implementation of this concept must overcome several problems, among which are a few whose solutions are greatly simplified by having a metaobject protocol. A list of problems that must be solved when implementing an ORB, which are relevant to this book, are as follows.

- setTarget takes an object reference. One could create a new class called, for example, *RemoteObjectReference*. Instances of such a class could be passed to setTarget, and the information contained in such instances could be used by dispatch to forward the invocation properly to the server.

- The class parameter of createProxyClass is an object reference, but the class object resides on another computer, the server. A different interface is required to create the proxy class. The client must ask the server for the interface of the target class (the class parameter of createProxyClass is used only to iterate over the supported methods). To ask the server for the interface implies that classes must be named, but in our object model classes are not named (in the sense that there is no instance variable in *Class* that contains the name of the class).[2]

---

2.   An interesting variation is to name the interface instead of the class. In Microsoft's COM, the interface for all classes has a universally unique identifier, with which the client can query the server for the information needed to construct the proxy class.

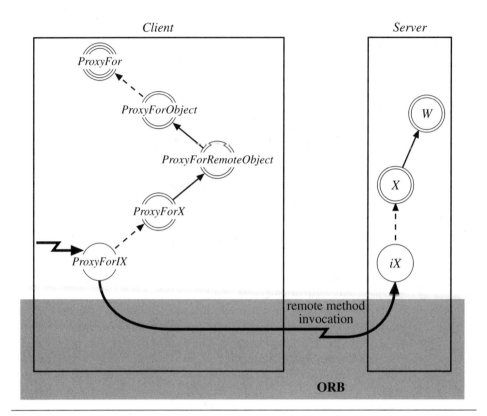

Figure 9-9. A design concept for proxies for remote objects.

- Methods are identified by the pair: introducing class and method name. The introducing class is a class reference. One must make these class references meaningful on the client computer. One approach is to create duplicate class objects on the client. This implies that the implementation of the target class and all of its ancestors must be duplicated on the client. This can be optimized by the recognition that one can place an abstract class on the client (which is a class object with a null code pointer in its method table). By doing so, the implementation of the target class is not required on the client side.

- The override of dispatch in *ProxyForRemoteObject* must perform the following functions.

    1. Marshall the actual parameters.
    2. By using ORB services, send the invocation to the server.
    3. Bring back the values returned by the remote invocation.
    4. If the returned value is a remote object reference, convert it to a proxy.

If a method returns a class reference, the last step yields a proxy for a class. Although proxies for classes can be created, most of the methods of our metaobject protocol take parameters that are meaningful only on the client (for example, code pointers and other class references).

This is a daunting set of problems to solve in addition to the usual set of reliability, robustness, and performance problems that are inherent in distributed systems design. It takes much skill and hard work to build a usable implementation of Common Object Request Broker Architecture (CORBA) with the proxy support we have described. However, it can be done, as attested to by the Distributed SOM framework for the IBM SOMobjects Toolkit.

9.5 Extent Managed Proxies

In this section, we present a nice bit of reusability. In Section 6.9, we introduced *ExtentManaged*, a metaclass for keeping track of the instances of a class. This metaclass can be combined with *ProxyFor* to create a facility for changing the targets of existing proxies. Figure 9-10 shows that one new class method is added.

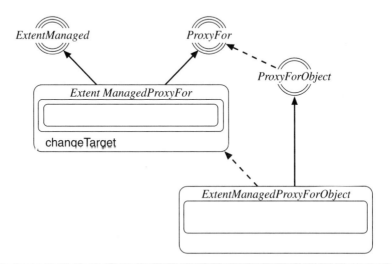

Figure 9-10. The design concept for *ExtentManagedProxyForObject*.

The class declarations are as follows.

```
class ExtentManagedProxyFor : public virtual ExtentManaged, public virtual ProxyFor {
    public:
        void changeTarget( Object* oldTarget, Object* newTarget );
}
class ExtentManagedProxyForObject : public virtual ProxyForObject
                                          : ExtentManagedProxyFor /*metaclass*/{
}
```

The new class method iterates through the extent of the proxy class to change the target of any proxy whose target is oldTarget.

```
void ExtentManagedProxyFor :: changeTarget( Object* oldTarget, Object* newTarget )
{/* Specification */
Precondition:
    newTarget.class isDescendantOf oldTarget.class
Action:
    ObjectList extent = getExtent( ); // This is a list of proxy objects.
    for ( int i = 0; i < #length; i++ ) {
        ProxyForObject* aProxy = extent[i];
        if ( aProxy->getTarget() == oldTarget )
            aProxy->setTarget( newTarget );
    }
}
```

Retargeting proxies can be a useful technique in system evolution.

9.6 Summary

To construct a proxy class, one needs the interface of the target class (that is, the set of methods supported by the target class). A proxy for an object provides a useful abstraction of the object reference. It is a testimonial to the efficacy of our metaobject protocol that such a fundamental notion as object reference can be abstracted.

9.7 Exercises

9.1   Write a Boolean function named isProxy that determines whether or not an object refer-
        ence is to a proxy.

9.2   In the code fragment below, is the proxy or the target returned by function test?

```
class X : public virtual Object {
        Object* returnThis() { return this; }
}
class XProxy : public virtual X, public virtual ProxyForObject {
}
Object* test() {
        X* iX = X->makeInstance();
        ProxyFor* proxyClass;
        proxyClass = XProxy->createProxyClass(X);
        ProxyForObject* proxy;
        proxy = proxyClass->makeInstance();
        proxy->setTarget( iX );
        return proxy->returnThis();
}
```

9.3   Analyze the following code fragment, which is similar to the one used to produce Figure
        9-6. Can one successfully create a proxy for a proxy in this manner?

```
class X; // an arbitrary class
...
        X* iX = X->makeInstance();
        ProxyFor* proxyClass;
        proxyClass = ProxyForObject->createProxyClass(X);
        ProxyForObject* proxy;
        proxy = proxyClass->makeInstance();
        proxy->setTarget( iX );
        ProxyForObject* proxyOfTheProxy;
        proxyOfTheProxy = proxyClass->makeInstance();
        proxyOfTheProxy->setTarget( proxy );
```

Chapter 10
Metaclasses for Frameworks

This chapter introduces several metaclasses that are useful for engineering of class frameworks. When a class framework is engineered, there are class properties that one wishes to enforce, but object-oriented programming languages do not support the granularity of enforcement that is really needed. All of the metaclasses introduced in this chapter are variants of the idea that some property of a class or set of classes must be enforced. In all cases, if the property does not hold when checked, execution terminates. Our objective is to demonstrate that it is possible to make these checks.

10.1 Invariant Checking

A **class invariant** is a condition that must always be true of the data in an object when no method is executing. This implies that the invariant must be true before any method is executed and that all method executions must ensure that the invariant is true on termination. This is an ideal application of the Before/After Metaclass. Figure 10-1 shows the design concept for a metaclass that checks invariants. This design concept uses a helper class, because we wish to introduce an instance method, named computeInvariant, that returns a Boolean value indicating whether or not the invariant is true.

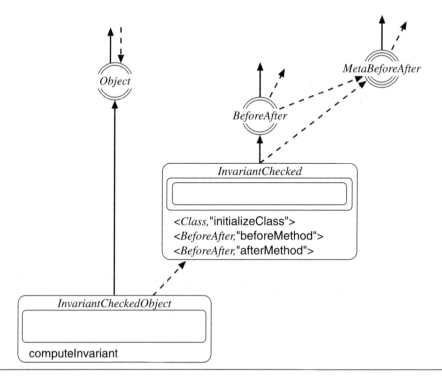

Figure 10-1. Design concept for the *InvariantChecked* metaclass.

The implementation of the metaclass and its helper are presented below. The implementation assumes that if the invariant is not true, execution should be terminated immediately. To do so, we assume that the operating system provides a primitive named osAbort, which is used in beforeMethod and afterMethod.

```
class InvariantChecked : public virtual BeforeAfter {
    boolean initializeClass( ObjectList aParentList, DataSegment aDataSegment );
    long beforeMethod(  Object*  target,
                        Class* introducingClass,
                        string methodName,
                        ObjectList vaList );
    void afterMethod(  Object*  target,
                        Class* introducingClass,
                        string methodName,
                        ObjectList vaList,
                        void** returnValue );
}
```

```
class InvariantCheckedObject : public virtual Object {
    cooperative boolean computeInvariant ( );
}
```

```
boolean InvariantCheckedObject :: computeInvariant( ) {
    return TRUE;
}
```

The metaclass InvariantChecked is meant to be used only with the helper class InvariantCheckedObject, which is enforced by a special check. The class initialization below ensures that instances have the proper interface — that is, respond to the method computeInvariant. This is done by ensuring that each instance of InvariantChecked is a descendant of InvariantCheckedObject. In our metaobject protocol, this is an easier check than asking if the class supports the method computeInvariant, because initializeClass is called on InvariantCheckedObject itself before the method computeInvariant has been added.

```
boolean InvariantChecked :: initializeClass( ObjectList aParentList,
                                            DataSegment aDataSogment ) {
{ /* Specification */
Action:
    if ( __parent->initializeClass( aParentList, aDataSegment ) ) {
        return this->isDescendantOf( InvariantCheckedObject );
    }
    else
        return FALSE;
}
```

The invariant is both a precondition and a postcondition for method execution. An excellent discussion of this topic can be found in [61]. If the before method for *InvariantChecked* finds the invariant false, this indicates that encapsulation of the object has been broken. If the after method for *InvariantChecked* finds the invariant false, this indicates that the method has not been properly implemented.

```
long InvariantChecked :: beforeMethod( Object* target,
                                       Class* introducingClass,
                                       string methodName,
                                       ObjectList vaList )
{
    if ( !((InvariantCheckedObject*)target)->computeInvariant( ) ) {
        // Encapsulation is violated.
        osAbort();
    }
    return 0;
}
```

```
void InvariantChecked :: afterMethod( Object*  target,
                                      Class* introducingClass,
                                      string methodName,
                                      ObjectList vaList,
                                      void** returnValue )
{
    if ( !((InvariantCheckedObject*)target)->computeInvariant( ) ) {
        // Class implementation does not maintain the invariant.
        osAbort();
    }
}
```

Below is a very simple example of the use of the invariant checking metaclass.

Example.
```
class Point {
protected:
    double x;
    double y;
}
class PointOnUnitCircle : public virtual Point, public virtual InvariantCheckedObject
{
    boolean computeInvariant();
}
boolean PointOnUnitCircle :: computeInvariant() {
    return __parent->computeInvariant() && ( (x*x+y*y) == 1 );
}
```

☐

Invariants should always be written down. An invariant that is written down is almost never violated. But an invariant trusted to a programmer's memory is quickly forgotten and intermittently violated. Having executable invariant checking is useful during testing to ensure that no programmer has made a mistake. With proper system design, one can avoid performance costs in the production version of the system. Consider the following example.

Example.

In the following code fragment, the class X is conditionally compiled so that if the symbol TESTMODE is defined, X is a subclass that is invariant checked.

```
class X // Any class of your application program
#ifdef TESTMODE
        : InvariantCheckedObject
#endif
{
...
#ifdef TESTMODE
   boolean computeInvariant();
#endif
}
#ifdef TESTMODE
boolean X :: computeInvariant() {
   return __parent->computeInvariant() &&
           // Boolean expression for the invariant of X
       ;
}
#endif
...
```

☐

The technique above is useful but a bit cumbersome. In addition, once a program has been distributed to its users, there is no way to turn the invariant checking on to aid in problem diagnosis. This can be done if one dynamically chooses the class for which instances of X are created, as illustrated in the following example.

Example.

In the following code fragment, two classes are created, a "normal" version and an invariant checked version. Some indicator (in this case, isProgramInTestMode) is checked to determine whether or not the system is being run in test mode. This indicator controls which class reference is placed in the variable XClassObject. All instances of X are created by using the class reference in that variable. This means that in test mode, invariant checked instances of X are created, whereas normal instances of X are created when not in test mode.

```
class X; // Any class of your application program
class InvariantCheckedX : public virtual X, public virtual InvariantCheckedObject {
    boolean computeInvariant();
}
boolean InvariantCheckedX :: computeInvariant() {
    return __parent->computeInvariant() &&
            ... // Boolean expression for the invariant of X
            ;
}
...
    Class* XClassObject:
...
    if ( isProgramInTestMode ) { // A condition set dynamically.
        XClassObject = InvariantCheckedX;
    else
        XClassObject = X;
...
    X* anX = XClassObject->makeInstance();
...
```

☐

The example above seems to be a "have one's cake and eat it, too" solution. That is, there is a negligible performance cost for having the capability to turn on invariant checking dynamically. However, there is a programming cost in that the technique above must be used for all classes in the application program. Our metaobject protocol supports dynamic creation of classes, so if all of an application program's classes are derived from a single base, we should be able to impart properties to that base class, which in turn (by inheritance of metaclass constraints) imparts the property to all of the classes in the application program. In trying to do this, we are frustrated by the fact that DTS C++ does not allow us to change the parentage of a class dynamically.[1] For example, one cannot write

```
class BaseClass;
class BaseClassWithProperty : public virtual BaseClass, public virtual Property;
class TopOfApplicationProgram : ( mode ? BaseClass : BaseClassWithProperty );
```

where mode is a variable set dynamically (say, from the command line). Here is evidence that in the future our model will be used with languages more dynamic than DTS C++.

---

1. It is true that with a metaclass the list of parents used in initializeClass can be changed. However, the list of parents used for the call to solveMetaclassConstraints is fixed at compile time. Therefore, statically declared classes cannot have dynamically changing strict ancestors.

10.2 Single-Instanced Property

A **single-instanced class** is one that can have at most one instance. This specification requires the makeInstance method to create an object only if none exists; otherwise, the existent object is returned. In addition, the class must keep a reference count of the number of times makeInstance is called; the instance is destroyed only when deleteInstance is called an equal number of times. This would seem to have the following direct implementation.

```
class BadSingleInstanced : public virtual Cooperative {
    private:
        Object* singleInstance = NULL;
        long referenceCount = 0;
    public:
        Object* makeInstance( );
        void deleteInstance( Object* anObject );
}
```

```
Object* BadSingleInstanced :: makeInstance( )
{ /* Specification */
```
Action:
```
    referenceCount++;
    if ( singleInstance == NULL )
        return __parent->makeInstance();
    else
        return singleInstance;
}
```

```
void BadSingleInstanced :: deleteInstance( Object* anObject )
{ /* Specification */
```
Precondition:
    class (anObject) *isDescendantOf SingleInstanced*
Action:
```
    referenceCount--;
    if ( referenceCount == 0 ) {
        __parent->deleteInstance( anObject );
        singleInstance = NULL );
    }
    return;
}
```

The implementation above is inadequate because the overrides of makeInstance and deleteInstance change the actual parameters of the call (makeInstance controls the return parameter and deleteInstance may or may not invalidate its parameter as an object reference). Recall the discussion in Section 7.5. This means that the overrides must request the first cooperative method to each of makeInstance and deleteInstance. This must be done by the class of *SingleInstanced*, which is another metametaclass. Figure 10-2 shows the design concept for the *SingleInstanced* metaclass.

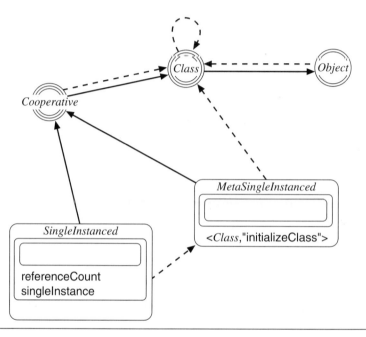

Figure 10-2. The design concept for *SingleInstanced* metaclass.

Following our standard technique for being cooperative (see Figure 7-4), the class declaration must appear as follows.

```
class MetaSingleInstanced : public virtual Cooperative {
    public:
        boolean initializeClass( ObjectList aParentList, DataSegment aDataSegment );
}

class SingleInstanced : public virtual Cooperative : MetaSingleInstanced {
    private:
        Object* singleInstance = NULL;
        long referenceCount = 0;
}
```

The method implementations are given below.

```
boolean MetaSingleInstanced :: initializeClass( ObjectList aParentList,
                                                DataSegment aDataSegment ) {
{ /* Specification */
Action:
    if ( __parent->initializeClass( aParentList, aDataSegment ) &&
        this->requestFirstCooperativeMethodCall(  Class,
                                                  "makeInstance",
                                                  SingleInstanced_makeInstance ) &&
        this->requestFirstCooperativeMethodCall(  Class,
                                                  "deleteInstance",
                                                  SingleInstanced_deleteInstance ) ) {
        this->satisfyRequests();
        return TRUE;
    }
    else
        return FALSE;
}
```

Presented below are the method implementations that cooperate on makeInstance and deleteInstance. Neither is a method of a class, and thus they are declared with the appropriate signatures for procedures that are to be called from method tables. That is, the target object appears in the signature as an explicit formal parameter. In addition, in the specification of the action, the full expressions for instance variable access are used.

```
Object* SingleInstanced_makeInstance( Class* self )
{ /* Specification */
Action:
    self.SingleInstanced.referenceCount++;
    if ( self.SingleInstanced.singleInstance == NULL ) {
        CodePtr nextMakeInstance
            = getClass(self)->getNextCooperative(  Class,
                                                   "makeInstance",
                                                   SingleInstanced_makeInstance );
        self.SingleInstanced.singleInstance = (*nextMakeInstance)( self );
    }
    return self.SingleInstanced.singleInstance;
}
```

```
void SingleInstanced_deleteInstance( Class* self, Object* anObject )
{ /* Specification */
```
Precondition:
      class (self) *isDescendantOf SingleInstanced and class*(anObject) == self
Action:
```
        self.SingleInstanced.referenceCount--;
        if ( self.SingleInstanced.referenceCount == 0 ) {
            CodePtr nextDeleteInstance
                = getClass(self)->getNextCooperative(   Class,
                                                        "deleteInstance",
                                                        SingleInstanced_deleteInstance );
            (*nextDeleteInstance)( self, anObject );
            self.SingleInstanced.singleInstance = NULL;
        }
        return;
}
```

Often one sees a program in which class variables are used as shared storage for the instances of a class. We do not believe that this is a proper use of class variables, because it confuses the function of the class with that of its instances. When shared storage among instances is desired, it is more appropriate to use a single-instanced class for the shared portion of the instances.

10.3 The Abstract Property

An **abstract class** is a class that is not allowed to have instances, because some of its methods do not have implementations (when added to the method table, method implementation is the NULL pointer). Such methods are usually called **abstract methods.** An abstract class is used to specify a class with a parameter that is a method. The parameter is supplied by subclassing the abstract class and overriding the abstract methods.

The design concept for the metaclass *Abstract* is shown in Figure 10-3. The class declaration for *Abstract* is as follows.

```
class Abstract : public virtual Class {
    private:
        boolean isAbstract = FALSE;
    public:
        Object* makeInstance( );
        void readyClass();
}
```

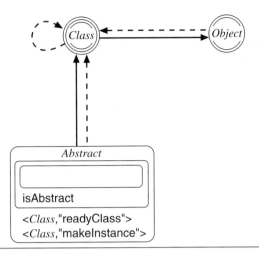

Figure 10-3. The design concept for the *Abstract* metaclass.

The overrides for readyClass and makeInstance are shown below. The override for readyClass checks to see if any method has a NULL implementation pointer. If so, the class variable isAbstract is set to TRUE. The implementation pointer is retrieved with resolveTerminal rather than resolveMethod because resolveTerminal always returns the implementation that would be used for the method without the modification of any metaclass. For example, if *Abstract* were composed with *Redispatched*, resolveMethod would be returning pointers to redispatch stubs for abstract methods.

```
void Abstract :: readyClass()
{ /* Specification */
Action:
    __parent->readyClass();
    MethodList methods = this->getSupportedMethods();
    Method* mp;
    for ( mp= methods; mp != NULL; mp++ )
        if ( this->resolveTerminal(mp->introducingClass,mp->methodName) == NULL )
            isAbstract = TRUE;
    }
}
```

The override of makeInstance merely checks to see if the class is abstract, and if so, terminates execution. Because this terminates execution, a simple override is in order. The behavior of makeInstance is not cooperative, but it does not really matter because the program is terminated. Further, there is a parent method call on all paths, because for convenience osAbort looks like any other procedure call (if this were not the case, a warning message would be issued by our DTS C++ compiler). On the other hand, throwing an exception (if one is using a programming language that implements exceptions) is not the same as terminating the program (with osAbort), because the exception can be caught. In this case, the metametaclass has to be used.

```
Object* Abstract :: makeInstance()
{ /* Specification */
Action:
    if ( isAbstract ) {
        osAbort();
        }
    return __parent->makeInstance();
}
```

This version of the notion of an abstract class is that of the C++ object model, which states

if any method is abstract, the class cannot be instantiated.

But it is not the only one possible. The abstract metaclass developed in [96] enforces the property

the class cannot be instantiated.

This alternative specification can be implemented in our model but is not very useful. Because of inheritance of metaclass constraints, no descendant of an abstract class (enforcing this alternative specification) can be instantiated. The lack of usefulness of the abstract metaclass used in [96] with unconditional prohibition against instantiation is not a great loss when viewed in light of the benefits of inheritance of metaclass constraints.

10.4 The Final Property

Prohibiting a class from having subclasses is another useful property for framework programming. An appropriate adjective for this property is "final." The design concept is given in Figure 10-4, which shows that all we need do is override initializeClass.

The class declaration for *Final* is as follows.

```
class Final : public virtual Class {
    public:
        boolean initializeClass( ObjectList aParentList, DataSegment aDataSegment );
}
```

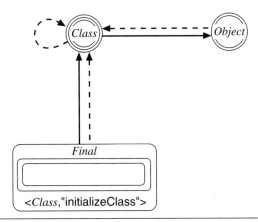

Figure 10-4. The design concept for the *Final* metaclass.

This design is a bit subtle. Because of inheritance of metaclass constraints, any attempt to create a subclass of a final class is an attempt to create a final class. Therefore, in initializeClass, all we need do is check that no parent class is final.

```
boolean Final :: initializeClass( ObjectList aParentList, DataSegment aDataSegment )
{ /* Specification */
Action:
    if ( __parent->initializeClass( aParentList, aDataSegment )) {
        ObjectList X;
        for ( X=this->getParents(); X!=NULL; X++ ) {
            if ( getClass(*X)->isDescendantOf( Final ) )
                osAbort();
        }
        return TRUE;
    }
    else
        return FALSE;
}
```

It is worth repeating that *Final* is easy to program because of inheritance of metaclass constraints. If metaclass declarations are treated as imperatives, a metaclass that embodies the final property cannot influence the construction of descendants of its instances.

10.5 Mixins

A **mixin** is a class that is meant to be combined through multiple inheritance with other classes to impart an implementation of some property to a subclass. Normally, the methods defined by a mixin class (called "mixin" methods) participate in the implementation of some specific property. The mixin methods may be introduced or inherited, and the mixin class provides an implementation of the corresponding property by defining and then participating in the execution of these methods. We are following the general definition of mixin, the likes of which can be found in [12] or [47].

In [15], a mixin class is described as differing from a normal base class in that a mixin class can make parent method calls to methods that its descendants must inherit from elsewhere in the hierarchy (that is, it is not necessary that the method be introduced by an ancestor of the mixin). Such mixins can be created with our metaobject protocol. However, with our linearized inheritance model, there seems to be no reason not to simply declare the class that introduces the mixin method as a parent of the mixin, which allows overrides to be programmed as usual. Also, as we will see below, an interesting category of mixin class enabled by our model defines no methods (a metaclass is used to contribute the property).

Mixins usually are not intended to be instantiated, which makes them similar to abstract classes, but mixins are normally perceived in terms of the methods they define, whereas abstract classes are often most interesting in terms of the methods they do not define. In one typical pattern that combines both kinds of classes, mixins implement methods introduced but left undefined (or with a useless "default" implementation) by an abstract class.

To support the programming of mixins, we introduce the metaclass *Noninstantiable*, which prevents its instance classes from being instantiated. The design concept is shown in Figure 10-5 and the specification is given below.

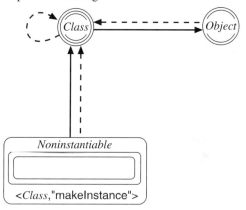

Figure 10-5. The design concept for the *Noninstantiable* metaclass.

```
class Noninstantiable : public virtual Class {
    public:
        Object* makeInstance( );
}


Object* Noninstantiable :: makeInstance()
{ /* Specification */
Action:
    ObjectList X;
    for ( X=this->getMRO(); *X!=Object; X++ ) {
        if ( *X != Class )
            if ( !getClass( *X )->isDescendantOf( Noninstantiable ) )
                return __parent->makeInstance();
    }
    osAbort();
}
```

In the method implementation above, every ancestor of a noninstantiable ordinary class must be an instance of *Noninstantiable* or must be *Object* itself in order for the implementation to stop instantiation. The implication of this design is that the set of noninstantiable ordinary classes is positioned directly below *Object*.

Note that if the class being created (*X in the method implementation) is a metaclass, then *Class*, which is also in *MRO(*X)*, must not be counted as an ancestor that is not *Noninstantiable*. This metaclass is included for use with mixins when it is appropriate. Again, it is not necessary for a mixin to be noninstantiable.

The relationship between noninstantiability and mixins is subtle. Remember that a mixin is a class that captures the implementation of a property, so it can be characterized using an adjective. Consider an adjective such as "blue." Although it may make sense to create the mixin class *BlueObject* by implementing a color attribute with the value "blue," this class may not be intended by its designer to exhibit any other useful behavior. In such cases, the mixin class contains only partial knowledge concerning the desired implementation of a functionally useful object, and use of *Noninstantiable* may be appropriate. However, one can make a counterargument based on software engineering concerns. For example, for software testing it may be useful to create an instance of *BlueObject*. For this reason and to the credit of our metaobject protocol, the instantiability of a mixin is a choice left to the designer of the mixin.

Historically, the concept of a mixin originated with the idea that properties could be isolated with classes and reused by multiple inheritance. Ordinary multiple inheritance is a fairly weak form of combination (because it is a union-like operation on methods and instance variables). This weakness in multiple inheritance caused mixins to have little consequence for reusable software (although there has been some effort to define mixin as an abstraction separate from classes [40]). One solution to this weakness is provided by our multiple inheritance model, which includes inheritance of metaclass constraints. This allows use of our metaobject protocol to program a property mixin.

Such mixins are very useful with respect to creating a library (or libraries) of properties with our metaobject protocol. Figure 10-6 depicts two alternative ways for a metaclass to impart a property to a class (Y in the figure). The first alternative (on the left) shows the metaclass being directly used in the construction of Y. The second alternative (on the right) shows a mixin that has a metaclass constraint (but defines neither methods nor instance variables) being used to impart the property of the metaclass to Y. Because of inheritance of metaclass constraints, the use of the mixin in the definition of Y ensures that the metaclass for Y is a descendant of *AMetaclass*. This illustrates an important implication for class frameworks programmed using our object model and metaobject protocol:

The functionality of a class framework can be exported entirely with classes.

This means that one can create a uniform interface for the framework with exported classes. One does not have to explain to the customer of the framework implementation details such as what is implemented with a class and what is implemented with a metaclass. This aspect of inheritance of metaclass constraints means that the customers of the framework may not even be aware that there are metaclasses in the programming system at all. This valuable consequent of our metaobject protocol has implications for the support of separate compilation, which is explained in Chapter 11.

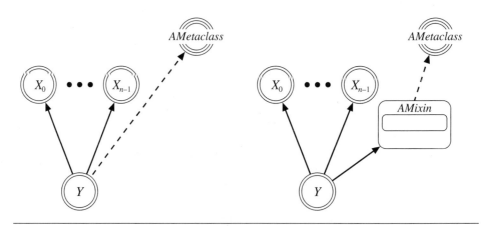

Figure 10-6. Two equivalent ways for Y to obtain the property of *AMetaclass*.

10.6   Preventing Parent Method Calls

In Chapter 8, beforeMethod and afterMethod are specified not to make parent method calls because the dispatcher handles the problem of invoking the proper before methods and after methods. Let us create a metaclass that enforces this part of the specification.

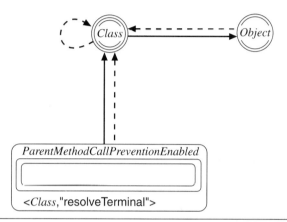

Figure 10-7. Design concept for the *ParentMethodCallPreventionEnabled* metaclass.

Figure 10-7 shows the design concept for this metaclass. The specification is written below and is quite simple. All parent method calls use resolveTerminal. Therefore, we override resolveTerminal with an implementation that checks for the methods that should be prevented from making a parent method call.

```
class ParentMethodCallPreventionEnabled : public virtual Class {
    public:
        CodePtr resolveTerminal( Class* introducingClass, string methodName );
}
```

The override below completes successfully only for methods that are not beforeMethod or afterMethod. We choose to abort if these methods are called, because calling them is a programming error and any test case will uncover the error. (Theoretically, a better solution is to make a check for a parent method call in the implementation of beforeMethod or afterMethod during class construction. However, our object model does not have the metadata to support such a check, and so we do it at runtime.)

```
CodePtr ParentMethodCallPreventionEnabled :: resolveTerminal(
                                        Class* introducingClass,
                                        string methodName )
{ /* Specification */
Action:
    if ( !(introducingClass == BeforeAfter and
        (methodName == "beforeMethod" or methodName == "afterMethod")) ) {
      return __parent->resolveTerminal( introducingClass, methodName )) {
    else {
      osAbort();


}
```

Figure 10-8 is a modification of Figure 8-5, which was the original design concept for the *BeforeAfter* metaclass. Figure 10-8 depicts how *ParentMethodCallPreventionEnabled* can be used to enforce the check on implementation of overrides of beforeMethod and afterMethod. Note that *ParentMethodCallPreventionEnabled* is being used as a metametaclass, although it is not programmed in any special way; such is the generality of our metaobject protocol.

Clearly, *ParentMethodCallPreventionEnabled* is specified to work only with *BeforeAfter*. This is not a very general approach. Exercise 10.7 asks you to specify a generally useful version of *ParentMethodCallPreventionEnabled*.

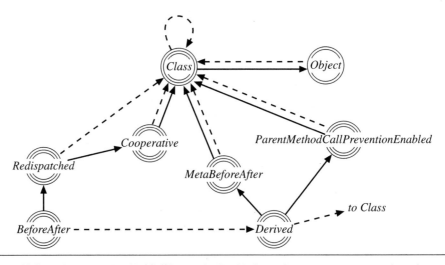

Figure 10-8. Using *ParentMethodCallPreventionEnabled* to enforce proper programming of *BeforeAfter* metaclasses.

10.7 Summary

This chapter has introduced several metaclasses that aid the engineering of class frameworks. Additional ideas for metaclass support for engineering of class frameworks can be found in [92]. These metaclasses are generally easy to write for several reasons.

- The property that each metaclass embodies is a property of a class.

- Starting with our metaobject protocol, we have created a basis sufficient to make such problems easy to program.

- Inheritance of metaclass constraints ensures that properties of classes flow to descendants with no additional effort.

An additional reason is that whenever a check of a property fails, execution is terminated. Termination of execution may not be the best choice in all cases, most notably in fault-tolerant systems. This is where a good exception facility would come to the rescue. Exception facilities are not language neutral; introducing one would not contribute to our goal of showing how to put metaclasses to work.

10.8 Exercises

10.1   Select a class that you have written sometime during your career as a programmer. What is a useful invariant for that class? Are you able to write the invariant in the language in which you wrote the class?

10.2   Suppose Abstract::makeInstance is specified to return NULL if the class is abstract. Does the implementation have to request the first cooperative method? If not, does it compose with SingleInstanced?

10.3   The default implementation for computeInvariant returns TRUE. Redefine InvariantCheckedObject so that it is an abstract class. Show how the metaclass Abstract can be employed in Figure 10-1.

10.4   It is tempting to implement the override of initializeClass in *Final* by simply checking the parent list parameter. Why is this an incorrect implementation?

10.5   The *MixinEnabled* metaclass does not check that the required base implementations exist for the parent method calls made by its instances, because it has no metadata with which to do so. Add an interface to the *MixinEnabled* metaclass to provide this metadata and override initializeClass to make the appropriate check.

10.6   Write a metaclass that allows the programmer of a class to prohibit descendants from overriding particular methods.

10.7   Specify a general version of *ParentMethodCallPreventionEnabled* that allows one to specify at class construction time the methods that are to be prevented from making parent method calls.

Chapter 11
Release-to-Release
Binary Compatibility

The cover of the May 1994 issue of *Byte* Magazine declared: "Object-oriented computing has failed." However, Udel's story inside [114] is not nearly as inflammatory. It describes the situation as we know it: despite all of its promise, software reuse in object-oriented programming has yet to reach its full potential. We recognize that a major impediment to reuse is the inability to evolve a compiled class library without abandoning the support for the already compiled applications. The underlying cause of this problem is that the typical object-oriented model has elements that are not part of the interface model of the linkage editor/loader. Therefore, the implementation of an object-oriented model must be carefully designed so that class-library transformations that should not break already compiled applications do not indeed break such applications. This leads us (at the conclusion of this chapter) to a new criterion for the correctness of separate compilation for all programming systems. The ability to evolve class libraries is essential to our objective of putting metaclasses to work, because programming with metaclasses is not useful if libraries that use metaclasses cannot evolve. As we shall see, inheritance of metaclass constraints is an essential ingredient.

11.1 The Library Compatibility Problem

An **API (application programming interface)** is the interface that a programmer uses, whereas an **ABI (application binary interface)** refers to the specific conventions on which running programs depend. API compatibility ensures that applications can be recompiled successfully; ABI compatibility ensures that compiled applications continue to run successfully.

Let us consider the predicament of a software vendor that is selling a software library; the customers of the library vendor use the library to develop applications. The library vendor gives the customers a description of the API for the library (for example, header files or OMG IDL [99,102]) and the compiled library in the form of a **dynamically linked library (DLL)**. The interface to the (compiled) DLL is the ABI. The advantage of using a DLL (to both the library vendor and the application producer) is that multiple applications can run with one copy of the DLL present, which vastly reduces the memory requirements and improves response time. This chapter focuses on one very important facet of software flexibility; an excellent overview of software flexibility can be found in [6].

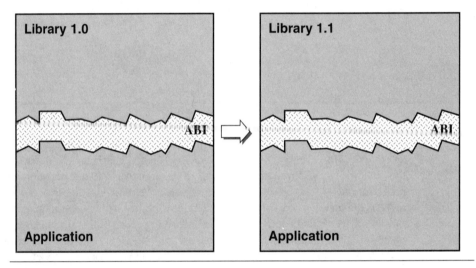

Figure 11-1. A release-to-release binary compatible library revision supports compiled applications.

A problem arises when the library vendor wishes to evolve the library (Figure 11-1). The library vendor must maintain release-to-release binary compatibility, because it is impossible for the application producer to recompile the already distributed copies of the application.

This problem is couched in the terms of a library vendor, an application producer, and dynamically linked libraries, because we wish to emphasize the relevance of our work to this area. In reality, the problem and our solution are much more general. The granularity goes down to the individual programmer who provides libraries for others or even for herself or himself. Whenever a library is changed, one must consider the impact on the applications that are already using the library.

Pragmatically, a revision in a library is release-to-release binary compatible if all the applications that depend on the library still work. Because of a lack of precise specifications for both the library and the application, this is a subjective judgment. For example, one can repair a defect in the library only to find that application programmers consider it a feature.

Let us be a bit more concrete by examining an example of how C++ fails to support release-to-release binary compatibility. Figure 11-2 depicts the situation in which class X (from the class library) is subclassed in the application with class Y. With release 1.0 of the library, the application runs perfectly; in particular, fmethod can be invoked on iY, an instance of class Y. Now let us consider what happens when the library vendor makes the seemingly innocuous change of adding a new method (hmethod) to class X, which is invoked from fmethod. Now, because the application was built with the old library definition, the C++ method table for Y has a code pointer to gmethod in its second entry. However, when fmethod is invoked on iY, it subsequently tries to invoke hmethod, which in class X is the second entry in the method table. The result is that gmethod is called when hmethod was specified.

This situation is both familiar and frustrating to the users of C++. What makes this problem even more insidious is the fact that it appears that the problem is in class X, which is called the base class in C++. Because of this example and others like it, the myth of the "fragile base class problem" has arisen. The poor base class is blamed, diverting our attention from the real problem: the compiler/linker combination does not properly support subclassing across the binary interface.

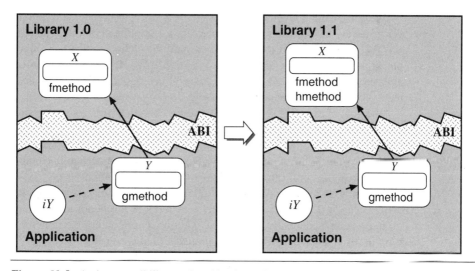

Figure 11-2. An incompatibility produced by the typical C++ compiler.

11.2   Defining Release-to-Release Binary Compatibility

Creating an effective definition of release-to-release binary compatibility is not simple. Consider this direct attack on the problem. Let

A ∞ L mean that application A is combined with library L

and let

SAT(P, S) mean that program P satisfies specification S

where P, A, and L represent compiled modules.

> **Definition 24.** L_1 is an **RRBC-successor** to L_0 if
>
> SAT(A ∞ L_0, S) implies SAT(A ∞ L_1, S)
>
> for all reasonable functional specifications S and for all applications A using library L.

The problems with this definition characterize the difficulties of supporting the evolution of binary class libraries. First, the operator ∞ symbolizes many different implementations (one for each compiler/linker/loader combination). Second, there is no satisfactory definition of "reasonable functional specification." Third, establishing the implication of the definition is tantamount to proving program equivalence, an unsolvable problem. Fourth, even if program equivalence were not unsolvable, defect removal implies that some functions of the new library are not equivalent. Fifth, even if "reasonable functional specification" could be satisfactorily defined, real software products rarely have satisfactory functional specifications. Sixth, for a generally available class library product, one cannot know the set of applications using the library (this simply means that for generally available libraries, a successor must support all possible applications).

In light of the abovementioned difficulties, the only recourse is to develop an engineering discipline for software libraries. This discipline should be based on transformations that are guaranteed to preserve compatibility. This means that a library revision is compatible if only these transformations are used to derive it from the old library. The engineering discipline, then, requires a careful justification for those revisions that are not attained by the transformations.

The goal of this engineering discipline for compiled libraries can be stated as follows:

Only application alteration necessitates recompilation.

This implies that if the evolution of the class library does not require changes in the application source, the application should not require recompilation.

In terms of our straw-man definition, these transformations produce compatible RRBC-successors. But because the straw-man definition is not formal, each transformation must be independently justified. In addition, enumerating the transformations of this discipline is not enough. Because compiled libraries must be accommodated, we must require that the technology for binding applications to libraries must support the transformations. Now, as we shall see, current linkage editors are adequate for procedural programming, but for object-oriented programming a larger set of transformations is required.

11.3 Procedural Programming

For procedural programming (the style that preceded object-oriented programming), the constituents of an application programming interface are procedures, as depicted in Figure 11-3. Applications make procedure calls, and linkage editors ensure that each procedure call is bound to the appropriate procedure implementation.

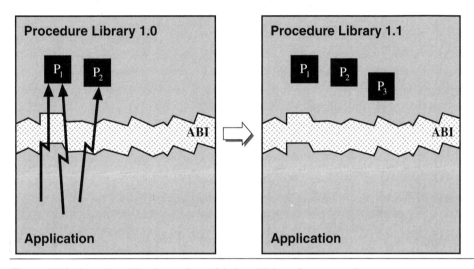

Figure 11-3. Procedure libraries evolve safely by addition of new procedures.

With this ABI, the problem of release-to-release binary compatibility reduces to the following question:

Is each procedure of the new library a more complete implementation of its predecessor?

This implies that there are five transformations available to our engineering discipline.

Transformation 0:   The procedure can be reimplemented to provide better performance for the same functional interface. (Note that we ignore any pathological real-time situation where a better-performing implementation fails to meet its specification.)

Transformation 1:   The domain of the procedure can be enlarged to return values for inputs for which it previously aborted or failed to return (infinite loop or deadlock).

Transformation 2:   On systems where the calling conventions indicate the number of parameters, the number of parameters of a procedure can be increased.

Transformation 3:   Addition of new procedures

Transformation 4:   Retraction of private procedures

Our engineering discipline says that as long as only these transformations are applied, the new procedure library is a release-to-release binary compatible revision of the old library.

Of course, there are good reasons for making changes that are outside these transformations; these changes must be carefully analyzed for their impact on applications using the old libraries. By "private" we mean the generic notion of an entity not being known outside of its compilation unit.

11.4 Object-Oriented Programming

The richness of object-oriented programming adds new facets to the ABI. Besides the ABI of procedural libraries, applications subclass the classes of the library (see Figure 11-4). The new aspects of the problem give rise to additional transformations needed to ensure release-to-release binary compatibility of a class library and thus the continued functioning of the dependent applications.

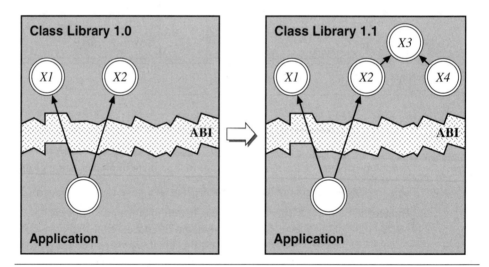

Figure 11-4. Applications subclass from class libraries, which evolve by addition of new classes.

The additional transformations required to support our engineering discipline are as follows.

Transformation 5:   Introduction of new instance variables to objects

Transformation 6:   Introduction of new methods to classes

Transformation 7:   Insertion of new classes into the hierarchy

Transformation 8:   Migration of a parent class downward in the class hierarchy

Transformation 9:   Migration of a method upward in the class hierarchy

Transformation 10:   Retraction of private classes

Transformation 11:   Retraction of private methods

Transformation 12:   Retraction of private instance data

Transformation 13:   Reordering of the methods of a class

Transformation 14:   Reordering of the instance variables of an object

Transformation 8 means that a descendant of a parent class can be used in place of that parent class (in the list of parents). Transformation 8 is included in the list for clarity. It is attainable as a combination of Transformation 6 and Transformation 7. In addition, it may seem counterintuitive that migration of a parent *downward* leaves the library compatible, but moving the parent downward simply means that the new parent supports the functionality of the old parent.

The need for these additional transformations is directly caused by permitting subclassing across the ABI.

11.5 When Classes Are First-Class Objects

Because of the use of metaclasses, our engineering discipline requires an additional transformation.

Transformation 15:   The metaclass constraint can be moved downward
                      in the class hierarchy.

This means that if a class X is an instance of the metaclass *XMeta* in one release of a class library, then in a subsequent release class X can be made an instance of a descendant of *XMeta*. This transformation is similar to Transformation 8 in that when migrating the metaclass downward, the new metaclass supports all the functionality of the old metaclass.

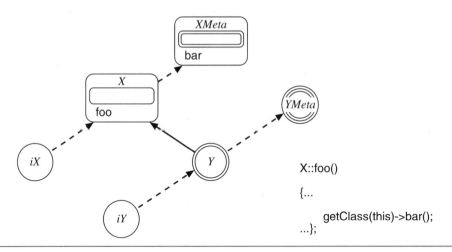

Figure 11-5. Example of a metaclass incompatibility.

To understand the importance of Transformation 15, Figure 11-5 depicts a metaclass incompatibility (which we introduced in Section 3.2). This is not allowed to occur in our object model because of inheritance of metaclass constraints. But if this were not the case, we could fall into the situation depicted in Figure 11-6. The application and the two libraries in the upper part of the figure work together correctly. If Library A evolves by insertion of a new metaclass (which should be acceptable because it is moving the metaclass constraint downward) and foo is reimplemented, the metaclass incompatibility depicted in Figure 11-5 is attained.

Figure 11-7 shows how the lower half of Figure 11-6 looks when the system is built dynamically according to our class construction protocol with inheritance of metaclass constraints. This example makes one further point. The metaclass incompatibility can arise across libraries. There is no way for a metaclass programmer to know about how metaclasses are used in applications. Without the notion of the derived metaclass, there is no way for the application programmer to avoid this situation.

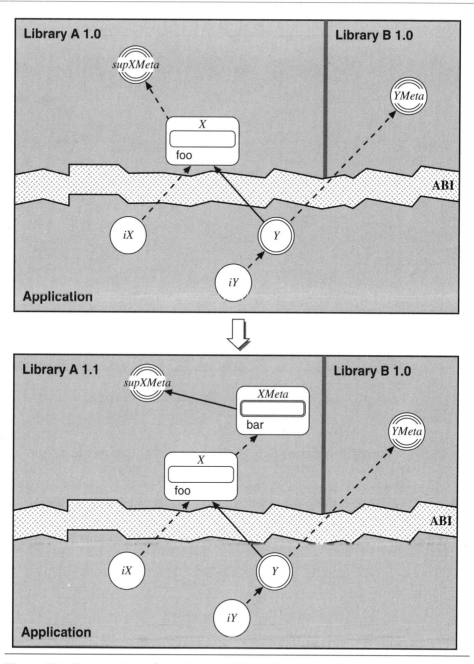

Figure 11-6. Example of a metaclass incompatibility arising in library use if Postulate 10 were not enforced.

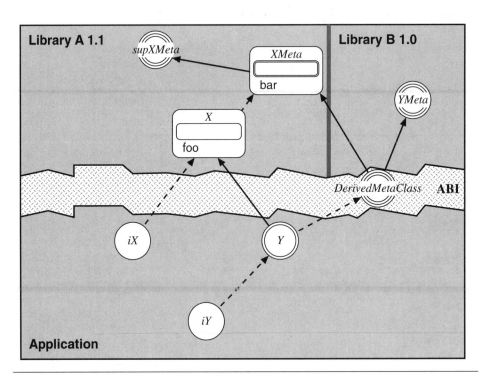

Figure 11-7. Derived metaclass prevents the metaclass incompatibility.

11.6 A Comparison of Support in Several Object Models

Now, when choosing a programming system in which to produce compiled libraries, one needs to consider which transformations are supported. Table 11-1 gives such a comparison for several object models.[1] The Smalltalk and C++ columns are generic, but the Delta/C++ column refers to the C++ compiler from Silicon Graphics [105] and the OBI column refers to the research work of Sun Microsystems [51].

---

1. We exclude Microsoft's COM [93] because it is an interface model rather than an object model and because its ABI forbids subclassing between library and application. If our analysis technique is applied to COM, one sees that it supports only Transformations 0, 1, 3, and 4, which places it in the category of procedural programming rather than object-oriented programming.

In Table 11-1, "Yes" means that the transformation is supported and "No" means that it is not. In cases where the transformation has no meaning in that technology, Table 11-1 has an "n/a" entry.

Note that none of these technologies supports Transformation 2. This is not an impediment to the evolution of a class library, because one can define a new method (with a new name) having the expanded signature while retaining the old method. Now, the compiled applications run as expected while new applications use the new method.

Our presentation has been informal — for instance, we have not defined the criteria for a complete set of transformations that are compatibility preserving (and, for that matter, neither has "compatibility preserving" been formally defined). Lack of completeness of a transformation set usually implies lack of sufficiency. For the problem of evolution of class libraries, however, this is not the case. Clearly, IBM SOM is not complete, because Transformation 2 is not supported. But as we argue above, this is not a serious impediment to evolution of a class library.

11.7 Completeness of a Set of Transformations

A programming system is a programming language together with the tools that support it (for example, compilers, linkers, and loaders). For any programming system, the definition of an RRBC-successor (Definition 24) is sufficient to determine what *are* the safe transformations (transformations T such that, for all libraries L_0, $T(L_0)$ is an RRBC-successor for L_0). However, this definition does not tell us what *should be* the safe transformations in any particular programming system. In this section, we propose such a definition based on the programming language alone. We argue that the current criterion for the correctness of separate compilation is too weak. This weakness has led to the dismal situation in C++ that Table 11-1 summarizes. A stronger criterion for the correctness of separate compilation is proposed.

Definition 24 is about binary compatibility, because each of the symbols A, L_0, and L_1 represents a compiled module. Let us be explicit about the compilation process; let the symbol τ represent the compilation process and let $P \oplus Q$ represent the joining of the source code of two modules P and Q. With these two symbols, we can represent the usual criterion for the correctness of separate compilation.

Weak Correctness Criterion for Separate Compilation
The separate compilation of a program A and a library L_0 is correct if

$$\text{SAT}(\ A \oplus L_0,\ S\ )\ \text{implies SAT}(\ \tau(A \oplus L_0{}^{\text{def}})\ \infty\ \tau(L_0),\ S\ )$$

for all functional specifications S, where $L_0{}^{\text{def}}$ represents the definitions that the language requires for the compilation of A.

Table 11-1. Comparison of Support for Compiled Class Libraries

Transformation	Compiled Smalltalk	Compiled CLOS	Generic C++	IBM SOM	Delta/ C++	OBI	Objec- tive-C	Java
0: improve performance	Yes	Yes	Yes	Yes	Yes	Yes	Yes	Yes
1: eliminate failures	Yes	Yes	Yes	Yes	Yes	Yes	Yes	Yes
2: add parameter	No	No[a]	No[b]	No[c]	No	No	No	No
3: add procedure	n/a	Yes	Yes	Yes	Yes	Yes	Yes	n/a
4: retract private procedure	n/a	n/a	Yes	Yes	Yes	Yes	Yes	n/a
5: introduce instance variable	No[d]	Yes	No	Yes	Yes	Yes	No	Yes
6: introduce new method	Yes	Yes	No	Yes	Yes	Yes	Yes	Yes
7: insert new class	Yes	Yes	No	Yes	Yes	Yes	No	Yes[e]
8: migrate parent downward	Yes	Yes	No	Yes	Yes	No[f]	No	Yes
9: migrate method upward	Yes	Yes	No	Yes	Yes	Yes	Yes	Yes
10: retract private class	n/a	n/a	No	Yes	Yes	Yes	Yes	Yes
11: retract private method	n/a	n/a	No	Yes	Yes[g]	Yes	n/a	Yes
12: retract private data	n/a	n/a	No	Yes	Yes	Yes	n/a	Yes
13: reorder methods	n/a	Yes	No	Yes	Yes	No[f]	Yes	Yes
14: reorder instance variables	No	Yes	No	Yes	Yes	No[f]	No[h]	Yes
15: migrate metaclass constraint downward	No	No	n/a	Yes	n/a	n/a	No	n/a

a. This transformation is supported for functions in compiled LISP but not for generic methods in CLOS.

b. Because of overloading in C++, this box gets a formal "No," because addition of new parameters defines a new method. One might think that this is not a problem, because overloading allows multiple procedures with the same name. However, this causes an answer for procedures that is different from that for methods.

c. IBM SOM supports procedures and methods that are defined to have variable numbers of parameters.

d. With compiled Smalltalk, addition of instance variables requires recompilation of applications.

e. Some early implementations of Java do not support these transformations, but the new specification makes it clear that all of our transformations must be supported (see [65], pages 206-214).

f. One should bear in mind that OBI is a research project that had the additional goal of supporting multiple versions of a class.

g. Because this is a C++ approach, one must ensure that private members have not been exposed by friend specifications.

h. Objective-C supports a direct access interface to instance data, making the entry in this box a "No." Brad Cox informs us that wise Objective-C programmers avoid use of this facility (and, by doing so, turn the entry in this box to a "Yes").

For example, in C or C++, $L_0{}^{def}$ represents the header files for the library L_0. On the other, for LISP libraries $L_0{}^{def}$ always contains an empty set of statements. The asymmetry in the formula is a result of the expectation that the program knows about the library, but the library must contain no references to the program (in order for the library to be reusable). Again, we have waved our hands at several important issues — particularly the fact that in some languages separate compilation may require more work than merely separating the source code into different files. (The use of the symbols τ, $\oplus$, and so on is intended to clarify the presentation. We understand that we are not proving a mathematical result, and we hope you understand this, too.)

The weak correctness criterion is the origin of the release-to-release compatibility problem. If the library L_0 is changed, the application must be recompiled if the definitions change. As we have seen in the earlier sections of this chapter, it is not sufficient for a programming system to support such a weak notion.

So let us rewrite Definition 24 using τ and letting A, L_0, and L_1 represent source code.

Definition 25. L_1 is an **RRBC-successor** to L_0 if

$$\text{SAT}(\ \iota(A \oplus L_0{}^{def})\ \oslash\oslash\ \tau(L_0),\ S\ )\ \text{implies SAT}(\ \tau(A \oplus L_0{}^{def})\ \oslash\oslash\ \tau(L_1),\ S\ )$$

for all reasonable functional specifications S and for all applications A using library L.

This more precise definition explicitly shows that the application program is compiled with the definitions of the old library. Definition 25 is an improvement; however, the definition still relies on the notion of a reasonable functional specification. Let us define a "reasonable functional specification" as one that does not constrain or reference the structure of the program that implements the specification (that is, either the structure of the source program or the structure of the compiled program). This definition of reasonable functional specification has a deficiency in that reflective programs (programs that have outputs based on the structure of the program) do not have functional specifications that are reasonable. This is not a concern here; this definition of reasonable functional specification is adequate for defining what should be the safe transformations and strengthening our notion of correctness of separate compilation.

Now let us assume that $L_1 = T(L_0)$, where T is a correctness-preserving transformation on the library alone when the library and the application program are compiled as a single unit.

Definition 26. A transformation T (on a library L_0) is **correctness preserving** if

$$\text{SAT}(\ A \oplus L_0,\ S\ )\ \text{implies SAT}(\ A \oplus T(L_0),\ S\ )$$

for all reasonable functional specifications S and for all programs $A \oplus L_0$.

We claim (and our experience confirms) that a programming system is much easier to use when the correctness-preserving transformations (on the library) are not invalidated by separate compilation. This is very natural for LISP programming (where $L_0{}^{def}$ is empty) and C programming (where $L_0{}^{def}$ is not empty). Thus, the definition of RRBC-safe transformations can be based on that of correctness-preserving transformations.

Definition 27. If SAT($A \oplus L_0$, S), then a transformation T is **RRBC safe** if

SAT($A \oplus T(L_0)$, S) implies SAT($\tau(A \oplus L_0^{def})$ ⚭ $\tau(T(L_0))$, S)

for all reasonable functional specifications S and for all applications A using library L_0.

If Definition 27 is rearranged so that its central formula looks like this:

[SAT($A \oplus L_0$, S) implies SAT($A \oplus T(L_0)$, S)]
implies SAT($\tau(A \oplus L_0^{def})$ ⚭ $\tau(T(L_0))$, S)

then it is evident that an RRBC-safe transformation must be correctness preserving. Note that transformations that change both the application program and the library may be correctness preserving, but are not RRBC safe. Also note that Transformation 2 is not considered RRBC safe for C++ programs, because the antecedent of the definition is not fulfilled (if T changes the signature of a method, $A \oplus T(L_0)$ is not a valid C++ program).

Combining Definition 27 with the weak correctness criterion for separate compilation yields a stronger criterion for the correctness of separate compilation for all programming systems.

Strong Correctness Criterion for Separate Compilation

The separate compilation of a program A and a library L_0 is correct if

SAT($A \oplus L_0$, S) implies

[SAT($\tau(A \oplus L_0^{def})$ ⚭ $\tau(L_0)$, S)
and
SAT($A \oplus T(L_0)$, S) implies SAT($\tau(A \oplus L_0^{def})$ ⚭ $\tau(T(L_0))$, S)
]

for all functional specifications S, where L_0^{def} represents the definitions that the language requires for the compilation of A.

This stronger criterion says:

> Any library transformation that preserves correctness when the library is compiled with an application program as a single unit should preserve correctness when the library and the application program (with the old definition context) are separately compiled.

Thus far, we have simply restated our definitions in preparation for defining the completeness of a set of transformations for a programming system. A programming system is **RRBC complete** if all correctness-preserving transformations on libraries are RRBC-safe transformations. In procedural programming, a programming system that is not RRBC complete would be deemed faulty and would not be tolerated. For object-oriented programming, the same should be true. We further assert the following:

All programming systems should be RRBC complete.

Note that we have not proved nor do we claim that the set of transformations in Table 11-1 is RRBC complete for DTS C++. The problem of proving a set of transformations RRBC complete for any particular programming system seems quite difficult and should be the subject of further study. Our study covers only transformations on the library. One may also consider transformations that cover the library and the application jointly. This was done in [94] for a single-inheritance object model without metaclasses; this study is recommended reading.

11.8 Summary

Release-to-release binary compatibility is a valuable property of a programming system; this statement is based on experience with the IBM SOMobjects Toolkit. The paper from which this chapter was derived [43] contains a section that describes that experience. This experience strongly indicates that separate compilation must be properly supported by a programming system in order to put metaclasses to work. Proper support means being RRBC complete, which implies that Transformation 15 (moving of the metaclass constraint downward) must be supported.

Chapter 12
Conclusion

Although this chapter is titled "Conclusion," this book is part of the beginning of a new epoch in the evolution of computer programming. It may seem pretentious to write about "a new epoch in the evolution of computer programming," but we mean this in a modest sense. We are tired of reading about "programming revolutions" that are mere tempests in teapots. A careful reading of the history of computer programming shows that our object model is built on the hard work of many other researchers and as such is part of the "evolution" of computer programming. The term "epoch" is chosen for its geological context, because in the technology of computer programming our progress is glacial compared with that of our colleagues in hardware. Be that as it may, we must recognize that introduction of metaobject protocols (and, more generally, other reflective computing facilities) into computer programming makes a dramatic change in which reuse becomes a reality.

Reusability of programs has been disappointing; this is especially true in the area of object-oriented programming in light of its early promise. The goal of this book is to establish the basis (an object model with metaclasses, inheritance of metaclass constraints, and a supporting metaobject protocol) for greater reuse and to demonstrate greater reuse (a reasonable set of metaclasses that compose with one another). There are three synergistic aspects of our work that lead to greater reuse.

- First, a metaclass can embody a class property. This concept is totally inexpressible in any object-oriented programming language without a metaobject protocol.

- Second, because metaclasses can examine the structure of class as it is constructed, metaclasses can be programmed independently of any class that uses them, and vice versa.

- Third, because of inheritance of metaclass constraints, metaclass composability reduces to addition of the appropriate cooperative features during the class construction process. That is, if the class initializations of two metaclasses compose, the metaclasses compose.

The system of metaclass programming that we have demonstrated has been limited by the metadata that we have chosen to put into our object model and to make accessible through our metaobject protocol. For example, no metadata was included about method signatures, the types of instance variables, or the implementation of a method (beyond the code pointer). Despite this, we have demonstrated a wide range of useful metaclasses that compose with one another. Additional metadata only increases that efficacy of metaclass programming.

12.1   Contributions of This Book

12.1.1   Inheritance of Metaclass Constraints

In mathematics, **monotonic** is an adjective that means that a function is always increasing or always decreasing. Computer science has adopted this term in its positive sense (always increasing) to talk about reasoning — the set of conclusions grows monotonically with increasing information, as long as the information is not contradictory. In object-oriented programming, a monotonic class hierarchy means that all that is true of a class is true of its descendants — as a subclass adds structure to its parents (increasing information), any statement that is true for any parent remains true. This kind of monotonicity is highly prized by programmers using frameworks. Put in another way, nonmonotonicity in a class framework means that the knowledge one has about a class cannot be reused when subclassing a descendant. Frameworks that are monotonic are easy to use; when they are not, it is easy to get into trouble. Our introduction of inheritance of metaclass constraints is a direct consequence of prizing monotonicity. The metaclass for a class contributes to the properties of all descendants; that is, inheritance of metaclass constraints is necessary for monotonicity (but is not sufficient). For this reason, our foremost contribution is inheritance of metaclass constraints.

12.1.2   Cooperation

Even with inheritance of metaclass constraints, metaclasses would have limited use if they often conflicted with each other so as to fail to build the desired class object. By introducing the notion of cooperation, we change the granularity of the main resource (method table entries) over which metaclasses contend. This makes it possible for metaclasses to cooperate on method implementations; the cumulative effect is that metaclasses can compose[1] where previously composition was difficult to achieve and impossible to guarantee.

With this facility (including inheritance of metaclass constraints), we have designed a framework of useful metaclasses that compose. We designed Before/After Metaclasses (Chapter 8), proxies (Chapter 9), and a set of metaclasses for programming frameworks (Chapter 10). These metaclasses can be composed. Remember the fable of George the programmer, which opened this book: we promised a large reduction in the number of classes that he must understand (the $n2^p$ versus $n+p$ argument at the end of Section 1.1). We have fulfilled this promise.

12.1.3 Monotonicity of Implementation Chains

Either single inheritance or monotonic linearization has been the approach proposed to tame method behavior in the presence of overrides. Neither is suitable for our purposes. We relaxed the constraint for monotonic linearization in Chapter 4 so that the method resolution order is computed even when order disagreements exist, but only when the order disagreements are not serious. This part of our object model changes the focus of concern from the linearization to its semantic impact on object behavior.

12.1.4 Definition of Release-to-Release Binary Compatibility

Before we defined it, release-to-release binary compatibility was an ill-understood concept. By defining it, we see that it is another manifestation of monotonicity, but in another dimension. Here, although the ordering relation of the classes is temporal succession rather than descendant in the inheritance hierarchy, the desired effect is the same: the knowledge one has of a class does not decrease. Release-to-release binary compatibility is a general topic in programming, but we had to interpret it for our object model with metaclasses. Release-to-release binary compatibility needed to be addressed in order to make our metaclass framework as valuable as possible. Our approach has levied requirements for programming systems that should never be relaxed.

12.1.5 Demystification of Metaclasses

Our introduction to object models from first principles is novel. The circuit in the instance-of relation that occurs in all finite object models seems mysterious, especially if it is introduced after inheritance. Our presentation shows that this is the direct consequence

---

1. We have not precisely defined "composition of metaclasses." It can be understood to be an operation that creates a new metaclass (the composite) from a set of metaclasses such that the composite is highly useful. Note that monotonicity is not necessary. However, it is hard to imagine a more useful composition operation than one that is monotonic.

of "All objects have a class" and "Every class is an object." Subsequently, there are implications for the creation of the environment, once the structure of a class is determined.

Our object model is described in terms of a metalanguage (*O*, *C*, *M*, *class*, *supportedMethods*, and so on). When our metaobject protocol is introduced, the primitives of the model are reflected in the metaobject protocol. We know our colleagues around the world understand this concept well and do not think it is novel. We believe this to be the correct pedagogical technique for reflective object models.

Our drawing conventions assist demystification by making class relationships easy to understand. The shape used to draw the boundary of an object is inconsequential, but our invention of single, double, and triple boundaries for ordinary object, ordinary class, and metaclass is not arbitrary. This convention is based on the fundamental structure inherent in all models with metaclasses.

12.2 Summary

A metaclass can be viewed as a transformation that imparts a property to a class object during class construction. In this sense, a metaclass is also a reusable entity that embodies a property without identification of the objects or classes of objects that have the property. The composition of metaclasses is the composition of the transformations they embody. When two classes are composed (using multiple inheritance), the resulting class should have the conjunction of the properties. Thus, the inheritance of metaclass constraints (which implies the composition of the metaclasses as transformations) is a necessary condition for monotonic class hierarchies. Metaclass transformations can compose or conflict; by appropriately lowering the granularity of the resources over which metaclasses conflict, we make metaclasses more composable and consequently more useful. Ultimately, the level of programming is raised, because the units with which one programs are classes and metaclasses that hopefully compose with one another. Linguistically, a property is often represented by an adjective, whereas a class is represented by a noun. Composition of metaclasses should be as easy as putting a sequence of adjectives in front of a noun when we speak.

Appendix A
Advanced Linearization

Given a class Z, a **linearization** is a list of the ancestors of Z.[1] Two uses of linearization have been made in this book.

- First, for inheritance, a linearization provides a precedence for resolving conflicts that arise when two ancestor classes define the same attribute (Section 2.5).

- Second, when doing parent method calls, a linearization provides the order for the implementation chain (Section 4.7).

The discussion below deals exclusively with the second use of linearization because it is the most difficult to master, in that the second use has a dynamic aspect (the order of execution of overrides), and dynamic aspects are always the most difficult to address.

A.1 Properties of Linearizations

Let us begin by considering the properties that are desirable for a linearization. There are four properties of interest: language independence, consistency, monotonicity, and stability. This section and the next two are based on the pioneering work in [34,35].

---

1. CLOS [104] and Dylan [2] use the term "class precedence list." IBM SOMobjects Toolkit 3.0 [62,63] uses the term "method resolution order."

A.1.1 Language Independence

Definition 28. Two classes have **isomorphic ancestor hierarchies** if the graphs of the ancestor hierarchies are isomorphic, including the order of the parent list.

An excellent explanation of graph isomorphism can be found in [57]. The additional phrase about the parent list means that if an isomorphism matches two classes, it also matches classes in the parent lists.

Definition 29. A **language-independent** linearization produces the same results for isomorphic ancestor hierarchies.

Example.

In Figure A-1, the subgraph of the ancestors of X_3 is isomorphic to the subgraph of the ancestors of Y_3. The isomorphism matches the classes as follows.

$$\text{Object } X_0 \ Y_0 \ X_1 \ X_2 \ X_3$$
$$\quad | \quad | \quad | \quad | \quad | \quad |$$
$$\text{Object } Y_0 \ X_0 \ Y_1 \ Y_2 \ Y_3$$

Note that X_0 in the subgraph of the ancestors of X_3 is matched with Y_0 in the subgraph of the ancestors of Y_3, and vice versa. The language independence of a linearization means that by knowing the linearization for X_3, we can use the isomorphism to compute the linearization for Y_3.

☐

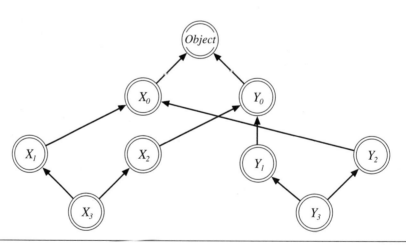

Figure A-1. Ancestor subgraph of X_3 is isomorphic to that of Y_3.

Definitions 28 and 29 may seem to be pedantic mathematics, but actually they are quite practical and quite important. The use of isomorphism establishes what information can and cannot be used to determine the linearization. The definitions combine to say that language-independent linearizations are determined solely on the basis of the structure of the class hierarchy. That is, by requiring a language-independent linearization to produce the same results for isomorphic ancestor hierarchies, we are saying that all other information is irrelevant. For example, forming the linearization by lexicographically sorting the set of topological sorts and choosing the first one is not language independent. Also, determining the linearization by position of the class declaration in the source code is not language independent.

These two definitions are motivated by pragmatic software engineering concerns. We have already stated that the linearization must be one of the topological sorts. Using information other than that contained in the class hierarchy tends to make programs (that declare the class hierarchy) harder to understand, because more information needs to be acquired to determine the linearization. Another aspect of this issue is that by limiting themselves to language-independent linearizations, programmers develop understanding that is highly transferrable among programs. The notion of language-independent linearizations is important to understand and is a basic principle for the design of all object-oriented programming languages. Language-independent linearization is an ideal way to limit the set of linearizations without mentioning the syntax of any programming language.

Language-independent linearizations are also related to release-to-release binary compatibility (see Chapter 11). Using language-dependent linearizations leaves open the possibility that the linearization might change when the new library is released even if the class hierarchy has not changed.

A.1.2   Consistency

Definition 30. Let $\propto$ be a precedence relation on the classes in a class hierarchy. A linearization of the ancestors of Z is said to be **consistent with precedence relation** $\propto$ if no entry in the linearization for Z is preceded by a $\propto$-successor.

Example.

Consider the class Z and its ancestors as depicted in Figure A-2. The ancestor set of class Z has five topological sorts.

$\square$

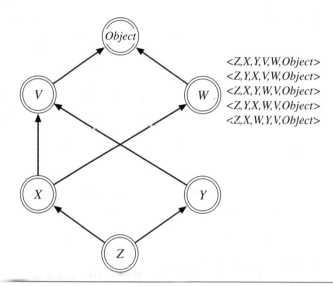

$<Z,X,Y,V,W,Object>$
$<Z,Y,X,V,W,Object>$
$<Z,X,Y,W,V,Object>$
$<Z,Y,X,W,V,Object>$
$<Z,X,W,Y,V,Object>$

Figure A-2. A class hierarchy and its linearizations.

Sometimes this lack of specificity can be resolved by considering the additional precedence relations implied by the order of the parent lists. This relation is called **local precedence.** If two classes in the same parent list appear in a topological sort in the reverse order, then the topological sort is eliminated from consideration. Figure A-3 shows this explicitly by displaying the indices of the parents and having lightly drawn arrows showing the precedence that the parent order implies. By considering only linearization consistent with local precedence, there is exactly one possible linearization for Figure A-3 — namely, $<Z,X,Y,V,W,Object>$.

Consistency with local precedence is not sufficient to produce unique linearizations for all class hierarchies. With a slight change of parentage (as Figure A-4 shows), there can be multiple linearizations that respect both the class hierarchy and the local precedence. In Figure A-4, multiple linearizations arise because V and Y are unrelated in the transitive closure of the two precedence relations (subclass and parent order).

Ideally, one would like to invent a precedence relation such that linearization consistent with that relation totally orders all class hierarchies. Unfortunately, after introducing the next important property of linearizations, we will see that no such precedence relation exists (see Theorem 10 in Section A.2).

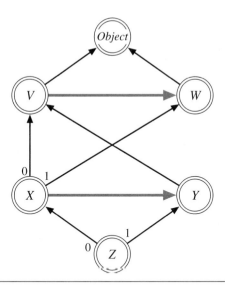

Figure A-3. This hierarchy for Z has only one topological sort consistent with local precedence.

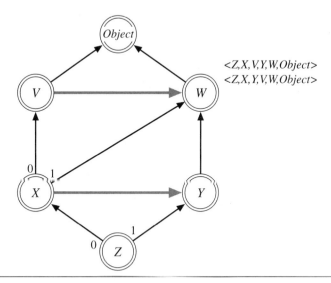

Figure A-4. The two linearizations of the ancestors of Z that respect parent list precedence.

A.1.3   Monotonicity

Definition 31. A linearization function L_H is **monotonic** if, for all pairs of classes X and Y such that X is an ancestor of Y, $L_H(X)$ is a subsequence of $L_H(Y)$.

Monotonicity is an important property, because it states that property inheritance cannot skip a generation. This may seem hard to imagine, but as reported in [34,35], CLOS linearization does not have this property. More recently, language designers are ensuring that their linearizations are monotonic [7].

Monotonicity solves a very important problem. Consider the situation in Figure A-5. Suppose that the metaclass *Persistent* has some state that it adds to an ordinary object, so that when persistent objects are used in a multithreaded environment, they must be in the critical region. We would like to do this with the *ThreadSafe* metaclass (one semaphore makes both the object state and the state added by *Persistent* thread safe). This can be done with *ThreadSafePersistent*, if monotonicity holds, because monotonicity guarantees that all descendants of *ThreadSafePersistent* have the state added by *Persistent* in the critical region.

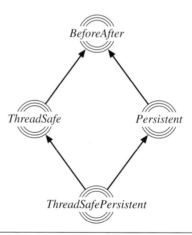

Figure A-5. Example that attests to the importance of monotonicity.

A.1.4   Stability

Suppose that a new class is inserted into the hierarchy between two classes. Our intuition says that this insertion should not affect the inheritance of any property not changed by this new class. This intuition is captured by the property of a linearization being stable.

Definition 32. A linearization is **stable** if the insertion of a class between two classes does not change the linearization other than to add the new class.

Stability of linearization is a consequence of the desire for release-to-release binary compatibility. In Chapter 11, we assert that one should be able to insert new classes into the class hierarchy (Transformation 7) without breaking release-to-release binary compatibility. If a linearization is not stable, the way a compiled application executes may change when the library changes.

A.2 The Limits of Linearization

Theorem 10. [35] There are no language-independent linearizations that are monotonic for all inheritance hierarchies.

Proof.

Figure A-6 shows a class hierarchy H. The classes X_3 and Y_3 have isomorphic ancestor hierarchies. One is composed of the set
$$\{Object, X_0, Y_0, X_1, X_2, X_3\}$$
and the second is composed of the set
$$\{Object, X_0, Y_0, Y_1, Y_2, Y_3\}$$
Any language-independent linearization must order X_0 and Y_0 in reverse for the linearization for X_3 and the linearization for Y_3. But a monotonic linearization is required to preserve both X_0 before Y_0 and Y_0 before X_0. This implies that a monotonic language-independent linearization cannot produce a value for the linearization for Z.

$\square$

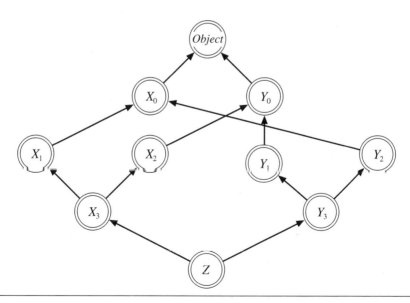

Figure A-6. Counterexample that proves Theorem 10.

A.3 Summary

Theorem 10 sets a limit on our expectations. Monotonicity cannot be attained without giving up the property of language independence. Because neither language independence nor monotonicity can be abandoned, there is only one possibility remaining — to abandon support for all hierarchies. This is one way to rationalize the algorithm in Section 4.5 in which all order disagreements are considered serious. Once one accepts the fact that some class hierarchies are not supported, the next step is to look carefully at the cases of order disagreement (that is, where monotonic merge is not possible) to see if it really matters. Those cases in which it matters are the serious order disagreements of Section 4.9.

A.4 Exercise

A.1   Consider the following linearization algorithm: For a class hierarchy, compute all of the topological sorts, order them alphabetically, and the first one is the linearization. Prove that this algorithm is not language independent. Prove that it is not monotonic.

Appendix B
Handling Apply and
Redispatch Stubs

The purpose of this appendix is to look more deeply at the underlying implementation of interpretive facilities provided by our metaobject protocol (Chapter 6). This involves a general understanding of procedure call linkage conventions. A linkage convention specifies low-level details for how procedure or method arguments are passed. For example, a simple linkage convention would be to place arguments onto an execution stack in the order of their declaration. Owing to the desire for efficiency, however, arguments are normally placed in general and special-purpose registers when possible. Linkage conventions can be complex and are closely tied to the instruction sets and register architectures of specific processors. The syntax employed for procedure and method calls insulates users of a high-level programming language from these details.

Based on the statically known name of the procedure to be called as well as the declared number and types of the arguments, a linkage convention allows a compiler to generate code at the calling site that puts arguments in the "right" places as expected by the compiled code to be called. However, there are times when it is useful to call a procedure whose name or arguments are not statically known. Some high-level languages provide facilities for this, which enables enhanced flexibility in application solutions. To enable portability of code, however, it is still essential that such facilities hide the procedure call linkage convention.

One solution to this problem is illustrated by C, which supports function pointers and variable argument lists as data types, and which provides a special syntax for declaring functions that can be called with a variable number of arguments. The data type used to hold a variable number of arguments is called a va_list, and the special syntax used to declare a procedure that accepts a variable number of arguments employs an ellipsis ... as a final parameter. The caller of such a procedure uses normal procedure call syntax, passing the desired number of arguments, but the called procedure is written in a special way. It declares a va_list as a local variable and "starts" it. This loads the va_list with the arguments represented by the ellipsis and is the standard way to construct a va_list in C, C++, and DTS C++.

The need for interoperability between different compilers typically leads to a standardized va_list representation defined by an operating system platform. In such cases, the utility of va_lists transcends individual languages and compilers.

B.1 Enhanced Control over Method Dispatch

To provide enhanced control of the method dispatch process, our DTS C++ metaobject protocol integrates and extends the use of va_lists discussed above in two important ways.[1]

First, the primitive apply function is available to invoke an arbitrary method implementation (identified by the code pointer returned by resolveMethod) using a va_list as an argument. An important aspect of this process is that the code to be called (a method implementation) does not receive a va_list — arguments are declared and processed as usual by the method implementation. To support this, resolveMethod does not actually return the address of a method implementation, but instead returns the address of a small piece of code, an **apply stub** that first moves arguments from the provided va_list into their correct locations (according to the procedure call linkage convention expected by the method implementation). Once this has been done, the apply stub calls the desired method implementation. The information necessary to allow resolveMethod to return an appropriate apply stub for a given method is provided by the method's introducing class when the method is registered using addMethod.[2] For simplicity, these details were omitted from the version of addMethod described in Chapter 6.

The second way relates to the creation of va_lists that are passed to apply. When they are created by programmers, the standard approach described in the introduction to this appendix is used. See Section B.2 for an example that illustrates this. In practice, however, most va_lists used by metaclass programmers are created by a second important extension that enables specialized control of method dispatch: a **redispatch stub.** The purpose of a

---

1. If we were representing our metaobject protocol using some other language without support for va_lists, we would model our intentions using whatever primitives seemed most appropriate in that language. What we represent with DTS C++, however, has actually been achieved, and can be viewed as the best effort yet at incorporation of these ideas into the C/C++ language heritage.

2. In early versions of SOMobjects Toolkit, individual apply stubs were defined and registered for each method introduced by a class. Later, in SOMobjects Toolkit 3.0, a single generic apply stub implementation was used, based on method signature information registered using addMethod.

redispatch stub is to act as a simple method implementation that creates a va_list, places the method arguments onto the va_list, and then invokes the method <*Object*,"dispatch">, which receives the va_list as an explicit argument.

Section B.3 shows how a redispatch stub can be implemented using standard language facilities. However, the fact that va_list representation is normally an operating system standard enables the use of low-level, platform-specific code to implement redispatch stubs. As with apply stubs, redispatch stubs in the SOMobjects Toolkit are supported on the basis of information registered using addMethod.[3]

In summary, a redispatch stub for a method is an implementation of the method that receives arguments of the declared number and type, uses these arguments to create a va_list, and then invokes <*Object*,"dispatch"> on the target object. A corresponding apply stub can receive this va_list, extract the arguments, and then call a different method implementation (as chosen by either resolveMethod or resolveTerminal), passing the required number and type of arguments. Both kinds of stubs depend on the linkage convention and the representation of va_lists, and therefore vary among operating system platforms.

As illustrated by numerous examples throughout this book, redispatch stubs are placed in method tables by the method putRDStub to implement specialized instance-level behavior required by a metaclass. The reason for the name "redispatch stub" is that dispatch normally uses apply at some point to invoke some other dynamically chosen implementation for the method — in effect, redispatching the method.[4] This explains the utility of the resolveTerminal method when implementing cooperation; if the method table entry for the indicated method contains a redispatch stub, resolveTerminal returns what would have been in the method table if a redispatch stub had not been placed there.

A simple way to understand the overall pattern enabled by the combination of apply and redispatch stubs in our metaobject protocol is as follows. Redispatch stubs are used by a metaclass to intercept the method dispatch process for objects of which it is a metaclass, and to invoke metaclass-defined instance behavior. When class-defined instance behavior is subsequently appropriate, an apply stub is used to return control to class-defined code.

---

3. In SOMobjects Toolkit 1.0, redispatch stubs were defined much as in Section B.3 and registered using addMethod. Later, in SOMobjects Toolkit 3.0, they were generated dynamically when required by putRDStub, using method signature information registered by addMethod.

4. Note that the va_list passed to apply in this case is normally the one provided to dispatch as an argument (by the redispatch stub). Thus, the implementor of dispatch rarely needs to construct a va_list.

B.2 Example of an Apply Stub

Imagine that we want to use apply to implement an interpreter for DTS C++ method calls. How would we use standard va_list capabilities provided by DTS C++ for this purpose?

Without loss of generality, assume that the interpreter invokes methods on a single object (created by the interpreter) by prompting the user for the method's name and introducing class, for the number of arguments to be passed, and for the argument values. For simplicity, assume there are at most two arguments, and that the method arguments and result are of type long. Also, assume that there is a method findClass introduced by *Class*, whose purpose is to locate and return a reference to a class with the indicated name. The interpreter can be implemented along the lines suggested by the following code.

```
// Define the code that will create a va_list and call apply. Given a target object, an
// apply stub, the address of a buffer to hold the result, and a variable number of
// arguments, invoke the method implementation represented by the apply stub.
void callApply( Object* obj, CodePtr applyStub, long* result, ... ) {
    va_list args;
    va_start(args, result);
    apply( obj, applyStub, args, (void**)result );
    va_end(args);
}
```

```
// Define the code used for interpretive method resolution. Given the name of
// a method and the name of its introducing class, return an apply stub for the
// implementation of this method appropriate for use on the given target object.
CodePtr lookupMethod( char* icName, char* methodName, Object* target)
{
    Class* ic = getClass(target)->findClass(icName);
    if (ic)
        return getClass(target)->resolveMethod( ic, methodName );
    else
        return NULL;
}
```

```
// Define the main body of the interpreter for this example. Determine the method
// to be called and the arguments to be passed. Resolve the method on the target
// and invoke the appropriate method implementation.
```

```
void main() {
    Object *obj = ...;  // create/access the object on which the method will be invoked
    char *ic, *mName;
    long argc, a1, a2, a3, a4, a5, result;
    cout << "what's the method name?" << endl;
    cin >> mName;
    cout << "what is the introducing class?" << endl;
    cin >> ic;
    CodePtr appStub = lookupMethod(ic, mName, obj),
    cout << "how many arguments?" << endl;
    cin >> argc;
    if (argc > 0) cout << "input the arguments" << endl;
    switch (argc) {
        case 0:  callApply(obj, appStub, &result);
                break;
        case 1: cin >> a1;
                callApply(obj, appStub, &result, a1);
                break;
        case 2: cin >> a1;
                cin >> a2;
                callApply(obj, appStub, &result, a1, a2);
    }
    cout << "the result is " << result;
}
```

B.3 Example of a Redispatch Stub

Imagine that addMethod requires as an argument a redispatch stub for the method. How can we use the approach introduced in Section B.2 to define a redispatch stub for a method M introduced by class C, where the method accepts two long arguments and returns a float value? Assume that method implementations (which is what redispatch stubs are) can be defined as extern "C" functions that receive the target object as their first parameter. The desired redispatch stub can be implemented as follows.

```
void callDispatch( Object *obj, Class* ic, char *mName, float *result, ... ) {
    va_list args;
    va_start(args,result);
    obj->dispatch( ic, mName, args, (void**)result );
    va_end(args);
}
```

```
extern "C" float rdStubforCM( Object *obj, long a1, long a2 ) {
    float result;
    callDispatch( obj, C, "M", &result, a1, a2 );
    return result;
}
```

Appendix C
Rationale for
Drawing Conventions

An object is depicted with some shape. The shape is arbitrary: a circle, a square, or a cloud are equally good possibilities. We use a rectangle with rounded corners.

which degenerates into a circle

when we draw a small one. Our intention is that the rectangle with the rounded corners is an **open representation** whereas the circle is a **closed representation.** The open representation is used to show what is inside the object; the closed representation means either that the content of the object is arbitrary or that there is an earlier open representation.

By Postulate 1, every object has an object reference. This object reference is written across the center of a circle or at the top of a rounded rectangle, which provides ample space for writing other annotations. For example, here are two objects.

We must remember that iX and iY are the object references, not the names of the objects. Objects are given names in various programming systems. Two different objects can have the same name but never the same object reference. Admittedly, this may seem overly precise, but we wish to reserve "object name" for dealing with the way a programming language can be bound to our model.

When one is dealing with an open representation, the data table of the object is written inside. For example,

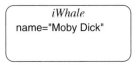

Usually it is sufficient to write only the instance variable name; the introducing class is written only if the disambiguation is necessary. A **part-of relation** between objects is represented by using an object reference as the value of an instance variable. For example,

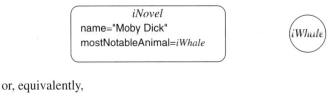

or, equivalently,

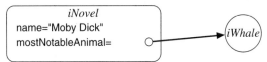

which is intended to depict the idea that $iWhale$ is in some sense inside $iNovel$.

Although the relation between an object and its class might be thought of as a part-of relation, it gets special treatment, because the class slot is not an instance variable. Following the convention that was introduced by Smalltalk [50], we draw a dashed arrow to indicate the class of an object (an arrow because the relation is asymmetric). For example,

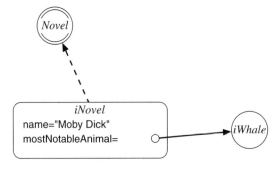

The double boundary arises because a class contains the template for its instances. The outer boundary is for the class (because it is an object, too) and the inner boundary is for the template. In our object model, that template is formally represented by the ivs instance variable that is present in all class objects, although only the content of the ivdefs instance variable is written inside the template boundary. For example,

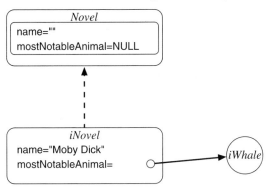

This convention permits a simple distinction between instance variables and class variables when viewing a class object; instance variables are written inside the template and class variables are written outside the template. Class variables, of course, are also instance variables — that is, they are the instance variables of the metaclass for the class.

The other instance variables of a class get special treatment, too. The subclass relation that is implied by the parents instance variable of a class is drawn with solid arrows from one class to another (also following the convention introduced by Smalltalk [50]). The left-to-right orientation of the arrows emanating from a class is the order in the parents list. For example,

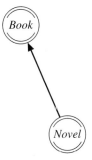

The method table is not drawn. Introduced methods of a class are written outside the template. For example,

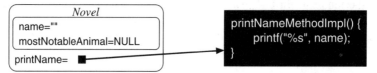

where the little black box indicates a code pointer and the large black box indicates a method implementation. Usually, we are not this precise and either write a code pointer name with the method name or write nothing with the method name. Again, we write only the introducing class associated with the method name when disambiguation is needed.

Curiously, this is always the case when a method is being overridden (otherwise, simply writing a method name would mean that a new method was being introduced).

The convention for drawing a metaclass is a consequence of the above conventions. The instance template for a metaclass must contain an instance template. Therefore, a metaclass is drawn with three boundaries. The makeInstance method makes a copy of the template of the class.

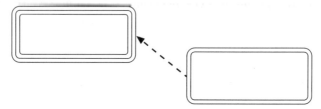

When a class inherits from a metaclass, it inherits a template in its template — that is, it adds a boundary that indicates that its instances are classes, too.

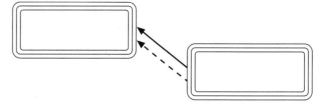

Appendix D
Answers to Selected Exercises

Chapter 1

Exercise 1.8:

No. The list produced by topSort has all vertices of equal distance from the minimal vertices grouped together. The order within each group is nondeterministic.

Chapter 2

Exercise 2.1:

The value of Z is

```
{   "class" = Class,
    Class       = {   "parents" = < X, Y >,
                      "ivdefs" = { Z = {      "zvar1" = 0,
                                             "zvar2" = 0 }
                                 },
                      "ivs" = {   X   =  {   "xvar" = 0 },
                                  Y   =  {   "yvar" = 0 },
                                  Z   =  {   "zvar1" = 0,
                                            "zvar2" = 0 }
                                },
                      "mdefs" = { },
                      "mtab" =   {   X = { "xmethod" = xcodePtr },
                                     Y = { "ymethod" = ycodePtr }
                                 }
                  }
}
```

Exercise 2.6.

The correct answer is given by the following diagram:

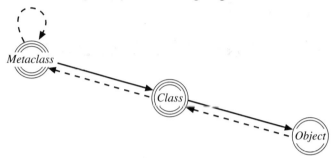

But this yields four types of metaclasses:

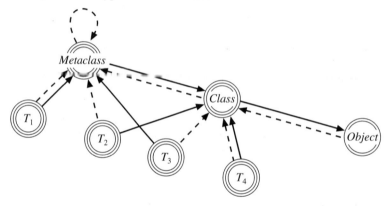

Because a metaclass is a class whose instances are classes, all four are metaclasses.

T_1 is for extensions of *Metaclass* (that is, it is used to add methods to which only metaclasses respond).

T_2 is the preferred technique for creation of a metaclass. It responds to the methods supported by *Metaclass* and its instances respond to the methods of *Class*.

T_3 seems to be an anomaly — it should be illegal.

T_4 is problematic because it is a metaclass that does not respond to the method of *Metaclass*. T_4 probably should be illegal (the programmer should be subclassing *Metaclass*).

An example of a use of this capability is the method createPrimary, which creates an instance of the target metaclass that is a subclass of *Object*. In effect, the method is creating a mixin class for the property embodied by the target metaclass. The target for createPrimary can only be a metaclass.

Exercise 2.9:

If there is a loop in the inheritance graph, the equations of Definition 16 still converge as long as no two classes on the loop override a method with different code pointers.

Exercise 2.10:

Here is a partial answer for the first eight postulates.

Postulate 1:

O is a nonempty, finite set.

Postulate 3:

$$C \subseteq O$$

Postulate 2:

class is a total function mapping O to C.

Postulate 6:

ancestors is a total function mapping C to subsets of C
(note: the empty set is in the range).

Postulate 4, Postulate 5, Postulate 7:

N is a set.
definedIVs is a total function mapping C to subsets of $C \times N$.
containedIVs is a total function mapping O to subsets of $C \times N$.

$$containedIVs(X) = \bigcup_{W \in ancestors(class(X))} definedIVs(W)$$

definedMethods is a total function mapping C to subsets of $C \times N$.
respondsTo is a total function mapping O to subsets of $C \times N$.

$$respondsTo(X) = \bigcup_{W \in ancestors(class(X))} definedMethods(W)$$

Postulate 8:

makeInstance $\in N$
there is an $X \in O$ such that
  $<X,$"makeInstance"$> \in respondsTo(X)$ and $class(<X,$"makeInstance"$>(X)) = X$,
where $<X,$"makeInstance"$>(X)$ is the result of invoking the method on X.
(Note: this is not quite right in that it does not accurately model the idea that a new object is created, for which we would need a model of the environment.)

This can be completed by assuming that getClass is introduced by *Object*.

Chapter 4

Exercise 4.1:

> The value of Z is

$$
\begin{aligned}
\{\text{"class"}= \ &Class, \\
Class \qquad = \ \{ \ &\text{"parents"} \ = \ <X,Y>, \\
&\text{"ivdefs"}=\{\,\}, \\
&\text{"mdefs"} = \ \{\ \}, \\
&\text{"ivs"} \quad = \ \{\}, \\
&\text{"mtab"} = \ \{ \quad U \ = \ \{ \ \text{"umethod"} = \text{ucodePtr} \,\}, \\
&\qquad\qquad\qquad\ W \ = \ \{ \ \text{"wmethod"} = \text{wcodePtr} \ \} \ \} \\
&\} \\
\} &
\end{aligned}
$$

> Note how the method resolution order for Z determines that the implementation for $<U, \text{"umethod"}>$ in Z is provided by the Y override.

Exercise 4.4:

> If the algorithm is run against the figure below, the linearization produced is
> $$<Z, X_3, X_1, Y_3, Y_1, Y_0, Y_2, X_2, X_0, Object>$$
> This is a bad linearization, because it puts Y_0 ahead of X_2 even though X_2 is a subclass of Y_0.

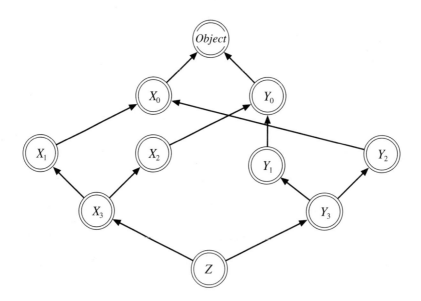

Exercise 4.5:

> There is no serious order disagreement in the construction of Z. There is an order disagreement between W_2 and W_4, but it is not serious because the sets of methods defined by these two classes are disjoint. Consequently,
> $$MRO(Z) = <Z, X_1, Y_1, X_2, Y_3, Y_4, W_3, W_4, Y_2, W_1, W_2, V>$$
> and Z can be constructed.

Chapter 5

Exercise 5.1:

> X and Z are metaclasses because they are descendants of *Class*.

Exercise 5.4:

> (a) Collect only the first response (note: there are alternatives for what "first" means); collect all responses into a list; collect the dominant responses into a list.
> (b) To collect dominant responses, express search responses as a pair <responding class, response> and use an inout argument to collect search responses. When a class is able to respond (because the search criterion is matched), add to the response list only if the list includes no descendants of the class (because a class is dominated by its descendants). Why the inout argument? Because this allows descendants to pass information to ancestors when making parent calls.
> (c) Event processing.

Exercise 5.5:

> (a) Without loss of generality, consider tree inheritance with a single multiply inherited instance variable. Move the multiply inherited instance variable from its original introducing class into the descendant classes that want to "own" the instance variable for their own purposes and introduce the instance variable in these classes. This creates multiple instance variables of the same name, distinguished by their introducing classes. Add an additional argument of type Class to all method definitions in the original introducing class that use the migrated instance variable. When a method needs the instance variable that was migrated, use its new class argument as a match criterion and search descendants for a value of the instance variable (employing a cooperative-override search pattern as in Exercise 5.4). A class responds to the search (returning the instance variable) if it introduces the instance variable and the class search argument is a descendant of the introducing class. Client code that invokes the methods to which the new class argument was added pass as the value of this argument the ancestor class to which the target object was typecast in the original program (as was necessary to select a branch of the original tree inherited object, in order to avoid ambiguity).
> (b) There cannot be multiple search responses, because otherwise the original tree inheritance program would have been ambiguous, and therefore illegal in C++.

Exercise 5.6:

(a) It is useful because it enables additional reasoning about the code that is executed by the method. When such implementation categories are reflected within a type system, this can enable useful special cases for typechecking, as in the case of cooperative methods. (b) One good example is Java's "final." Also, in the context of our current model, one might consider the utility of adding "fully cooperative" to the type system, because this would allow typechecking to ignore such methods when searching for serious order disagreements among the parents of a class.

Exercise 5.7:

It is impossible for such a method invocation to occur in this case. The method bar would be programmed something like this:

```
MX :: bar( ... X* obj, ...)
{
    ...
    ((X*)obj)->hook();
    ...
}
```

where, as usual, MX and X are the names for the class objects *MX* and *X*. If obj has the value *iY*, an exception would be raised during a cast operation used in preparation for such an invocation, because *Y* is not a subclass of *X*. One can reasonably observe that a metaclass programmer who does not have special contextual knowledge guaranteeing the correctness of a cast operation can trivially write code to dynamically verify it before the cast is executed. However, the approach suggested in Chapter 3 provides exactly this contextual information.

Exercise 5.8:

1. Metaclass programmers would statically indicate that their instances must either inherit from or be some specific class. Call this the "instance class."
2. The default instance class for any metaclass would be *Object*.
3. When derived metaclasses are used by typechecking to represent the expected type of a new class, a "derived instance class" (defined in the obvious way) would also be used as follows. Typechecking would verify that the new class itself has as ancestors all of the nonderived ancestors of the derived instance class.

Chapter 6

Exercise 6.5:

```
boolean isMethodNameUniquelyIntroduced( Class* aClass, string methodName )
{ /* Specification */
```
Action:

```
            for ( ObjectList mro = aClass->getMRO(); mro != NULL; mro++)
                if ( (*mro)->isDefinedMethod( (*mro), methodName ) )
                    count = count + 1;
            return (count == 1);
    }
```

Exercise 6.7:

If having an ancestor ahead of a descendant on the parent list of a class does not change the method resolution order, the code of solveMetaclassConstraints can be optimized with the following:

```
    {   ObjectList anOptimalMCL = <>; // an optimal Metaclass Constraint List
        for ( i=0; i < #aMetaclassConstraintList; i++ ) {
            if ( isNotAncestorOfAnyOf( aMetaclassConstraintList[i],
                    tail( aMetaclassConstraintList, i+1 ) ) {
                anOptimalMCL = anOptimalMCL ◁ aMetaclassConstraintList[i];
            }
        aMetaclassConstraintList = anOptimalMCL;
    }
```

at the line that references this exercise on page 150.

Exercise 6.8:

```
    Class* Class :: join( Class* aClass ) {
        if ( aClass->getClass()->IsDescendantOf( Class ) ) {
            Class* aMetaclass = solveMetaclassConstraints( NULL, <this,aClass> );
            Class* aJoin = aMetaclass->makeInstance();
            aJoin->initMIClass( <this,aClass>, {} );
            aJoin->readyClass();
            return aJoin; }}
        else {
            return NULL; }
    }
    Class* Class :: endow( Class* aMetaclass ) {
        if ( aMetaclass->isDescendantOf( Class ) ) {
            Class* actualMetaclass = solveMetaclassConstraints( <aMetaclass>, <this> );
            Class* aClass = actualMetaclass->makeInstance();
            aClass->initMIClass( <this>, {} );
            aClass->readyClass();
            return aClass; }
        else {
            return NULL; }
    }
```

Exercise 6.10:

This is the essence of the protocol: you must think through the rest.

```
Object* makeInstance();
Object* makeInstance( list aParentLIst );
Object* makeInstance( list aMetaclassList, list aParentList );
void defineMethod( ic, nm, impl );
void defineIV( ic, nm, val );
void initializeClass( ); // compute mtab and ivs
void readyClass();
```

Note that the second two forms of makeInstance are acceptable only for metaclasses and that the path expression for this class construction protocol is

(defineMethod + defineIV) initializeClass readyClass

Exercise 6.11:

(a) The analysis results in the diagram in Figure D-1. Both X and Y introduce an instance variable named creationTime. The value of the prevailingCTSClass in the Z class object decides which instance variable is used.

(b) Our metaobject protocol allows the introduction of instance variables only in the data table slot of the class being constructed. If the protocol allowed for the introduction of instance variables with arbitrary class components, the time stamp could be stored in the instance variable <*CTimeStamped*,"creationTime">. The two methods for getCreationTime in Z must be present; each method is part of the public interface of either X or Y, and consequently both methods must be supported.

Chapter 7

Exercise 7.2:

```
ObjectList getCooperativeMRO()
{ /* Specification */
Action:
        for ( ObjectList mro = this->getMRO(); mro != NULL; mro++)
            if ( getClass(*mro)->isDescendantOf( Cooperative ) )
                coopmro = coopmro ◁ (*mro);
            }
        return coopmro:
    }
```

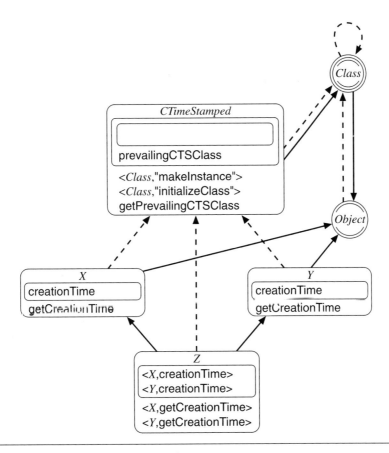

Figure D-1. Diagram for Exercise 6.11.

Exercise 7.5:

In CLOS, a generic function can have at most one implementation for any signature. The direct analog of our cooperation notion would require that a generic function have multiple implementations for a signature.

Chapter 8

Exercise 8.4:

> Hint: try starting with the following precondition for MetaBeforeAfter::readyClass:
> (this->definesMethod(*BeforeAfter*, "beforeMethod")
>   and this->definesMethod(*BeforeAfter*, "afterMethod"))
> or
> (not this->definesMethod(*BeforeAfter*, "beforeMethod")
>   and not this->definesMethod(*BeforeAfter*, "afterMethod"))
> or
> (this->definesMethod(*BeforeAfter*, "beforeMethod")
>   and (this->classResolve(*BeforeAfter*, "afterMethod")
>   = *BeforeAfter*->classResolve(*BeforeAfter*, "afterMethod")))
> or
> (this->definesMethod(*BeforeAfter*, "afterMethod")
>   and (this->classResolve(*BeforeAfter*, "beforeMethod")
>   = *BeforeAfter*->classResolve(*BeforeAfter*, "beforeMethod")))

Exercise 8.5:

> *BeforeAfter* is not suitable for use in a multithreaded environment because if any thread is executing inside the dispatcher, all other threads execute the primary method without executing the before/after behavior (because of the protection afforded by Section 0 of the dispatcher). This can be fixed by storing the object reference and thread identifier in the dispatchList.

Chapter 9

Exercise 9.1:

```
boolean isProxy( Object* objRef ) {
    return getClass(objRef)->isDescendantOf( ProxyForObject );
}
```

Exercise 9.2:

> The fragment creates the object structure depicted below. The dispatch used in *XProxyForX* is the one inherited from *ProxyForObject*, which forwards only methods that are not introduced by ancestors. returnThis is introduced by *X*, which is an ancestor of *XProxyForX*. Therefore, the invocation is not forwarded and returns the object reference to the proxy. That is, an invocation of test returns the value *ProxyFor_iX*.

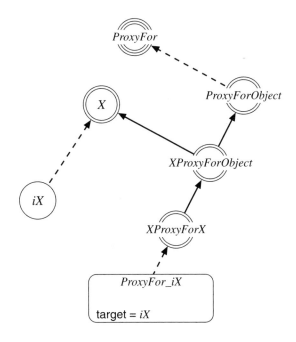

Exercise 9.3:

One might think that the fragment creates the object structure depicted below. However, there is a difference between the proxy objects *ProxyForProxyFor_iX* below and *ProxyForProxyForIX* in Figure 9-6. The precondition of setTarget is not true, if one tries to use *ProxyForX* as the class for *ProxyForProxyFor_iX*.

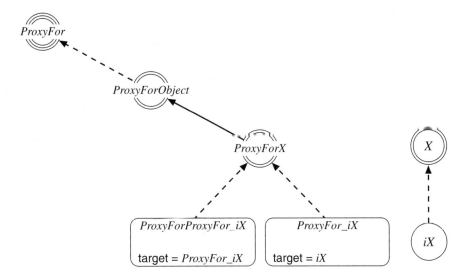

Chapter 10

Exercise 10.6:

The design concept for the metaclass is as follows.

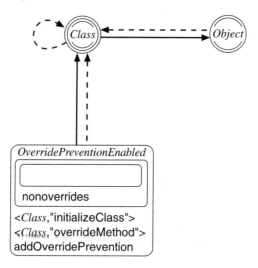

The class declaration and the method implementations are below.

```
class OverridePreventionEnabled : public virtual Class {
    protected:
        List nonoverrideableMethods = <>;
    public:
        boolean initializeClass( ObjectList aParentList, DataSegment aDataSegment );
        void overrideMethod( Class* introducingClass,
                             string methodName,
                             codePtr methodImpl );
        cooperative void addOverridePrevention(    Class* introducingClass,
                                                   string methodName );

}
```

```
boolean OverridePreventionEnabled :: initializeClass( ObjectList aParentList,
                                                      DataSegment aDataSegment ) {
```

{ /* Specification */
Action:

```
    if ( __parent->initializeClass( aParentList, aDataSegment ) ) {
        ObjectList realParents = this->getParents();
        for ( int i = 0; i < #realParents; i++ ) {
            nonoverrideableMethods =
                nonoverrideableMethods
                ◁
                realParents[i].OverridePreventionEnabled.nonoverrideableMethods;
        }
        return TRUE;
    }
    else
        return FALSE;
}
```

```
void OverridePreventionEnabled :: overrideMethod(  Class* introducingClass,
                                                   string methodName,
                                                   codePtr methodImpl )
```

{ /* Specification */
Action:

```
    if ( <introducingClass,methodName> ∈ nonoverrideableMethods )
        osAbort():

    __parent->overrideMethod( introducingClass, methodName, methodImpl );
}
```

```
void OverridePreventionEnabled :: addOverridePrevention(Class* introducingClass,
                                                        string methodName )
```

{ /* Specification */
Action:

```
    nonoverrideableMethods = nonoverrideableMethods
                                    ◁ <introducingClass,methodName>;
}
```

Note that this metaclass is always used with a helper metaclass as shown below.

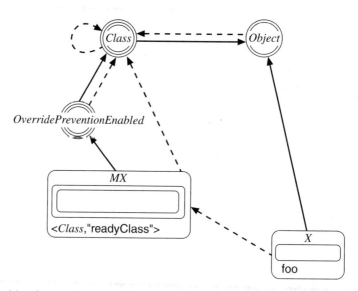

The override of readyClass in *MX* sets the override prevention for foo. Note that this kind of operation (setting some additional metadata) cannot be done during the writing of class *X*, because the class defines methods and variables that belong to the instances.

Bibliography

[1] Aksit, M., K. Wakita, J. Bosch, L. Bergmans, and A. Yonezawa, "Abstracting Object Interactions Using Composition Filters," in R. Guerraoui, O. Nierstrasz, and M. Riveill, eds., *Object-Based Distributed Processing*, LNCS 791, Springer-Verlag, 1993, 152–184.

[2] Apple Computer, *Dylan: An Object-Oriented Dynamic Language*, 1992.

[3] Arbadi, M., and L. Cardelli, *A Theory of Objects*, Springer-Verlag, 1996.

[4] Atkinson, C., *Object-Oriented Reuse, Concurrency and Distribution: An Ada-Based Approach*, Addison-Wesley, 1991.

[5] Ball, M., "The Joys of Stability," *C++ Report*, October 1995, 34–43.

[6] Banerji, A., D. Kulkarni, and D. Cohn, "A Framework for Building Extensible C++ Class Libraries," *USENIX C++ Technical Conference,* 1994.

[7] Barrett, K., B. Cassels, P. Haahr, D.A. Moon, K. Playford, and P.T. Tucker, "A Monotonic Superclass Linearization in Dylan," *OOPSLA '96 Conference Proceedings*, October 1996, 69–82.

[8] Beeri, C., "New Data Models and Languages — the Challenge," *Proceedings of the ACM SIGACT-SIGMOD-SIGART Symposium on Principles of Database Systems*, 1992, 1–15.

[9] Bergstein, P.L., "Object-Preserving Class Transformations," *OOPSLA '91 Conference Proceedings*, October 1991, 200–313.

[10] Berlin, L., "When Objects Collide: Experiences with Reusing Multiple Class Hierarchies," *OOPSLA '90 Conference Proceedings*, October 1990, 181–193.

[11] Bobrow, D.G., and G. Kiczales, "The Common Lisp Object System Metaobject Kernel: A Status Report," *ACM Conference on Lisp and Functional Programming*, July 1988.

[12] Booch, G., *Object-Oriented Programming with Applications*, Benjamin/Cummings, 1991.

[13] Borning, A.H., and D.H.H. Ingalls, "Multiple Inheritance in Smalltalk-80," *AAAI '82*, 1982.

[14] Bouraqadi-Saâdani, M.N., F. Rivard, and T. Ledoux, "Composition de Métaclasses," *Journées Francophones des Langages Applicatifs*, February 1998.

[15] Bracha, G., and W. Cook, "Mixin-Based Inheritance," *OOPSLA '90 Conference Proceedings*, October 1990, 303–311.

[16]   Bretthauer, H., J. Kopp, H. Davis, and K. Playford, "Balancing the EuLisp Metaobject Protocol," *LISP and Symbolic Computation,* 6(1–2), August 1993, 119–137.

[17]   Briot, J.-P., and P. Cointe, "Programming with Explicit Metaclasses in Smalltalk-80," *OOPSLA '89 Conference Proceedings,* October 1989, 419–431.

[18]   Broadbery, P., and C. Burdorf, "Applications of Telos," *LISP and Symbolic Computation,* 6(1–2), August 1993, 139–158.

[19]   Cardelli, L., and P. Wegner, "On Understanding Types, Data Abstractions, and Polymorphism," *ACM Computing Surveys,* 17(4), December 1985.

[20]   Castellanos, M., T. Kudrass, F. Saltor, and M. García-Solaco, "Interdatabase Existence Dependencies: A Metaclass Approach," *Proceedings of the International Conference on Parallel and Distributed Information Systems,* 1994.

[21]   Campbell, R.H., and A.N. Habermann, "The Specification of Process Synchronisation by Path Expressions," *Lecture Notes in Computer Science,* 16, Springer-Verlag, 1974, 89–102.

[22]   Chiba, S., "A Metaobject Protocol for C++," *OOPSLA '95 Conference Proceedings,* October 1995, 285–299.

[23]   Clarke, A.C., *Profiles of the Future,* Holt, Rinehart and Winston, 1984.

[24]   Cointe, P., "Metaclasses are First Class: The ObjVlisp Model," *OOPSLA '87 Conference Proceedings,* October 1987, 156–165.

[25]   Cook, W., and J. Palsberg, "A Denotational Semantics of Inheritance and Its Correctness," *OOPSLA '89 Conference Proceedings,* October 1989, 433–444.

[26]   Cook, W.R., W.L. Hill, and P.S. Canning, "Inheritance Is Not Subtyping," *Conference Record of 17th Annual ACM Symposium on Principles of Programming Languages,* January 1990, 125–135.

[27]   Copeland, G., personal communication, 1994.

[28]   Danforth, S., and C. Tomlinson, "Type Theories and Object-Oriented Programming," *ACM Computing Surveys,* 20(1), March 1988.

[29]   Danforth, S., "A Bird's Eye View of SOM," *IBM OS/2 Developer,* Winter 1992.

[30]   Danforth, S.H., and I.R. Forman, "Derived Metaclasses in SOM," *Proceedings of the 1994 Conference on Technology of Object-Oriented Languages and Systems,* April 1994.

[31]   Danforth, S.H., and I.R. Forman, "Reflections on Metaclass Programming in SOM," *OOPSLA '94 Conference Proceedings,* October 1994, 440–452.

[32]   Danforth, S., P. Koenen, and B. Tate, *Objects for OS/2,* Van Nostrand Reinhold, 1994.

[33] Davey, B.A., and H.A. Priestley, *Introduction to Lattices and Order*, Cambridge University Press, 1990.

[34] Ducournau, R., M. Habib, M. Huchard, and M.L. Mugnier, "Monotonic Conflict Resolution Mechanisms for Inheritance," *OOPSLA '92 Conference Proceedings*, October 1992, 16–24.

[35] Ducournau, R., M. Habib, M. Huchard, and M.L. Mugnier, "Proposal for a Monotonic Multiple Inheritance Linearization," *OOPSLA '94 Conference Proceedings*, October 1994, 164–175.

[36] Deubler, H.-H., and M. Koestler, "Introducing Object Orientation to Large and Complex Systems," *IEEE Transactions on Software Engineering*, 20(11), November 1994, 840–848.

[37] Eliëns, A., *Principles of Object-Oriented Software Development*, Addison-Wesley, 1995.

[38] Ellis, M.A., and B. Stroustrup, *The Annotated C++ Reference Manual*, Addison-Wesley, 1990.

[39] Ferber, J., "Computational Reflection in Class-Based Object Oriented Languages," *OOPSLA '89 Conference Proceedings*, October 1989, 317–326.

[40] Flatt, M., S. Krishnamurthi, and M. Felleisen, "Classes and Mixins," *Conference Record of POPL '98*, January 1998, 171–183.

[41] Foote, B., and R.E. Johnson, "Reflective Facilities in Smalltalk-80," *OOPSLA '89 Conference Proceedings*, October 1989, 327–335.

[42] Forman, I.R., S.H. Danforth, and H.H. Madduri, "Composition of Before/After Metaclasses in SOM," *OOPSLA '94 Conference Proceedings*, October 1994, 427–439.

[43] Forman, I.R., M.H. Conner, S.H. Danforth, and L.K. Raper, "Release-to-Release Binary Compatibility in SOM," *OOPSLA '95 Conference Proceedings*, October 1995, 426–438.

[44] Forman, I.R., and S.H. Danforth, "Inheritance of Metaclass Constraints in SOM," *Reflection'96*, 1996.

[45] Francez, N., *Program Verification*, Addison-Wesley, 1972.

[46] Francez, N., and I.R. Forman, *Interacting Processes: A Multiparty Approach to Coordinated Distributed Programming*, Addison-Wesley, 1996.

[47] Gamma, R., R. Helm, R. Johnson, and J. Vlissides, *Design Patterns: Elements of Reusable Object-Oriented Software*, Addison-Wesley, 1994.

[48] Gibbs, S., D. Tsidhritzis, E. Casals, O. Nierstrasz, and X. Pintado, "Class Management for Software Communities," *Communications of the ACM*, 33(9), September 1990, 90–103.

[49] Göers, J., and A. Heuer, "Definition and Application of Metaclasses in an Object-Oriented Database Model," *Proceedings of the 9th International Conference on Data Engineering*, 1993.

[50] Goldberg, A., and D. Robson, *Smalltalk-80: The Language and Its Implementation*, Addison-Wesley, 1983.

[51] Goldstein, T.C., and A.D. Sloane, "The Object Binary Interface — C++ Objects for Evolvable Shared Class Libraries," *USENIX C++ Technical Conference*, 1994.

[52] Graube, N., "Metaclass Compatibility," *OOPSLA '89 Conference Proceedings*, October 1989, 305–316.

[53] Gries, D., and F.B. Schneider, *A Logical Approach to Discrete Math*, Springer-Verlag, 1993.

[54] Gunter, C.A., and J.C. Mitchell, *Theoretical Aspects of Object-Oriented Programming: Types, Semantics, and Language Design*, The MIT Press, 1994.

[55] Hamilton, J., R. Klarer, M. Mendell, and B. Thomson, "Using SOM with C++," *C++ Report*, July/August 1995.

[56] Hamilton, J., "Reusing Binary Objects with DirectToSOM C++," *C++ Report*, March 1996, 42–51.

[57] Harary, F., *Graph Theory*, Addison-Wesley, 1972.

[58] Harrison, W., and H. Ossher, "Subject-Oriented Programming (A Critique of Pure Objects)," *OOPSLA '93 Conference Proceedings*, September 1993, 411–428.

[59] Hecht, M.S., *Flow Analysis of Computer Programs*, North-Holland, 1977.

[60] Helm, R., I.M. Holland, and D. Gangopadhyay, "Contracts: Specifying Behavioral Compositions in Object-Oriented Systems," *OOPSLA '90 Conference Proceedings*, October 1990, 169–180.

[61] Hoare, C.A.R., "Proof of Correctness of Data Representations," *Acta Informatica*, 1, 1972, 271–281.

[62] IBM, *SOMobjects Developer Toolkit Reference Manual, Version 2.1*, October 1994.

[63] IBM, *SOMobjects Developer Toolkit User's Guide, Version 2.1*, October 1994.

[64] Johnson, R., and M. Palaniappan, "MetaFlex: A Flexible Metaclass Generator," *Proceedings of the Seventh European Conference on Object-Oriented Programming*, July 1993, 502–527.

[65] Gosling, J., B. Joy, and G. Steele, *The Java Language Specification*, Addison-Wesley, 1996.

[66] Kathuria, R., "Improved Modeling and Design Using Assimilation and Property Modeling," *Journal of Object-Oriented Programming*, January 1997, 15–24.

[67]   Katz, S.M., "A Superimposition Control Construct for Distributed Systems," *ACM Transactions on Programming Languages and Systems*, 15(2), April 1993, 337–356.

[68]   Khoshafian, S., and R. Abnous, *Object Orientation*, John Wiley, 1990.

[69]   Kiczales, G., J. des Rivieres, and D.G. Bobrow, *The Art of the Metaobject Protocol*, The MIT Press, 1991.

[70]   Kiczales, G., and J. Lamping, "Issues in the Design and Specification of Class Libraries," *OOPSLA '92 Conference Proceedings*, 1992, 435–451.

[71]   Kifer, M., G. Lausen, and J. Wu, "Logical Foundations of Object-Oriented and Frame-Based Languages," *Journal of the ACM*, 42(4), July 1995, 741–843.

[72]   Kim, W., *Introduction to Object-Oriented Databases*, The MIT Press, 1990.

[73]   Kim, W., ed., *Modern Database Systems: The Object Model, Interoperability, and Beyond*, Addison-Wesley, 1995.

[74]   Kishimoto, Y., N. Kotaka, and S. Honiden, "Adapting Object-Communication Methods Dynamically," *IEEE Software*, May 1995, 65–74.

[75]   Klas, W., G. Fischer, and K. Aberer, "Integrating Relational and Object-Oriented Database Systems Using a Metaclass Concept," *Journal of Systems Integration*, 4, 1994, 341–372.

[76]   Kristensen, B.B., O.L. Madsen, B. Møller-Pedersen, and K. Nygaard, "The BETA Programming Language," in B.D. Shriver and P. Wegner, eds., *Research Directions in Object Oriented Programming*, The MIT Press, 1987.

[77]   Lange, D.B., and Y. Nakamura, "Program Explorer: A Program Visualizer for C++," *Proceedings of USENIX Conference on Object-Oriented Technologies*, June 1995, 39–54.

[78]   Lau, C., *Object-Oriented Programming for SOM and DSOM*, Van Nostrand Reinhold, 1994.

[79]   Lee, A.H., and J.L. Zachary, "Using Metaprogramming to Add Persistence to CLOS," *Proceedings of the 1994 IEEE International Conference on Computer Languages*, May 1994, 16–19.

[80]   Lee, A.H., and J.L. Zachary, "Reflections on Metaprogramming," *IEEE Transactions on Software Engineering*, 21(11), November 1995, 883–893.

[81]   Lieberherr, K.J., and C. Xiao, "Object-Oriented Software Evolution," *IEEE Transactions on Software Engineering*, 19(4), April 1993, 313–343.

[82]   Lieberherr, K.J., *Adaptive Object-Oriented Software*, PWS, 1996.

[83]   Linger, R.C., H.D. Mills, and B.I. Witt, *Structured Programming: Theory and Practice*, Addison-Wesley, 1979.

[84]   Lippman, S.B., and J. Lajoie, *C++ Primer*, Third Edition, Addison-Wesley, 1998.

[85]   Maes, P., "Concepts and Experiments in Computational Reflection," *OOPSLA '87 Conference Proceedings*, October 1987, 147–155.

[86]   Manna, Z., *Mathematical Theory of Computation*, McGraw-Hill, 1974.

[87]   Matsuoka, S., and A. Yonezawa, "Analysis of Inheritance Anomaly in Object-Oriented Concurrent Programming," in G. Agha, P. Wegner, and A. Yonezawa, eds., *Research Directions in Concurrent Object-Oriented Programming*, The MIT Press, 1993.

[88]   Meyer, B., "Lessons from the Design of the Eiffel Libraries," *Communications of the ACM*, 33(9), September 1990, 68–89.

[89]   Meyer, B., *Reusable Software: The Base Object-Oriented Component Library*, Prentice-Hall International, 1990.

[90]   Meyers, S., *Effective C++: 50 Specific Ways to Improve Your Programs and Designs*, Second Edition, Addison-Wesley, 1997.

[91]   Meyers, S., *More Effective C++: 35 New Ways to Improve Your Programs and Designs*, Addison-Wesley, 1996.

[92]   Mezini, M., "Dynamic Metaclass Construction for an Explicit Specialization Interface," *Proceedings of Reflection '96*, April 1996.

[93]   Microsoft, *OLE 2 Programmer's Reference Volume One*, Microsoft Press, 1994.

[94]   Mikhajlov, L., and E. Sekerinski, "The Fragile Base Class Problem and Its Solution," Turku Centre for Computer Science, Technical Report 117, June 1997.

[95]   Mohindra, A., G. Copeland, and M. Devarakonda, "Dynamic Insertion of Object Services," *Proceedings of USENIX Conference on Object-Oriented Technologies*, June 1995, 3–20.

[96]   Mulet, P., J. Malenfant, and P. Cointe, "Towards a Methodology for Explicit Composition of MetaObjects," *OOPSLA '95 Conference Proceedings*, October 1995, 316–330.

[97]   Murer, S., S. Omohundro, D. Stoutamire, and C. Szyperski, "Interaction Abstraction in Sather," *ACM Transactions on Programming Languages and Systems*, 16(1), January 1996, 1–15.

[98]   Mylopoulos, J., A. Borgida, J. Matthias, and M. Korbarakis, "Telos: Representing Knowledge About Information Systems," *ACM Transactions on Information Systems*, 8(4), October 1990, 325–362.

[99]   Object Management Group, *The Common Object Request Broker: Architecture and Specification*, OMG Document No. 91.12.1, 1991.

[100]   Orlafi, R., and D. Harkey, *Client/Server Programming with OS/2 2.1*, Van Nostrand Reinhold, 1993.

[101] Ossher, H., M. Kaplan, W. Harrison, A. Katz, and V. Kruskal, "Subject-Oriented Composition Rules," *OOPSLA '95 Conference Proceedings*, October 1995, 235–250.

[102] Otte, R., P. Patrick, and M. Roy, *Understanding CORBA*, Prentice-Hall, 1996.

[103] Paepcke, A., "PCLOS: A Critical Review," *OOPSLA '89 Conference Proceedings*, October 1989, 221–237.

[104] Paepcke, A., ed., *Object-Oriented Programming: The CLOS Perspective*, The MIT Press, 1993.

[105] Palay, A.J., "C++ in a Changing Environment," *USENIX C++ Technical Conference*, 1992.

[106] Pascoe, G.A., "Encapsulators: A New Software Paradigm in Smalltalk-80," *OOPSLA '86 Conference Proceedings*, September 1986, 341–346.

[107] Pree, W., *Design Patterns for Object-Oriented Software Development*, Addison-Wesley, 1995.

[108] Russinoff, D.M., "Proteus: A Frame-Based Nonmonotonic Inference System," in W. Kim and F.H. Lochovsky, eds., *Object-Oriented Concepts, Databases, and Applications*, ACM Press, 1989, 127–150.

[109] Snyder, A., "Encapsulation and Inheritance in OOP Languages," *OOPSLA '86 Conference Proceedings*, September 1986, 38–45.

[110] Stein, A.S., "Delegation Is Inheritance," *OOPSLA '87 Conference Proceedings*, October 1987, 138–146.

[111] Stroustrup, B., *The C++ Programming Language*, Third Edition, Addison-Wesley, 1997.

[112] Taivalsaari, A., "On the Notion of Inheritance," *ACM Computing Surveys*, 28(3), September 1996, 438–479.

[113] Touretzky, D.S., *The Mathematics of Inheritance Systems*, Morgan-Kaufmann, 1988.

[114] Udel, J., "Componentware," *Byte*, May 1994, 46–56.

[115] Ungar, D., and R.B. Smith, "Self: The Power of Simplicity," *OOPSLA '87 Conference Proceedings*, October 1987, 227–242.

[116] Wand, M., and D. Friedman, "The Mystery of the Tower Revealed," *Proceedings of 1986 LISP and Functional Programming Conference*, 1986.

[117] Wegner, P., and S. Zdonik, "Principle of Substitutability," *ECOOP '89*, 1989.

[118] Wegner, P., "Concepts and Paradigms of Object-Oriented Programming," *OOPS Messenger*, 1(1), August 1990, 7–87.

[119] Xu, J., B. Randell, A. Romanovsky, C.M.F. Rubira, R.J. Stroud, and X Wu, "Fault Tolerance in Concurrent Object-Oriented Programming through Coordinated Error Recovery," Technical Report 507, University of Newcastle on Tyne, 1995.

[120] Yang, Y., "A Metaobject Based Version Control Mechanism in Software Object Databases," *Proceedings of the Fifth Israel Conference on Computer Systems and Software Engineering*, May 1991, 120–125.

[121] Yelland, P.M., "Experimental Classification Facilities in Smalltalk," *OOPSLA '94 Conference Proceedings*, October 1994, 164–175.

[122] Zimmerman, C., ed., *Advances in Object-Oriented Metalevel Architectures and Reflection*, CRC Press, 1996.

Index

A

ABI 235
abstract class 224
abstract methods 224
abstract property 53, 224–226
access control 88
action (in a specification) 6, 119
addCooperativeMethod 154, 155, 157, 160–161, 187
addMethod 71, 117, 123, 128, 162, 197
addToDispatchList 182
afterMethod
  See also BeforeAfter
  composition problem 174–176
  correspondence between before methods and 187
  defined 173
  invariant checking 218
  specification of 182
AfterMethodType 183
afterTable 178, 179
ancestors 21
API 235
application programming interface 235
applications binary interface 235
apply 136–138, 199, 201
apply stub 264, 266–267
Aristotle 20
associativity
  of Before/After Metaclasses 188–189
  of metaclass composition 166–167

B

BadSingleInstanced 221
base implementation 71
base proxy class 197
befaftDispatch 184

BeforeAfter 178
  associativity of 188–189
  design of 177–185
  difference between cooperation and 187
  example 189–191
beforeMethod
  composition problem 174–176
  correspondence between after methods and 187
  defined 173
  invariant checking 217
  specification of 182
BeforeMethodType 183
beforeTable 178, 179
breaking encapsulation 63

C

C 12
C++
  See also DTS C++ 85
  basics 86–92
  breaking encapsulation 63
  metaclass incompatibility 42
  method invocation 60
  support for binary libraries 246
  typechecking 102–103
changeTarget 212
Class (class object) 14
  DTS C++ declaration for 117–118
class (function) 13
class libaries, comparison of support 244–245, 246
class(es)
  construction 70–71, 123–132
  defined 12
  defining methods of a 128–131
  definition in DTS C++ 92–93

Addison-Wesley Computer and Engineering Publishing Group

How to Interact with Us

1. Visit our Web site

http://www.awl.com/cseng

When you think you've read enough, there's always more content for you at Addison-Wesley's web site. Our web site contains a directory of complete product information including:

- Chapters
- Exclusive author interviews
- Links to authors' pages
- Tables of contents
- Source code

You can also discover what tradeshows and conferences Addison-Wesley will be attending, read what others are saying about our titles, and find out where and when you can meet our authors and have them sign your book.

2. Subscribe to Our Email Mailing Lists

Subscribe to our electronic mailing lists and be the first to know when new books are publishing. Here's how it works: Sign up for our electronic mailing at http://www.awl.com/cseng/mailinglists.html. Just select the subject areas that interest you and you will receive notification via email when we publish a book in that area.

3. Contact with Us via Email

cepubprof@awl.com
Ask general questions about our books.
Sign up for our electronic mailing lists.
Submit corrections for our web site.

bexpress@awl.com
Request an Addison-Wesley catalog.
Get answers to questions regarding
your order or our products.

innovations@awl.com
Request a current Innovations Newsletter.

webmaster@awl.com
Send comments about our web site.

cepubeditors@awl.com
Submit a book proposal.
Send errata for an Addison-Wesley book.

cepubpublicity@awl.com
Request a review copy for a member of the media
interested in reviewing new Addison-Wesley titles.

We encourage you to patronize the many fine retailers who stock Addison-Wesley titles. Visit our online directory to find stores near you or visit our online store: http://store.awl.com/ or call 800-824-7799.

Addison Wesley Longman
Computer and Engineering Publishing Group
One Jacob Way, Reading, Massachusetts 01867 USA
TEL 781-944-3700 • FAX 781-942-3076